NEGOTIATING SOCIAL RELATIONS

Tenor Resources in English

Every day we negotiate our social relations. This may involve small, seemingly inconsequential chats with friends, family, and colleagues that perform our relationships, or it may involve large, communal events that bring us together or tear us apart. In all cases, we negotiate these social relations through the language, paralanguage, and related systems of meaning that we use. This book introduces a new model for analysing how people negotiate social relations through the framework of Systemic Functional Linguistics (SFL). It focuses on SFL's conception of social context and in particular on the interpersonal component of context known as *tenor*. Drawing on decades of SFL research, tenor is reworked as a resource for meaning – with the aim of describing in some detail how we go about building and maintaining sociality.

The book begins by considering how language varies in relation to social context and the different perspectives we can take to explore this variation. It then introduces our model of tenor as a resource for negotiating social relations. The model comprises three main systems. *Positioning* considers how people put forward meanings, react to them, and position each other when we talk. *Orienting* looks at the nature of the meanings we negotiate, attending to the vast background of shared values that underpin our talk, help us build communities, and hold them together. *Tuning* deals with how we raise or lower the stakes of what is being said, how we broaden or narrow the scope of what it applies to, and how we vary the spirit in which the meanings are being put forward. Taken together, these systems provide us with resources for enacting social relations as we align and disalign with people and communities of various kinds. Examples focus in particular on a range of meanings associated with motherhood, including language and paralanguage (both gesture and emoji) in spoken, written, and social media texts.

(Key Concepts in Systemic Functional Linguistics)

Y.J. DORAN is an associate professor in language and literacy education at the Australian Catholic University.

J.R. MARTIN is a professor of linguistics at the University of Sydney.

MICHELE ZAPPAVIGNA is an associate professor in the School of Arts and Media at the University of New South Wales, Sydney.

Key Concepts in Systemic Functional Linguistics

Series Editors
Gerard O'Grady, Cardiff University
Rebekah Wegener, University of Salzburg
Tom Bartlett, University of Glasgow

Books in this series provide monographic treatments of core theoretical concepts within Systemic Functional Linguistics, together with coverage of more recent concerns in Systemic Functional Linguistic theory and important areas of application and trans-disciplinary collaboration.

Each monograph is organized around a description of the historical factors that led to the emergence of the concept within Systemic Functional Linguistics and a detailed theoretical description of the concept within the overall architecture of the theory.

Published

Neo-Firthian Approaches to Linguistic Typology
William B. McGregor

System in Systemic Functional Linguistics: A System-based Theory of Language
Christian M.I.M. Matthiessen

Systemic Functional Translation Studies: Theoretical Insights and New Directions
Bo Wang and Yuanyi Ma

Verbal Art and Systemic Functional Linguistics
Donna R. Miller

Word Phonology in a Systemic Functional Linguistic Framework: Phonological Studies in English, German, Welsh and Tera (Nigeria)
Paul Tench

Information Structure in Spoken English: A Systemic Functional Linguistics View
Gerard O'Grady

Negotiating Social Relations

Tenor Resources in English

Y.J. DORAN, J.R. MARTIN, AND MICHELE ZAPPAVIGNA

UNIVERSITY OF TORONTO PRESS
Toronto Buffalo London

Published by University of Toronto Press in 2026
Toronto Buffalo London
utppublishing.com
Printed in the USA

ISBN 978-1-4875-8488-7 (cloth)
ISBN 978-1-4875-5706-5 (paper)
ISBN 978-1-4875-9536-4 (EPUB)
ISBN 978-1-4875-9498-5 (PDF)

Library and Archives Canada Cataloguing in Publication

Title: Negotiating social relations : tenor resources in English / Y.J. Doran, J.R. Martin, and Michele Zappavigna.
Names: Doran, Yeagan J., author | Martin, J. R., 1950- author | Zappavigna, Michele, author
Series: Key concepts in systemic functional linguistics.
Description: Series statement: Key concepts in systemic functional linguistics | Includes bibliographical references and index.
Identifiers: Canadiana (print) 20250304139 | Canadiana (ebook) 2025030418X | ISBN 9781487584887 (cloth) | ISBN 9781487557065 (paper) | ISBN 9781487594985 (PDF) | ISBN 9781487595364 (EPUB)
Subjects: LCSH: Functionalism (Linguistics) | LCSH: Social exchange. | LCSH: Social interaction. | LCSH: Systemic grammar.
Classification: LCC P147 .D67 2026 | DDC 302.2—dc23 | 410.1/83—dc23

The manufacturer's authorised representative in the EU for product safety is Mare Nostrum Group B.V., Mauritskade 21D, 1091 GC Amsterdam, The Netherlands. Email: gpsr@mare-nostrum.co.uk

We wish to acknowledge the land on which the University of Toronto Press operates. This land is the traditional territory of the Wendat, the Anishnaabeg, the Haudenosaunee, the Métis, and the Mississaugas of the Credit First Nation.

University of Toronto Press acknowledges the financial support of the Government of Canada, the Canada Council for the Arts, and the Ontario Arts Council, an agency of the Government of Ontario, for its publishing activities.

Canada Council for the Arts
Conseil des Arts du Canada

Funded by the Government of Canada
Financé par le gouvernement du Canada

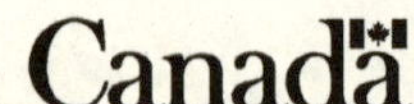

Contents

List of Figures vii

List of Tables ix

Preface xi

1 Negotiating Social Relations: A Systemic Functional Perspective 2
- *1.1 Introduction* 2
- *1.2 Language and Social Context* 3
- *1.3 Modelling Field, Mode, and Tenor* 8
  - 1.3.1 Classifying Registers 8
  - 1.3.2 Patterns of Usage 11
- *1.4 Tenor as a Resource* 20
- *1.5 Chapter Outline* 26
- *1.6 Resource Guide* 27
  - 1.6.1 Paralanguage 27
  - 1.6.2 Intonation and Rhythm 28
  - 1.6.3 Halliday's Functional Grammar 28
  - 1.6.4 Discourse Semantics 28
  - 1.6.5 Context 28

2 Negotiating Tenor: Rendering Meaning in Dialogue and Monologue 29
- *2.1 Introduction* 29
- *2.2 Engaging in Conversation* 31
- *2.3 Negotiating Meaning* 34
- *2.4 Rendering* 36
- *2.5 Building Dialogue* 40
- *2.6 Internal and External Rendering* 44
- *2.7 Rendering Other Voices* 48

2.8 Negotiating Monologue 54
2.9 Conclusion 60
3 Positioning Others: Tendering in Text 61
3.1 Introduction 61
3.2 Tendering Propositions and Proposals 62
3.3 Open and Complete Propositions and Proposals 68
3.4 Repositioning 74
3.5 Purview: Speaker and Listener Positioning 81
3.6 Purview in Spoken and Written Language 90
3.7 Conclusion 97
4 Building Values: Establishing Meanings to Share 99
4.1 Introduction 99
4.2 Underlying Values 101
4.3 Orienting Positions 106
4.3.1 Sourcing 108
4.3.2 Convoking 116
4.3.3 Opposing 120
4.3.4 Likening 131
4.3.5 Encapsulating 138
4.4 Orienting and Genre 144
4.5 Conclusion 150
5 Tuning: Adjusting the Meanings We Share 151
5.1 Introduction 151
5.2 Multilogue Communication 154
5.3 Guilt and Motherhood on Social Media 156
5.4 Tuning Positions: Scoping, Staking, and Spiriting #momguilt 159
5.4.1 Scoping Resources 162
5.4.2 Staking Resources 165
5.4.3 Spiriting Resources 173
5.5 Tuning in Dialogue 175
5.6 Conclusion 178
6 Resources for Negotiating Social Relations 180
6.1 Tenor and Systemic Functional Linguistics 180
6.2 Looking Below: Tenor, Language, and Paralanguage 183
6.3 Looking Around: Tenor, Field, and Mode 194
6.4 Looking Above: Tenor and Genre 201
6.5 Looking Across: Tenor, Social Relations, and the Social Semiotic 212

Glossary 215

Notes 221

References 233

Index 247

List of Figures

Figure 1.1 Language and social context as supervenient systems 4
Figure 1.2 Language, register (field, tenor, and mode), and genre 5
Figure 1.3 Outline of linguistic and contextual strata 6
Figure 1.4 Metafunctions – ideational, textual, and interpersonal 7
Figure 1.5 Discourse semantic systems and register variables 8
Figure 1.6 Poynton's (1990a) model of tenor relations 13
Figure 1.7 Hierarchy of instantiation 16
Figure 1.8 Major field systems 17
Figure 1.9 More delicate activity and item systems 18
Figure 1.10 More delicate property systems 19
Figure 1.11 Hierarchy of individuation 20
Figure 1.12 Key systems of tenor 26
Figure 2.1 Preliminary options for rendering 41
Figure 2.2 Network for rendering 47
Figure 3.1 Initial network of tendering 74
Figure 3.2 Options for tendering 95
Figure 3.3 Full POSITIONING system 96
Figure 4.1 System of ORIENTING 143
Figure 5.1 The TUNING system 178
Figure 6.1 Full system of tenor as a resource 182
Figure 6.2 Lowering stakes through language, voice quality, and facial expression 187
Figure 6.3 Rejection through language and facial expression, 1 187
Figure 6.4 Rejection through language and facial expression, 2 188
Figure 6.5 Tentative negotiation genre, with prosodic Sides followed by a Solution 207
Figure 6.6 Genre analysis of gossip 209
Figure 6.7 Genre analysis of chat 210

List of Tables

Table 1.1 Types of presence 13
Table 1.2 Types of mass 14
Table 2.1 Rendering Mashenka the lady and Mashenka the laundress in Kollontai (1916/1997, p. 128) 58
Table 2.2 Rendering options and their common realizations 60
Table 3.1 Speaker and listener purview 86
Table 4.1 Realizations of sourcing 115
Table 4.2 Sourcing and convoking in Kollontai's (1916/1997) text marking the exemplum genre stages 119
Table 4.3 Realizations of convoking 120
Table 4.4 Some oppositions in a primary school discussion 122
Table 4.5 Oppositions in a primary school discussion 124
Table 4.6 Some realizations for opposing 130
Table 4.7 Arguments for and against advertisements, including likening 133
Table 4.8 Likening and opposing in a conversation 135
Table 4.9 The constellation underpinning the arguments for and against advertisements 140
Table 4.10 Kristy and her mother's developing constellation, 1 141
Table 4.11 Kristy and her mother's developing constellation, 2 142
Table 4.12 Kristy and her mother's developing constellation, 3 142
Table 4.13 Kristy and her mother's developing constellation, 4 142
Table 4.14 Kristy and her mother's developing constellation, 5 143
Table 5.1 The 20 most frequent hashtags in the corpus (co-occurring with #momguilt) 159
Table 6.1 A biographical recount of Jarrad Madgwick (Commonwealth of Australia, 2023, pp. 339–340) 197
Table 6.2 Some genres, their stages, and their typical realizations through resources of tenor and field 202

Preface

It was almost a decade ago that Tom Bartlett, Gerard O'Grady, and Rebekah Wegener invited Jim to make a contribution to their Key Concepts in Systemic Functional Linguistics (SFL) series – asking him to focus on "identity, instantiation and individuation." Somewhat daunted by the task, Jim approached Michele to join the project, with a view to drawing on her ambient affiliation research; and soon after they drew Yaegan in, to take advantage of his twin training in SFL and Legitimation Code Theory.

Together we decided to work on "motherhood" discourse, which was a growing interest of Michele's at the time. Alongside the sets of web-based data Michele provided, we were of course reminded of Hasan's work on mother-child interaction and drew heavily on the invaluable recordings so generously provided in the *Semantic Variation* volume of her collected papers (Hasan 2009).

As our work progressed, it gradually became clear that we needed to scale down the project, and so we ended up with the current volume – which proposes a new conception of tenor as a resource for enacting social relations. This we came to see as a necessary step towards a more comprehensive social semiotic model addressing instantiation and individuation – one that takes seriously both the social and the semiotic. Full credit to Yaegan for the turn towards tenor as a resource, a turn he had already modelled for us through his work reconceiving field as a resource for construing phenomena.

Perhaps appropriately for our focus on motherhood, our work drew on and took inspiration in particular from a number of our female SFL colleagues, past and present, who have pioneered so much invaluable work. And so for this we thank Margaret Berry, Eija Ventola, Ruqaiya Hasan, Cate Poynton, Suzanne Eggins, Diana Slade, Sue Hood, Maree Stenglin, and Naomi Knight. We offer this monograph on interpersonal meaning as a tribute to their contributions.

Sydney, March 2024

NEGOTIATING SOCIAL RELATIONS

1 Negotiating Social Relations: A Systemic Functional Perspective

1.1 Introduction

Every day we negotiate our social relations. This may involve small, seemingly inconsequential chats with friends, families, and colleagues that help us stay in contact with and possibly get closer to them. Or they may be large, momentous events that bring us together or tear us apart. In all cases, we negotiate these social relations through the discourse we use – through language and a range of related semiotic resources.

In this book we introduce a new model for analysing how people negotiate social relations in discourse. We do so within the general theoretical framework of Systemic Functional Linguistics (SFL) by developing its conception of social context. The particular parameter of context we focus on is what is known in SFL as **tenor**. In SFL, tenor has typically been considered the contextual variable that organizes our social relations – the "roles played by those taking part" in a situation, "the values that the interactants imbue" the activity with (Halliday & Matthiessen, 2014, p. 33), and the relationships between addressees or interactants (Gregory, 1967; Hasan, 2020). Or, more broadly, it comprises the "general dimensions of social relations" (Poynton, 1990a, p. 70) and their negotiation (Martin, 1992, p. 523).

Grasping how we organize our social relations involves understanding how we build the sets of values that guide both our everyday life and the large decisions and communities that shape the way we engage with the world; it involves understanding how we put these values forward and react to them in ways that allow us to come closer together or perhaps to drift apart; it involves understanding how we position ourselves or each other as having control or not over the decisions we are making; and it involves understanding the wide range of nuanced ways in which we can present our meanings as heartfelt and warm or as direct and stern, as highly intense and significant or as tentative and low-stakes, as being for a wide range of people or just a very specific individual. It involves grasping many of the resources we use to go about our lives across a wide range of situations.

Understanding how social relations are enacted is thus crucial to understanding how language is used and how we build our social world itself. Accordingly, scholars in SFL (and related approaches) have worked hard to model tenor for upwards of half a century. However, as we will explain in this chapter, while these efforts have given us great insight into language in relation to its social context, they have often struggled to relate the internal organization of language to parameters proposed for tenor. The model presented in this book is our reconception of tenor as a resource for negotiating social relations. It is a new approach that aims to better link options in tenor to those of language.

In the following section, we introduce in broad terms the model of language and context we use to grasp such wide-ranging meanings taken up in our social world. Then, in Section 1.3, we briefly introduce the new perspective on tenor upon which we will elaborate in the subsequent chapters of this book.

1.2 Language and Social Context

In this book we will treat social context as a semiotic system realized through patterns of language (Figure 1.1). This model conceives of context and language as being intricately related and co-developed, with each continually impacting the other (what Martin [2011], adopting a term suggested by Chris Cléirigh, calls a "supervenient" perspective on social context). Such an approach contrasts with perspectives that treat social context either as an independent phenomenon alongside language (i.e., at best, correlated with language choices but otherwise having no co-genetic relation) or alternatively as a circumvenient phenomenon in which language is in some sense embedded in context but where there is only a one-way determination – so that context determines language choice, but language has no or minimal effect on context. Our project, in other words, involves working towards a model in which social context is realized through recurrent patterns of meaning – where realization involves a two-way process of mutual actualization between language and context. Accordingly, anything we say about social context is an abstraction from recurrent patterns of semantic choice (Martin, 2014) – a relationship Lemke (e.g., 1995) refers to as a metaredundancy.

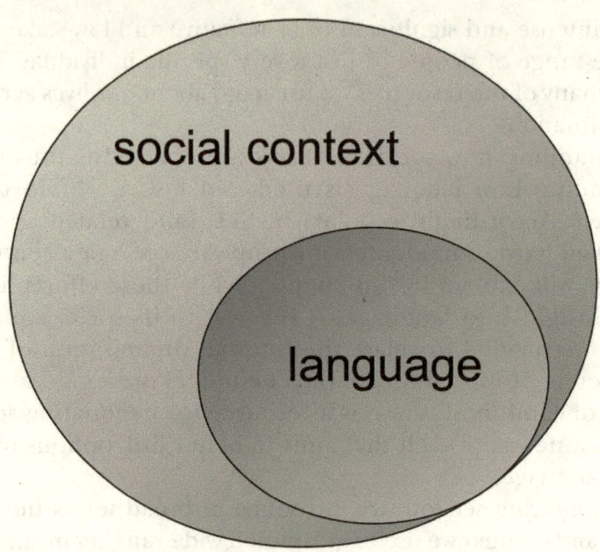

Figure 1.1 Language and social context as supervenient systems

In addition we will treat social context as involving two strata: genre and register. For practical purposes genre can be interpreted as modelling context as a system of staged, goal-oriented social processes realized through register – the latter comprising field, tenor, and mode (Martin, 1992; Martin & Rose, 2008). More technically, genre is a supervenient system realized through choices in register (after Martin, 1984, 1992, 1999, 2014).

Speaking in very general terms, field is concerned with what is going on, tenor addresses who is taking part, and mode deals with the role assigned to language (alongside attendant modalities of communication and behaviour). More specifically, following Halliday and Hasan (1985):

> **Field** is concerned with "what is happening . . . the nature of the social action that is taking place: what is it that the participants are engaged in, in which the language figures as some essential component?"
> **Tenor** addresses "who is taking part, to the nature of the participants, their statuses and roles, including permanent and temporary relationships of one kind or another . . . and the whole cluster of socially significant relationships in which they are involved."
> **Mode** deals with "what part the language is playing . . . including the channel (is it spoken or written or some combination of the two?)." (p. 12)

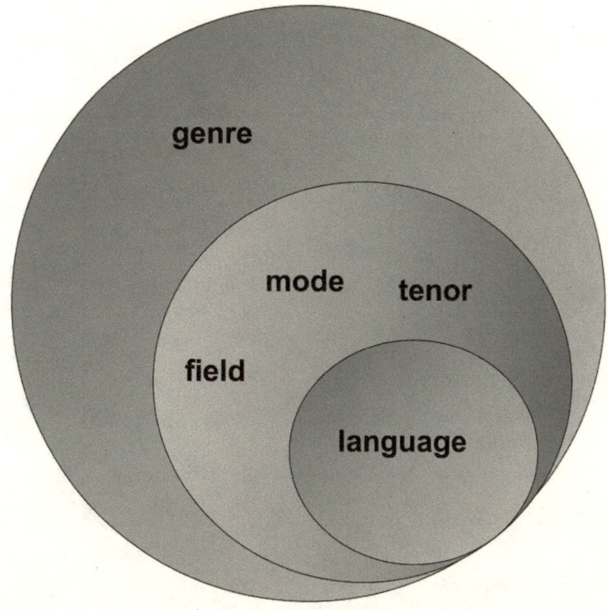

Figure 1.2 Language, register (field, tenor, and mode), and genre

In the model used in this book, *register* is the cover term for the stratum comprising field, tenor, and mode (Figure 1.2). This contrasts with Halliday's use of the term register to refer to the skewing of probabilities in semantic systems inside language by field, tenor, and mode (e.g., Halliday, 1991b, p. 48; 2006). Both concepts – field, tenor, and mode (what in this book we call register), and the language patterns that arise due to specific choices in field, tenor, and mode (what Halliday calls register) – occur within this model. The difference with Halliday in this regard is purely terminological.[1]

For language, this book assumes a model of language comprising the strata of phonology (or graphology for written language or the embodied signing of sign languages), lexicogrammar, and discourse semantics (Figure 1.3). We call the most abstract stratum of language *discourse semantics,* not semantics, to emphasize its orientation to larger text patterns (Martin, 1992; Martin & Rose, 2003/2007); this distinguishes it from the clause semantics of, say, Halliday and Matthiessen (1999) or Hasan (e.g., Hasan et al., 2005). For grammatical analysis of English examples, we rely on Halliday (1985 and subsequent editions); for phonological analysis, we draw on Halliday and Greaves (2008); and for paralanguage (body language, gesture, etc.), we reference Ngo et al. (2022).

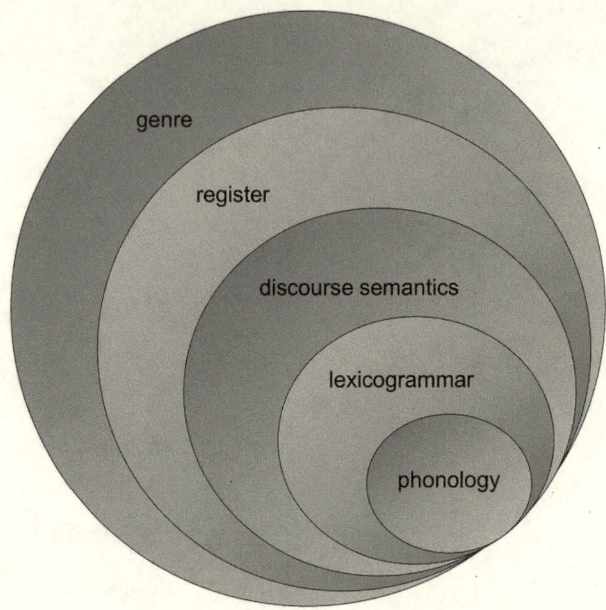

Figure 1.3 Outline of linguistic and contextual strata

The other main dimension of analysis we need to introduce here is metafunction. As developed by Halliday (e.g., 1973, 1978), this dimension refers to the different kinds of meaning that language can make – ideational resources for construing our world, interpersonal resources for enacting social relations, and textual resources for composing information flow (Figure 1.4). More technically, *metafunction* refers to the tendency of linguistic systems to bundle together, with some sets of systems highly interdependent on each other, and others highly independent of each other. For grammar, this is reflected in the fact that sets of options within the ideational system of TRANSITIVITY are relatively interdependent on each other, but they are relatively independent of those within the interpersonal system of MOOD or the textual system of THEME (Martin & Matruglio, 2013/2020; Matthiessen, 1995).

The significance of metafunctionality for this book and for the model of context in SFL in general has to do with their relation with field, tenor, and mode. As explored in Halliday (1978), the metafunctions of language (that we can describe as the "intrinsic" functionality of language) are said to *resonate* with the field, tenor, and mode variables of context (what we can describe as the "extrinsic" functionality of context) – with ideational meaning by and large responsible for construing

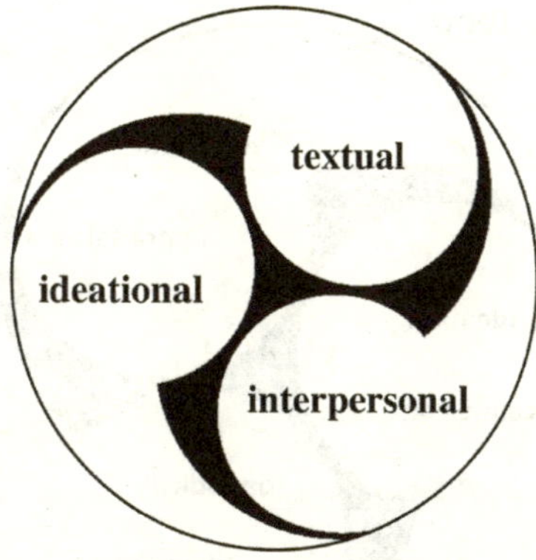

Figure 1.4 Metafunctions – ideational, textual, and interpersonal

field, interpersonal meaning by and large responsible for enacting tenor, and textual meaning by and large responsible for composing mode. This is a powerful claim, which suggests that language is not randomly correlated with context but in fact has evolved in a very definite relation with context, such that its overarching internal organization connects closely with the organization of context. It puts forward a model that suggests the organization of language and of our social system are intimately connected, with each dependent on the other – rather than being just superficially coordinated. Sustaining this resonance between language's intrinsic functionality conceptualized through metafunction and extrinsic functionality conceptualized through register (field, tenor, and mode) is a key motivation for the model of tenor offered in this book.

The model of discourse semantics we assume here is also organized by metafunction (Hao, 2020; Martin, 1992; Martin & Rose, 2003/2007; Martin & White, 2005). As outlined in Figure 1.5, its systems comprise the following: the ideational systems of IDEATION, which map how we construe our experience in terms of the occurrences, states, entities, and qualities of language, and CONNEXION, which articulate how we connect these ideational meanings and stretches of text together into larger sequences of experience or rhetoric; the textual systems of PERIODICITY, which are concerned with how we foreground and background information as waves of prominence, and IDENTIFICATION, which map how we introduce and track people, places, and things; and, most significantly for this book, the interpersonal systems of NEGOTIATION, which present the resources we have for dialogue, and APPRAISAL, which map the resources we have for evaluating, amplifying, and arranging interpersonal meanings. This perspective on discourse semantics has

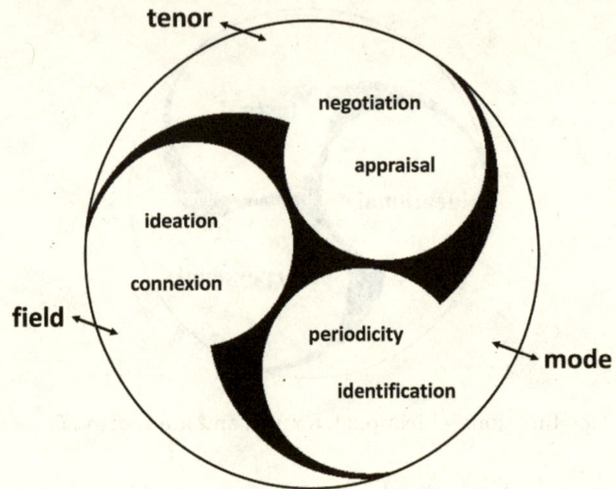

Figure 1.5 Discourse semantic systems and register variables

implications for the way we characterize register variables. For example, for tenor it means that discourse roles such as "questioner, informer, responder, doubter, contradictor and the like," which Halliday (1978, p. 144) locates within tenor as "second order social roles," would be handled as part of language, not register – via the discourse semantic system of NEGOTIATION.

Throughout the history of SFL, a range of scholars have tried to make tenor do a very wide range of things. But with a more elaborated model of language and context that includes discourse semantics, genre, and, as we will discuss in Section 1.3.2, instantiation and individuation, the division of semiotic labour can be more comfortably distributed across the model.

The resonance between discourse semantic systems and register variables is annotated in Figure 1.5 – with field skewing probabilities in the IDEATION and CONNEXION systems, mode skewing probabilities in the PERIODICITY and IDENTIFICATION systems, and tenor skewing probabilities in the NEGOTIATION and APPRAISAL systems.

1.3 Modelling Field, Mode, and Tenor

1.3.1 Classifying Registers

Since Halliday (1978), the basic approach to characterizing context has been that of classifying different fields, modes, and tenors. For example, with respect to field, Halliday notes the fields of personal toilet (p. 64), child at play (p. 115), games (p. 143), and buying and selling newspapers (p. 222) as goings on. With respect to mode, he notes speaking and writing (p. 33), monologue and dialogue (p. 115), and text written to be read aloud (p. 144) to characterize the part language is playing. And for tenor he notes examples "of role relationships, that would be reflected in the language used, are teacher/pupil, parent/child, child/child in peer group, doctor/patient, customer/salesman, casual acquaintances on a train, and so on" (p. 222). We will set aside field and mode at this point and concentrate on the classification of tenors.

Extending this, Eggins and Slade (1997/2004, pp. 52–53) suggest that tenors need to be co-classified along four dimensions:

Status relations (e.g., customer and salesperson)
Affective involvement (e.g., friends and lovers)
Contact (e.g., immediate family and one-off encounters)
Orientation to affiliation (e.g., fellow students and fellow passengers on a bus)

This approach is considerably elaborated by Hasan (2014; 2020, p. 274). Using an example of mother-child discourse, Hasan (2020, p. 294) provides examples of tenor analysis for four major dimensions of co-classification: AGENTIVE ROLE, TEXTUAL ROLE, SOCIAL ROLE, and SOCIAL DISTANCE:

First interactant (child):
AGENTIVE ROLE: care receiver
TEXTUAL ROLE: speaker/addressee present in mss [material situational setting]
SOCIAL ROLE: hierarchic: lower; invisible; offspring; Australian; female; child
Second interactant (mother):
AGENTIVE ROLE: caregiver
TEXTUAL ROLE: speaker/addressee present in mss
SOCIAL ROLE: hierarchic: higher; invisible; mother; Australian; female; mature
SOCIAL DISTANCE: minimal (p. 294)

Poynton (1990a, pp. 64ff) notes that analyses such as this characterize social roles at a range of different levels of abstraction. This analysis, for example, includes quite general categories such as *hierarchic* (*lower* or *higher*), *speaker/addressee present in mss [material situational setting]*, and SOCIAL DISTANCE*: minimal*, which can apply across a wide range of social positions. As we will discuss below, these offer a very useful starting point for understanding how social relations are developed through language. But the description above also includes considerably more specific social positions, such as *mother, child, female, mature,* and so on, that are tied to individual identities. As Poynton notes, these latter categories cannot easily be pinned down to specific patterns of realization through choices in language but rather encapsulate a wide range of possible strategies as to how they can "present" themselves in relation to these social positions. Using Poynton's example (1990a) as an illustration:

> A young male student wanting special consideration may attempt to charm an older female lecturer ('superior' with respect to two dimensions: generation and institutional standing), in an attempt to reconstitute the situation in purely gender terms, either as a (hetero)sexual game intended to put the lecturer in the weaker position (males conventionally being the ones who charm females into giving them what they want) or to recast the generational and status differences into the more familiar (and more manipulable) relational type of mother-son. A woman in such a situation can respond in various ways to such an attempt to constitute the situation in terms more likely to have a favourable outcome for the student. She can simply respond as a female to a male being charming; she can respond to the charm but let him know that she understands the game he's playing. Or she can refuse to participate in such a game and insisting on playing the encounter as one between institutional superior and subordinate. The way an individual lecturer negotiates such a situation is not predetermined in any simple sense by any particular aspect of their social identity, and certainly not by any assumption that she will simply step into the speaking position made available as a function of that adopted by the student. (p. 62)

Poynton's final note that the way a person "negotiates . . . a situation is not predetermined in any simple sense by any particular aspect of their social identity" (p. 62) is of particular importance. It suggests that we should be wary of descriptive models that take demographic categories such as *male, female, mother, daughter,* and the like as given and as being unproblematically linked to patterns in language.

At this point it is important to stop and ask where categories used to classify tenor relations such as this come from. It is not clear, for example, whether the categories arise from patterns in language. Neither is it clear how these categories can be clearly linked with choices in language – this is especially the case if we wish to keep some link between interpersonal systems and tenor. We can ask, for example, what interpersonal systems of language realize the category *female* or *offspring*.[2]

The distinctions also do not appear to be drawn from sociology – from, for example, the work of either Bernstein (e.g., 1996/2000) or Maton (2014), the two sociologists with whom SFL linguists have most closely collaborated.[3] Indeed Maton's work in particular has revealed major issues that arise when trying to classify aspects of social relations as distinct "types." Nor is it apparent that other academic disciplines have been brought to bear. One is left with the feeling that the demographic categories used to classify tenor relations are in fact simply drawing upon everyday commonsense understandings of social roles and relationships. Considering the enormously multifaceted and continually evolving nature of social identities and social relationships, such commonsense distinctions cannot offer a firm basis for a rich understanding of social reality. From a more pragmatic point of view, without there being any explicit links with language, it is difficult to see how any one classification can be motivated as more insightful than another. And it is hard to see where the proliferation of categories for classifying tenors might end. If we want a model of social semiosis that can show how language shapes and is shaped by context (and vice versa), we need something that can show the relation between them.

Accordingly, in this book we will take a different tack and think about how field, tenor, and mode can be characterized as **resources** for construing phenomena, enacting social relations, and composing information flow. In the next section, we review the work that has built up to this complementary perspective.

1.3.2 Patterns of Usage

As noted above we are treating register and genre (and thus tenor) as supervenient systems realized through recurrent patterns of meaning. The tenor specialist whose work most strongly reflects this orientation is Poynton (1984, 1985/1989, 1990a, 1996). In her PhD thesis (1990a) in particular, Poynton makes it clear that her model of tenor is based on patterns of realization in language. She refers to these patterns as reciprocity, proliferation, and amplification.

Considered in terms of the relative status between people, *reciprocity* refers to the tendency for people with equal status to take up the same kind of linguistic choices and for those with unequal status to draw on different ones (influenced by Brown & Gilman's [1960] canonical study of pronouns). Poynton's research focuses on naming and highlights the contrast between reciprocal usage (e.g., both using first names: *Kate* and *Gunther*) by those of similar status and non-reciprocal usage (e.g., one using a title + surname and the other using a first name: *Dr. Smith* and

Gunther) by those of different status. In terms of the relative social distance between people, *proliferation* refers to the tendency for people who know each other better to take up a wider range of choices (e.g., the names that a distant work acquaintance may use for one of the authors, e.g., *Yaegan Doran, Y.J. Doran,* and *Associate Professor Doran,* vs. the names his mother uses for him, e.g., *Yaegan, Yaegan John, Yaegan John Doran, Yaeg, Yaegy J, Yaegy JJ, Yaegy JJJ, Yaegy JJJJJ, B, BB, my B,* and *my BBBBB*) – with all the nuance in warmth or warning that each choice entails. Poynton also notes the concomitant tendency to prefer more contracted realizations (e.g., *Kat* vs. *Dr. Katherine Smith*) the more contact we have with one another. *Amplification* in turn refers to the tendency for interlocutors to ramp up or tone down degrees of positive or negative feeling (e.g., "You can be a bit of a bastard sometimes" vs. "You dirty rotten bastard"). In the case of naming, an example such as *Yaegy JJJJJ* contracts in terms of the truncated personal name *Yaeg,* highlighting the closeness, and then amplifies this with a diminutive suffix (*-y*) combined with a repeated initial (*JJJJJ*), thereby amplifying the warmth intended by the naming. In terms of status, while the author's mother has this wide range of names for him, his lower status means he would not be able to fully reciprocate with the same range: He cannot say the equivalent, *Susie QQQQQ* – it's just *Mum* with some small variations.

Based on these patterns of realization, Poynton recognizes three dimensions of tenor – POWER (realized by reciprocity of choice), DISTANCE (realized by proliferation of choice), and AFFECT (realized by amplification).[4] Her model is outlined in Figure 1.6; the slanted square brackets therein signal clined systems (e.g., POWER as more or less equal).[5]

Martin (1992) basically adopts this model of tenor based on realization principles, albeit with some changes to terminology (substituting STATUS for Poynton's power and CONTACT for her distance). But the later development of the APPRAISAL system in discourse semantics (Martin, 2000a; Martin & White, 2005) meant that Poynton's AFFECT was moved out of tenor to discourse semantics in language. The main reason for this was the influence that the principles of reciprocity as well as proliferation or contraction have on choices in APPRAISAL systems – a pattern of interaction that is more associated with stratified systems than with simultaneous systems in SFL (Martin & White, 2005, pp. 31–32).

To understand the complementary relation between Poynton's model and the model being presented in this book, we can turn to recent developments in field and mode. In recent years, Martin (Martin, 2017; Martin & Matruglio, 2013/2020; Martin & Unsworth, 2024) has revisited the register variables classifying modes and fields from the perspective

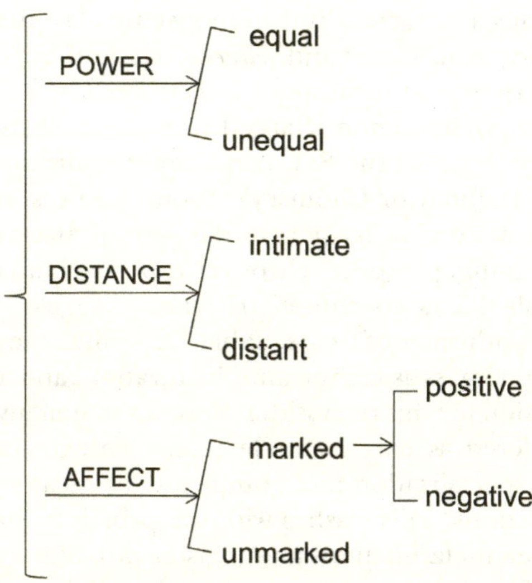

Figure 1.6 Poynton's (1990a) model of tenor relations

of metafunctions (i.e., ideational, interpersonal, and textual meaning). Influenced by Maton's (2014) concepts of semantic gravity and semantic density, he suggests that types of mode and field can in fact be associated with syndromes of choices from across all three metafunctions. For mode, from the perspective of textual meaning, the key variable is implicitness (e.g., to what extent does a text depend on reference to the physical situation?). From the perspective of interpersonal meaning, the key variable is negotiability (e.g., to what extent does a text engage people in the "to and fro" of dialogue, including the amount of emotion expressed?). From the perspective of ideational meaning, the key variable is iconicity (e.g., to what extent does a text unfold by mirroring what it is talking about?). Martin and Matruglio (2013/2020) suggest *presence* as a cover term for these syndromes of usage. Table 1.1 summarizes this metafunctional factoring of presence in language as implicitness, negotiability, and iconicity.

For field, from the perspective of ideational meaning, the key variable is technicality – in other words, to what extent is meaning distilled

Table 1.1 Types of Presence

Metafunction	Type of Presence
Textual	Implicitness
Interpersonal	Negotiability
Ideational	Iconicity

as technical terms arranged as uncommonsense classification, composition, and activity (e.g., *canine* and *feline* vs. *dog* and *cat*)? From the perspective of interpersonal meaning, the key variable is iconization – to what extent is a phenomenon charged with values shared by members of a community (e.g., for the SFL community, contrasting reactions to figures such as Halliday or Chomsky)? From the perspective of textual meaning, the key variable is aggregation – to what extent does a text consolidate meaning, prospectively or retrospectively, as it unfolds (e.g., the title of Table 1.2 vs. its contents)? Martin suggests *mass* as a cover term for these syndromes of usage. Table 1.2 summarizes this metafunctional factoring of mass as technicality, iconization, and aggregation.

A key motivation for this reconsideration was that many of the features typically considered as part of mode (e.g., context dependency) and field (e.g., the specialization and complexity of meaning) are realized across metafunctions. This clashes with the principle that there should be a link between metafunctions and register variables – field tending to be realized by ideational meaning and mode tending to be realized by textual meaning. The conceptualization of mass and presence as trans-metafunctional concepts allows for field and mode to be reconfigured in a way that maintains this register and metafunction hook-up (for what this looks like for field, see Doran & Martin, 2021).

Poynton's reciprocity as well as proliferation or contraction can be interpreted as comparable syndromes of usage in this regard, ranging across metafunctions. Indeed this is briefly suggested in Martin (1992), where he suggests *prominence* could be used as the cover term for differences in status with respect to mode, and *authority* for differences with respect to field (in addition to *control* for comparable patterns of genre), alongside *status* for tenor – though as far as we are aware, this suggestion has not been taken up. Although in his tables for these principles (Tables 7.10 and 7.12), Martin concentrates on interpersonal meanings (e.g., differential use of MOOD types, Vocatives, and exchange roles), the use or not of specialized and technical lexis (an ideational feature) is noted as an example of contraction. Such ideational features could just as well have been used as an example of reciprocity (for which variable ideational considerations such as agency and the source of projection

Table 1.2 Types of Mass

Metafunction	**Type of Mass**
Ideational	Technicality
Interpersonal	Iconization
Textual	Aggregation

could also have been brought into the picture). To illustrate this point, in an academic discipline, one aspect of both having higher status and speaking to someone else within your discipline (closer contact) is being able to use technical terminology in an appropriate manner – something that is not necessarily done by students of lower status, nor when speaking to someone from outside the academic discipline (more distant contact). So ideational meaning clearly has a role to play.

Similarly for textual meaning, Martin (1992, pp. 529–532) lists the textual features of marked tonality, marked tonicity, and homophoric reference as examples in the table for proliferation and contraction. And considerations such as who initiates identity chains or who manages higher level *Theme* and *New* could well have been included as enacting reciprocity. To clarify this point, if people are closer, they will tend to be able to refer to entities through shared knowledge (homophora) rather than having to introduce them; and if someone has higher status in a situation, they will often have control of having the first or last word on a topic (control of the *HyperTheme* and *HyperNews*) and can shift focus more comfortably (initiating and shifting identity chains). We won't attempt a more detailed discussion of metafunctional diversification and Poynton's principles here. Suffice it to say that it is very difficult to restrict these patterns of usage to interpersonal meanings alone. So, alongside mass and presence, Doran et al. (2024) suggest the cover term *association* to manage the metafunctional distribution of all the status and contact (reciprocity and proliferation–contraction) patterns in play.

What does this say about the resonance between register variables and metafunctions outlined in Figure 1.5? Part of the answer has to do with the distinction between realization and instantiation in SFL theory. Realization is a hierarchy of abstraction, with higher strata realized by patterns of meaning at lower ones. Instantiation, on the other hand, is a cline of generality, with higher rungs constituting a larger meaning potential than lower ones (a system-to-text relation). The realization hierarchy we assume here was outlined in Figure 1.3 (with genre as a more abstract pattern of register patterns, register as a more abstract pattern of discourse semantic patterns, etc.). This can be contrasted with the version of the instantiation cline presented as Figure 1.7 (cf. Martin, 2010, 2014). There, moving down from system, we have a cline of sub-potentialization (system, diatype, text type, and text); moving up, we have a concomitant cline of generalization (text, text type, diatype, and system).

Instantiation is typically considered in terms of the coupling of choices as conditioned by varying probabilities in different texts, text types, and diatypes. But recognizing the concepts of mass, presence, and association (i.e., status and contact) as metafunctionally diversified syndromes

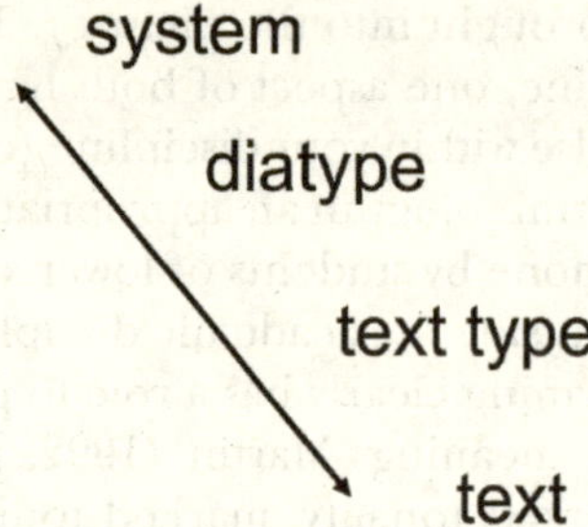

Figure 1.7 Hierarchy of instantiation

of choice offers a perspective on instantiation that can help explain why certain choices co-occur in certain situations. That is, mass, presence, and association can be considered principles of instantiation – principles underpinning the co-selection and arrangement of features across strata and metafunctions. This can help us move away from relatively ad hoc explanations as to why particular choices are taken up in particular texts or situations, and move us into considering different texts and the various domains they enter into in terms of a multidimensional set of principles. For example, scientific writing tends to involve significant interlocking networks of activity, taxonomy, and property, but relatively little evaluative language in comparison to other disciplines (e.g., Halliday & Martin, 1993). We could explain this in terms of science's aim for very strong ideational mass (technicality) but relatively weak interpersonal mass (iconization). We could also describe the fact that it regularly aims to link theory to data as illustrating a wide range of ideational presence (iconicity).

Reconsidering context in this way, in turn, opens up the possibility of reconceiving (from the perspective of instantiation) the *types* of field classifications pursued by previous models as syndromes of technicality, iconization, and aggregation (mass); of reconceiving types of mode as syndromes of implicitness, negotiability, and iconicity (presence); and of reconceiving types of tenor as syndromes of reciprocity and proliferation (association). And this, in turn, opens up the possibility of abandoning the classificatory approach to modelling field, tenor, and mode along the realization hierarchy – and replacing it with a social semiotic perspective on register variables as resources for construing phenomena (field), enacting social relations (tenor), and composing information flow (mode). Developing SFL along these lines, in turn, opens up the possibility of reconfirming the resonance between field, tenor, and mode and metafunctions that is put at risk by research dedicated to classifying fields, tenor, and modes in relatively commonsense terms.

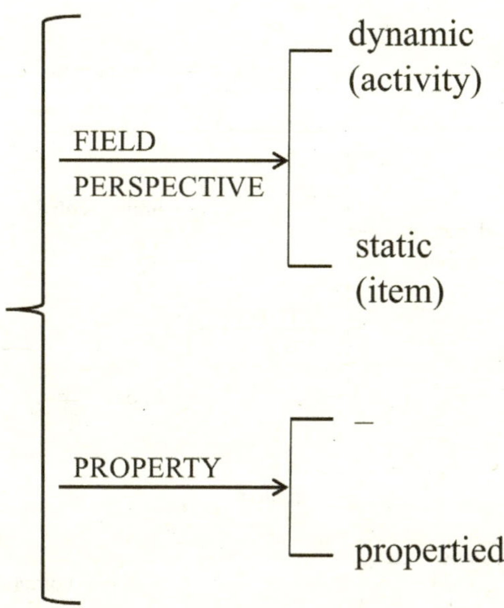

Figure 1.8 Major field systems[6]

This latter possibility of considering register variables as resources for meaning has recently been developed in Doran and Martin (2021) for field. In that model, field is mapped as a resource for construing phenomena – either statically as a set of relations between items, or dynamically as sets of activities and their moments, alongside their associated properties. These general systems are outlined in Figure 1.8. From a dynamic perspective, phenomena can be construed as goings on (e.g., *player serving* ^ *player volleying* ^ *point ends*); from a static perspective, phenomena are construed as things (e.g., a *point, game, match, player, umpire, ball,* and *racquet*). And either goings on or items can be propertied (e.g., *serve* ***hard*** and ***quick*** *game*).

For both the dynamic and static perspectives, there are further options in play (Figure 1.9). An activity can be presented as a single event (an *unmomented activity*, e.g., *Alcaraz won the match*), or it can be divided into moments of that activity (a *momented activity*, e.g., *Alcaraz won the first set, Ruud won the second, then Alcaraz won the third and also won the fourth*). If momented, the relationship can be one of implication where the unfolding activities are related by contingency where one necessarily follows another (e.g., *Djokovic hit the line judge with the ball between points and so was automatically defaulted*); alternatively they can be related by expectancy, where the unfolding is not born of necessity but

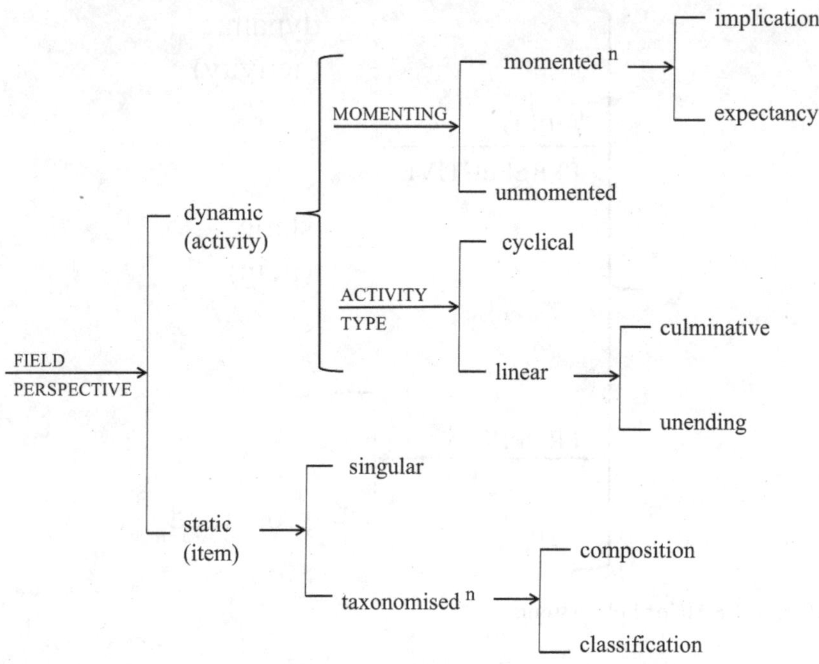

Figure 1.9 More delicate activity and item systems

is probabilistic or expectant (as in the 2022 US Open final example above, *Alcaraz won the first set, Ruud won the second, then Alcaraz won the third and also won the fourth*). For all these possibilities, there is also the option of construing an activity as cyclical (e.g., *Players play the Australian Open, then the French Open, then Wimbledon, then the US Open, before again playing the Australian Open*); or the activity can be linear, and if linear then culminative (e.g., *The serve hit the back wall*) or unending (e.g., *Tennis is played around the world*). Turning to a static perspective, an item can be noted individually (e.g., *ace*) or can be taxonomized via classification (e.g., *His second* ***serve*** *was an* ***ace***) or composition (e.g., *My first* ***racquet*** *was made of* ***wood*** *and* ***natural gut***).

Turning to properties, these can be qualitative (e.g., *He served* ***fast***) or spatiotemporal (e.g., *He served* ***to his opponent's backhand***). There is also the option of arraying properties (e.g., *He served* ***faster*** *in the first set*) and, if arrayed, then gauged (e.g., *He served on average* ***at 137 km/h***). These choices are outlined in Figure 1.10.

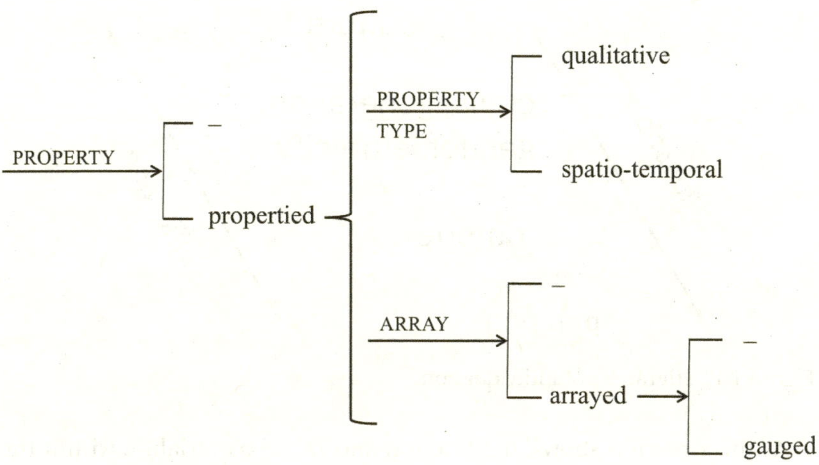

Figure 1.10 More delicate property systems

So instead of classifying fields as, say, horizontal or vertical; or as singulars or regions (as in Bernstein, 1996/2000); or as science, social science, or humanities (e.g., Martin, 1992, 2007a, 2007b); or as "personal toilet" or "games" (Halliday, 1978), field can be reconstrued as a resource for construing phenomena. These resources can then be tuned in to relevant ideational systems in language (across strata) as far as realization is concerned, and the results coupled with interpersonal and/or textual meanings as required from the perspective of instantiation (i.e., mass).[7]

Looking further afield this puts SFL in a stronger position to develop its third hierarchy, individuation (Martin, 2008a, 2008b, 2010, 2012; Zappavigna & Martin, 2018a, 2018b). A rough outline of the communion at stake is presented in Figure 1.11 as a scale of belonging. This time around we are looking at the relation of a culture to the personae who member it – in terms of the way semiotic resources are allocated to personae and the way they use these resources to affiliate along a cline ranging through smaller coteries of shared values and on to large ones engendered by bonds associated with what we think of as class, generation, gender, and ethnicity. Here we can consider how choices in the realization hierarchy and principles of instantiation are distributed across different communities, social fields of practice, and channels of communication, as well as how they are used to create, maintain, collaborate within, and struggle over these communities, social fields of practice, and channels of communication.

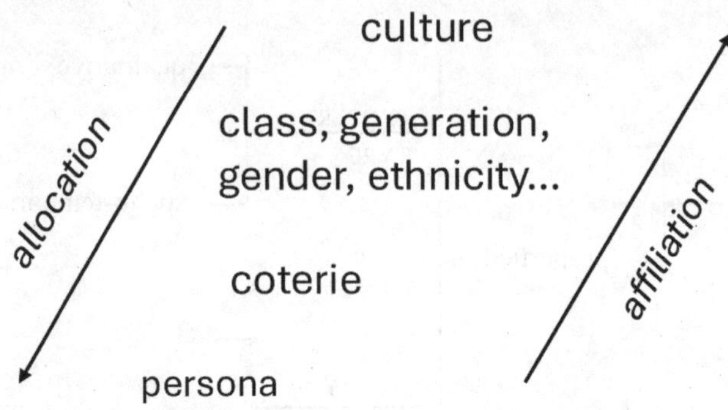

Figure 1.11 Hierarchy of individuation

As this overview shows, field, tenor, and mode as variables within the realization hierarchy are not the be-all and end-all of our view of social context. To take seriously the integration of semiosis and society, we need a much richer model. Our ultimate aim in this book is to develop a model of tenor (realization) that accounts for the contribution that interpersonal meaning makes to negotiating association (instantiation) by way of membering communities in culture (individuation) – so that we can move towards comprehensively appreciating the interaction of the social and the semiotic.

1.4 Tenor as a Resource

How, then, can we remodel tenor as a resource for enacting social relations? We can first look at how we put forward meanings and share them with others. In this book, we will suggest that a basic distinction in how we enact social relations is between resources for *tendering* meanings to be engaged with, and reacting to or *rendering* meanings that have been put forward. In Example (1.1) from a YouTube video, a six-year-old girl tries to convince her mother to take her to the pub. After her mother asks her, *What are you on about Jodie?*,[8] Jodie tenders a proposal about going to the pub, which is then rendered by her mother in terms of a rejection. An arrow indicates the direction of the rendering.

(1.1)	Jodie:	Going to the pub with Daddy, go and see Lauren and Leanne. Please!	tender
			↑
	Mother:	You're not going to the pub.	render: reject

When Jodie asks why, her mother explains that she cannot go to the pub because she is a child. In contrast to the first example, Jodie initially supports this statement, before trying another tack and tendering another position:

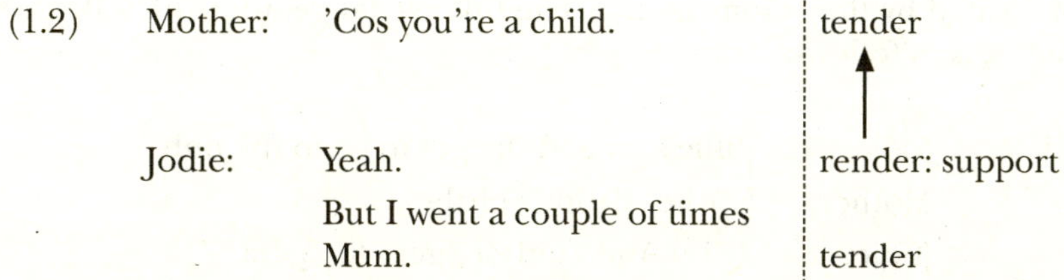

As we will see, in conversation it is relatively standard to both render something that has been said before and tender a new position at the same time (what Eggins [1990, p. 271] calls a "Janus" move). Jodie does this after her mother reiterates that she cannot go to the pub because she is little. Jodie retorts, *I'm six!* This both rejects the idea that she is little (because, after all, a six-year-old does not consider themselves little) and tenders that this is because she is six:

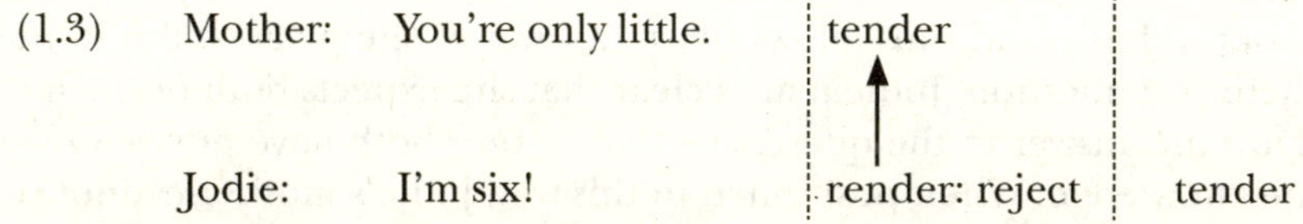

How we put forward positions and react to them is described in Chapters 2 and 3 within a system called POSITIONING. Chapter 2 focuses on resources for rendering meanings, and Chapter 3 focuses on resources for tendering. When we tender meanings, we will describe different ways in which we can position others to respond. For example, when Jodie's mother asks at the beginning of the conversation, *What are you on about Jodie?*, she asks this as a genuine question. With this question she positions Jodie as the one who has the knowledge for this exchange. By contrast, later on in the conversation, Jodie notes that her not being allowed to go to the pub contrasts with her friend Billie, who is also six, getting to go to the pub. Her mother notes that this is because it was her daddy's birthday. But Jodie is not convinced and insists by saying, *And did I get to go?* Although this is a question and grammatically an interrogative, Jodie is not genuinely asking for information – both Jodie and her mother know full well that she was not allowed to go to the pub. Rather, Jodie is using this to emphasize her point that she thinks there is a double standard at play. She indicates this by enunciating each word on its own beat (shown by each word bracketed by "/" in Example [1.4]), using a falling tone 1 (in contrast to the typical rising tone 2 of a question), and significantly lengthening the final *go* (indicated by the colons: *go:::*).[9] The full exchange, with the follow-up moves, is as follows:

(1.4)	Jodie:	Billie's six and she got to go to the pub.
	Mother:	For her daddy's birthday.
	Jodie:	//1 ^ And /did /I /get /to /**go:::**//
	Mother:	No.
	Jodie:	Well then, [CLAP] why do I not get to go to the Thatch?

In Chapter 3 we will describe the difference between the genuine question of *What are you on about Jodie?* and the rhetorical question of *And did I get to go?* in terms of a difference in *purview* that Jodie and her mother have over the knowledge. In the genuine question, Jodie's mother gives purview over the knowledge about what Jodie's talking about to Jodie and thus allows her to answer as she pleases. But in the rhetorical question, Jodie makes clear that she expects both of them to know the answer to the question – that is, they both have purview over the knowledge. When positioned in this way, Jodie's mother cannot really give an answer other than the one that is expected, because Jodie has positioned them both to agree. In Chapter 3, we will illustrate that we are regularly nuancing purview in this way to help position others to respond in particular ways. We will show that it is a rich resource for enacting social relations in terms of nuancing interpersonal control and responsibility.

POSITIONING and PURVIEW form the core of the tenor resources we will present in this book. Importantly, they are not just resources of dialogue but resources of monologue as well. This typically draws on resources of evaluative language, which in SFL are described in terms of ATTITUDE and ENGAGEMENT (Martin & White, 2005). This is illustrated by the following text, a paragraph from an opinion piece about the overturning of *Roe* v. *Wade* in the United States, upending rights to abortion across the country (Donegan, 2022). In this article, the author argues against the framing of this change as primarily being about the crumbling American institutions it reflects. Rather, following this excerpt, she argues that the real story is the effects it will have on everyday women. To make this argument, the author regularly renders support or rejection for different positions and different institutions. In the following excerpt, the positions and items being rendered (supported or rejected) are underlined, and the resources that render them are in italics for support and bold for rejection.

> The story is **not** about the supreme court. Today, **the sword that has long been hanging over American women's heads** finally fell: the supreme court overturned Roe v Wade, ending the nationwide right to an abortion. This has long been expected, and long **dreaded**, by those in the reproductive rights movement, and it has long been **denied** by those who wished to downplay the court's **extremist** lurch. The coming hours will be consumed with finger pointing and recriminations. But the story is **not** about who was *right* and who was **wrong**. (Donegan, 2022; emphasis added)

Through this excerpt, the author renders two broad things: the US Supreme Court decision overturning abortion rights in the United States and the framing of the story as being about the Supreme Court and related issues. The author's rejection of the Supreme Court decision primarily occurs through evaluative language resources called ATTITUDE (Martin & White, 2005). This includes the direct evaluative language of *dreaded* and *extremist,* as well as implied evaluative language through the metaphor *the sword that has long been hanging over American women's heads finally fell.* By contrast, the rejection of the framing of the story as being centred on the Supreme Court and the larger debate about abortion rights is developed through resources of ENGAGEMENT. More specifically, it is developed through negation: *The story is* ***not*** *about the supreme court* and *the story is* ***not*** *about who was right and who was wrong.* Throughout the opinion piece, the author puts forward and negotiates positions that were central to both the emerging story of the Supreme Court position and the larger history of abortion rights in the United States. She does this using a voice of expertise, with all of her statements being definitive with little room given to others to make up their own mind (i.e., she holds purview over these positions herself). We will see throughout this book that resources of tendering, rendering, and purview such as this are vital to how we negotiate the range of values that underpin our social world and the people who are associated with them.

This text also highlights that the meanings we put forward are not isolated positions that are negotiated separately. Rather, we are always speaking in relation to sets of background values that organize our points of view and how we react to things. In Chapter 4 we will illustrate how these values are built through a system called ORIENTING. In the opinion piece above, for example, whenever the author says what the story is *not*, she is putting forward two opposed positions so as to reject one of them. For example, when the author says, *The story is not about the supreme court*, she is opposing this to a possible position that the story *is* about the Supreme Court. In addition, the author attributes opposed positions to different groups of people, and in doing so, sets up different communities that she is engaging with: *This has long been expected, and long dreaded, by those in the reproductive rights movement, and it has long been denied by those who wished to downplay the court's extremist lurch; the story is not about who was right and who was wrong.* (Donegan, 2022; underlining added). The play of voices such as shown in this text has long been acknowledged within the APPRAISAL framework, through resources of ENGAGEMENT (Martin & White, 2005; White, 2003). But in Chapter 4, we will show that ENGAGEMENT works with a range of other resources, including CONNEXION and ATTITUDE and a wide range of paralinguistic resources, to build vast networks of values that can encapsulate significantly disparate realms of experience. In another paragraph of this opinion piece, for example, the author argues what the story is in fact about – it is about women. She uses this general statement to encapsulate a wide range of experiences women have in relation to pregnancy and abortion, such as the cancellation of abortion appointments, the financial implications of booking interstate appointments, the exhaustion of abortion providers, and the decisions that will be forced upon women and mothers. For the purposes of the opinion piece, all of these experiences are likened together as illustrating the same broad negative effect of the *Roe* v. *Wade* announcement:

> The real story is the women. The real story is the student whose appointment is scheduled for tomorrow, who will get a call from the clinic sometime in the next hours telling her that no, they are sorry, they cannot give her an abortion after all. The real story is the woman waiting tables, who feels so sick and exhausted these past few weeks that she can barely make it through her shifts, who will soon be calling clinics in other states, hearing that they're all booked for weeks, and will be asking friends for money to help cover the gas, or the plane, or the time off that she can't afford. The real story is the abortion provider, already exhausted and heartbroken from years of politicians playing politics with her patients' rights, who will wonder whether she can keep her clinic open for its other services any more, and conclude that she can't. The real story is the mom of two, squinting at her phone as she tries to comfort a screaming toddler, trying to figure out

what she will have to give up in order to keep living the life she wants, with the family she already has. (Donegan, 2022)

By relating these experiences together, the author reinforces a larger set of values that she aligns with regarding the real-world impacts on women of a lack of access to abortion services. In Chapter 4 we will show that building networks of values by likening and opposing experiences, sourcing them to different groups of people, and encapsulating these in generalized stances is a fundamental way in which we negotiate our social world.

Finally, this text illustrates the last set of resources we explore in this book. These are associated with a system we will call in Chapter 5 TUNING. Resources of TUNING concern how we adjust our meanings interpersonally: how we raise or lower the *stakes* of what is being said, how we broaden or narrow the *scope* of who the meanings relate to, and how we temper the *spirit* in which the meanings are being put forward. In this text, the author works hard to raise the stakes of what she is talking about by highlighting the massive significance and risk that this decision has produced. She does this primarily through resources of GRADUATION in discourse semantics: by upscaling her evaluations – *so sick and exhausted, a screaming toddler, long dreaded, extremist lurch, consumed with finger pointing and recriminations* – and by adding more and more examples – the student whose appointment will be cancelled, the woman who cannot afford interstate travel, the mother who needs to give up her way of life in order to have another child, and many more through the rest of the opinion piece. This repetition of examples also widens its scope: The values and renderings set up do not just orient to a small group of people, but are wide-ranging and all-consuming. And finally, the spirit in which this is written is serious – a warning. There is little sense of jovial light-heartedness that can be laughed off and taken with a smile. This opinion piece makes clear that what she is talking about is significant, wide-ranging, and grave. How we nuance our meanings to make clear the scope, spirit, and stakes of what we are saying is a vital part of how we engage with other people.

This book focuses on the resources we use to enact our social relations. It explores how we put meanings forward and react to them, it maps how we build vast networks of values that help us align or disalign with things and people, and it describes how we adjust all of these meanings so as to make clear how we feel about them. In short, it describes how we engage with the world interpersonally, and offers tools for being able to see this. An overview of the key systems that we will explore in this book is given in Figure 1.12.

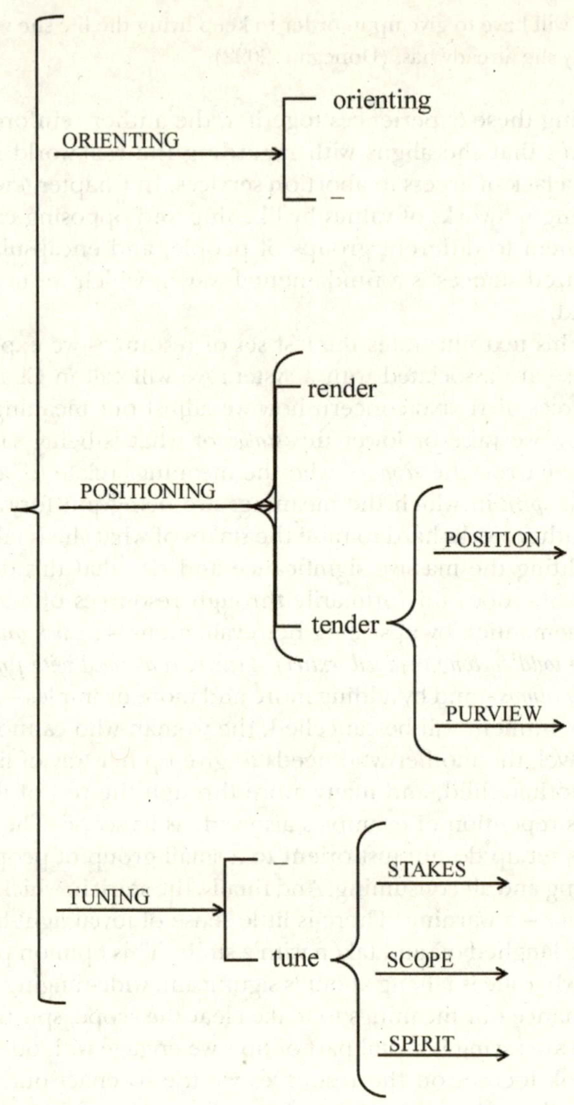

Figure 1.12 Key Systems of Tenor

1.5 Chapter Outline

Chapter 1 has surveyed SFL work on tenor, reviewing the model of language and social context assumed in this study and introducing in general terms the approach to modelling tenor as a resource for negotiating social relations we will outline in this book.

Chapters 2 and 3 spell out our approach to POSITIONING, as speakers tender and render propositions and proposals, negotiating as they do so the fine-grained roles of responsibility and control assigned by initiating and responding to moves.

Chapter 4 deals with points of view, showing how ORIENTING systems build networks of shared values and source stances to communing stakeholders. Then in Chapter 5 we consider how TUNING systems adjust the stakes, scope, and spirit of the meanings being negotiated.

Finally in Chapter 6 we address the implications of our proposals as far as research on tenor is concerned – looking up to considerations of genre; looking around to field and mode; below to realizations in lexicogrammar, phonology and graphology, and paralanguage; and across to the hierarchies of instantiation and individuation.

Throughout these chapters the thematic focus of our data is motherhood, as we canvass glimpses of the wide range of things it means to mother offspring – among all the other roles that women assume (with apologies to the related kith and kin who parent younger generations and care for elder ones).

While ours is a new approach to tenor, our sincere hope is that it can be read as a respectful one – making room across hierarchies for development of all the work on social relations that has been done. So thanks to our mentors; and our very best wishes to researchers building on the framework proposed here.

1.6 Resource Guide

As will be clear from this introduction, tenor is one module in the overall model of language and social context assumed here. Because of its position in the architecture of SFL (between genre and language and alongside field and mode), we draw on a wide range of descriptions of English – some of which may not be familiar to readers. Below we note some useful introductory resources for key descriptions, as well as the key reference books for each area.

1.6.1 Paralanguage

Martin, J.R., & Zappavigna, M. (2019). Embodied meaning: A systemic functional perspective on body language. *Functional Linguistics,* 6(1). https://doi.org/10.1186/s40554-018-0065-9.

Ngo, T., Hood, S., Martin, J.R., Painter, C., Smith B.A., & Zappavigna, M. (2022). *Modelling paralanguage using systemic functional semiotics.* Bloomsbury.

1.6.2 Intonation and Rhythm

Chapter 3 of Ngo, T., Hood, S., Martin, J.R., Painter, C., Smith B.A., & Zappavigna, M. (2022). *Modelling paralanguage using systemic functional semiotics.* Bloomsbury.

Albrow, K. (1968). *The rhythm and intonation of spoken English* (Program in Linguistics and English Teaching Paper 9). Longman.[10]

Halliday, M.A.K., & Greaves, W. S. (2008). *Intonation in the grammar of English.* Equinox.

1.6.3 Halliday's Functional Grammar

Halliday, M.A.K., & Matthiessen, C.M.I.M. (2014). *Halliday's introduction to functional grammar.* Routledge.

Thompson, G. (2013). *Introducing functional grammar* (3rd ed.). Routledge.

1.6.4 Discourse Semantics

Chapters 2 (appraisal) and 7 (negotiation) of Martin, J.R., & Rose, D. (2007). *Working with discourse: Meaning beyond the clause.* Continuum.

Martin, J.R. (1992). *English text: System and structure.* John Benjamins.

Martin, J.R., & White, P.R.R. (2005). *The language of evaluation: Appraisal in English.* Palgrave Macmillan.

1.6.5 Context

Halliday, M.A.K., & Hasan, R. (1989). *Language, context and text.* Oxford University Press.

Martin, J.R. (2010). Language, register and genre. In C. Coffin, T. Lillis, & K. O'Halloran (Eds.), *Applied linguistics methods: A reader* (pp. 12–32). Routledge.

Martin, J.R., & Rose, D. (2008). *Genre relations: Mapping culture.* Equinox.

2 Negotiating Tenor: Rendering Meaning in Dialogue and Monologue

2.1 Introduction

Talking with people helps us grow closer to them – it helps us share our feelings, check in with people, get them to do things for us, and learn from them. Talking with people also helps us push them away – to reject people's offers, to express our anger and frustration, and to insult and dominate people. Put in general terms, talking with people allows us to negotiate our social relations and develop our joint engagement with the world.

This negotiation happens in all texts and all situations. But it is most overt in conversation. In the following text (Text 2.1), taken from Hasan's work on interaction between mothers and children (Hasan, 2009), Kristy, who is yet to go to school, and Ruth, her toddler sister, are being dressed by their mother. As she is being dressed, Kristy tries to convince her mother that she shouldn't have to go out today. Kristy brings all her negotiatory and emotional resources to the task and semiotically engages her mother from all directions – by reasoning, by offering alternatives, and, most forcefully, by crying. Her mother, clearly skilled in negotiating Kristy's whims, is not convinced and successfully brings Kristy round. She does this by empathizing with her daughter while at the same time carefully massaging her proposals to lead Kristy towards the goal of getting dressed and going out.

Kristy opens by proposing that she fold some cardboard before her mother alternatively suggests that she get dressed – a suggestion that provokes tears.[1]

Kristy: what about I fold the cardboard
and then if I want some pieces um –
Mother: well how about I get you dressed instead
Kristy: no
don't want to go out today [CRYING]
Mother: you'll have a lovely day pet
I won't be home late either
I'll probably be home about the same time as Dee's big kids get home . . . maybe a little bit later, maybe a little bit earlier
oh dear oh dear . . . I don't think you're really upset about me going
[AS KRISTY CONTINUES CRYING] I think you're upset
because the TV wasn't working
Ruth wants to go on the potty [AS RUTH CALLS]
Kristy: [CRYING] I don't want to go away
Mother: come on . . . oh dear oh dear
Kristy: Mummy . . . I don't want to go away from you
Mother: you go away from me to kinder, don't you?
Kristy: yeah but –
Mother: and you like going away from me sometimes
Kristy: yeah
but then I meet not so many kids at kinder
and there's not only a big room
Mother: you mean you want to go to kinder
but you don't want to go to Dee's?
Kristy: Yeah
[TO RUTH] don't!
Mother: oh she's trying to be nice
don't get cranky

Text 2.1 Kristy and Ruth being dressed by their mother (adapted from Hasan, 2009, dialogue MK6A2)

In this text, Kristy and her mother are initially at odds in their goals – her mother wants Kristy to get dressed to go to kinder and then Dee's place, and Kristy most certainly does not want to do either. Yet despite these opposed positions, plenty of tears, and her younger sister Ruth doing things that toddlers do, by the end, her mother has managed to gradually bring Kristy around to her position (immediately following this excerpt, the conversation shifts from whether Kristy will get dressed to what she is going to wear). And she has hopefully done this without provoking any lasting emotional scars. But how did Kristy's mother do this? What resources does she use in this discussion to bring Kristy around? And what does Kristy use to try to get her way? Answering such questions involves coming to terms with the feelings at play, the kinds of positions Kristy and her mother put forward, and the way each attempts to pursue the ongoing conversation to minimize the risk of provoking any issues. That is to say, understanding how this conversation works involves understanding the interpersonal meaning at play – both the *inter* of the interpersonal, in terms of how Kristy and her mother propose and react to things being discussed; and the *personal* of the interpersonal, in terms of how they construe their feelings and thoughts (Poynton & Lee, 2009).

We will explore these questions by introducing a set of resources Kristy and her mother use to negotiate their feelings. In the model of tenor being developed in this book, these resources comprise a system called POSITIONING. As we introduce the resources being used, we will consider how they function and why they may have been used. In addition, we will consider how these resources can be used in different types of texts, both written and spoken, and the range of realizations available to speakers. In terms of SFL, this will involve discussing how speakers draw on the discourse semantic systems of NEGOTIATION and APPRAISAL; the grammatical, phonological, and gestural paralanguage resources that realize them; and how they are used in different genres and their stages.

In the following section, we will step through some issues that must be addressed in a model of the kind we are developing. Then we will establish the initial sets of resources for supporting and rejecting someone's position. Following this, we will explore how people negotiate positions both in dialogue and in monologue, in terms of what we will call *rendering*. In Chapter 3, we will additionally consider how speakers can position their listener to respond in particular ways, in terms of what we will call *tendering*.

2.2 Engaging in Conversation

As noted in Section 2.1, there are a number of key questions that need to be asked if we want to understand how social relations are enacted in a text like Kristy and her mother's:

- How do Kristy and her mother put forward their positions and accommodate each other's positions?

- How do they express their feelings and indicate whether they support or reject the other's feelings?
- How do they keep the conversation going until they have resolved the matter at hand?

These questions directly implicate recent work on affiliation emanating from Knight's (2008, 2010a, 2010b, 2013) studies of conversational humour. Knight describes how when friends chat with each other, they regularly react in ways that bring them together. But what they react to, and how, is not always understandable to an outsider. This is because friends laugh in places that to an outsider don't seem particularly funny, they support each other over seemingly insignificant things, and at times they reject or condemn things others have said but do so in ways that don't lead to lasting schisms. Knight describes this in terms of affiliation – noting that the acts of laughing, condemning, and communing around things bring people together.

The important features of Knight's work for this chapter are the strategies she describes that friends use to negotiate affiliation. Significant shared meanings that couple interpersonal evaluations with ideational content meanings (sometimes indicating shared *bonds*, drawing on Stenglin, 2004) were not just presented in conversation and left to freely float, but were actively engaged with – they were supported, rejected, or laughed at and with. In recent years, the affiliative strategies Knight described have been further developed in work on online communication, in particular by Zappavigna and colleagues (Logi & Zappavigna, 2022; Zappavigna, 2018; Zappavigna & Logi, 2024; Zappavigna & Martin, 2018a). This work has highlighted the centrality of affiliation to our everyday existence (Dreyfus, 2012), as well as key interactions between evaluative language (modelled in SFL as attitude – Martin & White, 2005) and dialogue (modelled as exchange – Berry, 1981a, 1981b; Martin, 1992; O'Donnell, 1990; Ventola, 1987; and as speech function – Halliday, 1985). Indeed, questions of how people engage with each other in conversation involve consideration of a wide range of interpersonal meanings (as described in detail, e.g., through Hasan's [1983] semantic networks). These discourse semantic resources in turn draw on the rich interpersonal grammar and phonology described by Halliday in Halliday and Matthiessen (2014) and Halliday and Greaves (2008), and consolidated for conversation in particular in Eggins and Slade (1997/2004).

Much of the focus of affiliation research has been on interaction. But, as White (2020) emphasizes, if we wish to understand how social relations are enacted in language, it is important that we understand how this occurs not just in dialogue but in monologue as well. Focusing in particular on news media, White draws attention to the crucial role of ENGAGEMENT (i.e., discourse semantic resources for managing different voices in text; Martin & White, 2005; White, 2003) in negotiating the range of positions at play in any text. This highlights the parallel between the dialogic resources of NEGOTIATION, where people can propose or react to positions put forward by another person in dialogue, and those of ENGAGEMENT, where people can do the same for purported or implied positions in both monologue and dialogue (Zhang, 2020a).

Finally, questions surrounding the negotiation of social relations implicate not just ENGAGEMENT and NEGOTIATION by themselves, but also their interplay as they work together in dialogue. Work by Muntigl (2009), Zhang (2020a, 2020b, 2021, 2024), and Kim et al. (2023) in particular highlight how speakers position each other through these resources as dialogue unfolds and speakers work towards consensus. Zhang's (2020c) work on Khorchin Mongolian in particular illustrates how a rich interpersonal grammar can be used for negotiating meanings as speakers commune. This latter concern will be explored in Chapter 3.

In short, to understand the linguistic enactment of social relations, we have to deal comprehensively with the interpersonal meanings available in discourse semantics, lexicogrammar, and phonology (as well as the concomitant interpersonal work done through gestural paralanguage [Ngo et al., 2022] and a range of other semiotic resources).

To begin, though, we will approach the dialogue between Kristy and her mother by viewing it "from above" – from the perspective of *genre*. Eggins and Slade (1997/2004) note that in conversation there are shifts between what they call "chat," which involves relatively continuous stretches of conversation that cannot be easily divided into distinct stages, and "chunks," which are relatively self-contained stretches that often realize various story genres (Martin & Rose, 2008). A long-standing issue in SFL is how to model the chat components of conversation. This is because chat tends to unfold prosodically, sliding between ideational topics as it goes, but being held together by interpersonal evaluations across exchanges (Martin, 2000b). Eggins (1990) sums up the goal of chat in this regard as simply to "keep the conversation going" (p. 16), which, following Knight's work (2010a), we can reinterpret as being oriented towards giving space for people to affiliate. Although Text 2.1 is relatively consistent in terms of its ideational focus, it does illustrate the issue of how we can model the gradual progression of conversation where there are few discrete stages. The following section will explore this by introducing resources in a tenor system known as POSITIONING.

2.3 Negotiating Meaning

As a general starting point, we will make a distinction between two choices available for speakers in dialogue. The first involves *tendering* meanings, where something is put forward to be negotiated or developed. This choice is in some sense prospective – it "looks forward" in conversation, tabling a position for others to react to. The second choice involves *rendering* by proffering some sort of opinion on what has been put forward. This option is in a sense retrospective – it "looks backward" by reacting to meaning.

In their simplest manifestations, tendering and rendering can be done in sequence in a dialogue. This is illustrated by Kristy and her mother in Example (2.1). Arrows are used to indicate the connection between tender and render pairs.

(2.1)	Mother:	you go away from me to kinder, don't you?	tender ↑
	Kristy:	yeah but –	render
	Mother:	and you like going away from me sometimes	tender ↑
	Kristy:	yeah	render

In the first line of Example (2.1), Kristy's mother tenders the proposition, *you go away from me to kinder, don't you?* Kristy then renders this by agreeing, *yeah* (she begins to counter this with an opposing statement introduced by *but*; however, she is cut off). Her mother then tenders another proposition, *and you like going away from me sometimes*, which Kristy renders once again through *yeah*. These examples illustrate that a key resource for rendering meanings is polarity – realized by the Mood Adjuncts *yes* and *no* (Halliday & Matthiessen, 2014, p. 175). These do not in themselves put forward an alternate proposition (i.e., they do not *tender* anything); they simply react by enacting a stance.

Another resource for rendering involves the use of positive or negative attitude that targets the tendered proposition. This is illustrated in the following sequence from a high school physics class in which a student tenders a description of a physics principle known as *Bohr's first postulate*. The teacher renders this move with the positive evaluation *Good* (what in a pedagogical context Rose [2018] calls an "Affirm" move).

(2.2)	Student:	An electron while in a stable energy state emits no radiation.	tender ↑
	Teacher:	Good.	render

In classrooms, teachers will often render support for a student's response simply by replaying it. Example (2.3) follows the teacher asking, *What did Maxwell say that accelerating charges do? They emit . . .*

(2.3)	Student:	Emit EMR.	tender ↑
	Teacher:	They emit EMR.	render

In conversational texts, someone can render a position by replaying the evaluative attitude rather than the ideational meanings themselves – as in the text message exchange in Example (2.4).

(2.4)	Father:	Good win. Great defence from Cronulla.	tender ↑
	Son:	Things are looking up.	render

These examples highlight the parallels between polarity in the lexicogrammar (Mood Adjuncts such as *yes* and *no*, *not* and *never*) and "polarity" in discourse semantics (realized through positive or negative attitude, e.g., *good* vs. *bad*; Martin, 2020). Both can be used to support or reject a tendered proposition.

Although we will not explore it in detail here, this analysis relates to what Berry (1981a, 1981b), in her influential model of exchange in dialogue, models as the "ideational" tier of exchange. Berry distinguishes between "proposition completion" moves, which present a full proposition (e.g., *An electron while in a stable energy state emits no radiation*), and "proposition-support" moves, which are used to support what has been put forward (e.g., *yes*). This distinction parallels the tendering-rendering distinction we have introduced so far, though there is not a one-to-one relation between the two models. For one thing, we are trying to cover both dialogue and monologue in this chapter; for another, we deal with certain aspects of dialogue such as questions differently from Berry. This difference arises due to the fact that we do not take the distinction between question and statement as fundamental to the description, but rather the negotiation of evaluation (i.e., as noted above, we take both the *inter* and the *personal* of the interpersonal into account).[2] Nonetheless, despite being relatively underexplored in comparison to her interpersonal tier of exchange, Berry's ideational tier is relevant to the interpretation of unfolding dialogue we develop in this chapter.

Tendering and rendering offer a basic choice for negotiating meaning in tenor – as speakers put a position forward or react to that position. Both tendering and rendering can be enacted in a number of ways to perform a wide range of functions. In the next section we explore the range of meanings offered for rendering; and in Chapter 3 we will turn to resources for tendering.

2.4 Rendering

So far, we have considered renderings that react positively to what is being tendered. We will say that these render *support*. But as Kristy shows in her conversation with her mother, we can also render *rejections* of something that has been put forward. In Example (2.5), Kristy *rejects* her mother's proposal that she get dressed.

(2.5)	Mother:	well how about I get you dressed instead	tender
			↑
	Kristy:	no	render: reject

And when Ruth does something to annoy Kristy, she also forcefully rejects this:

(2.6)	Ruth:	[DOES SOMETHING UNSPECIFIED TO KRISTY]	tender
			↑
	Kristy:	don't!	render: reject

Both of these moves are challenges (ch) in terms of Martin's (1992) model of exchange structure; they use negative polarity (*no* or *-n't*) to reject a proposal. In Example (2.5), the rejection derails the exchange, frustrating Kristy's mother's goal of getting Kristy dressed then and there (in Berry's terms, her mother puts forward a Da1, but Kristy derails the exchange before she could get to the A1 move). In Example (2.6), Ruth performs an action (the A1), and Kristy rejects it out of hand. In both cases, Kristy renders the position being tendered, but does so by rejecting it.

This gives us a distinction for types of rendering – opposing *support* to *reject.* This system allows us to make clear our thoughts and feelings about what people are saying, and thus plays a major role in terms of how we affiliate and disaffiliate with one another.

Alternatively we can choose to make a response that is not explicit about whether we are supporting or rejecting what is being said, but simply *noting* it. In dialogue, this is often done through backchannelling, as we acknowledge what has been said but do so in a way that does not give away our feelings. This is illustrated in Example (2.7) from a conversation between two mothers.

(2.7)	Renee:	It's that whole letting him be a kid, like	tender ↑
	Michele:	Mm[3]	render: note

Another possibility is to show our feelings by laughing at what is being put forward. Knight (2010a, 2010b) highlights the crucial importance of laughter in building solidarity in conversation. She argues it is a way of responding to something that pushes against shared values or knowledge – but in a "fun" way (i.e., not in a way that requires outright rejection or condemnation). Laughing allows us to acknowledge that what is being said is "unacceptable" in some sense, but that we all know it is unacceptable and so it's not an issue. By implicating this shared knowledge, laughter in fact reinforces affiliation – we come closer. To put this more technically, Knight describes laughter as occurring when a person puts forward a coupling of attitude and ideation that wrinkles against assumed shared-bond networks that align the speakers in the conversation. Rather than refusing to bond around an unacceptable coupling and so condemning the speaker, laughter allows the listener to "defer" a direct reaction to what has been said, and express their understanding of alternative unspoken "real" bonds that underpin the conversation.

We can exemplify this by looking at an interaction where Kristy and her mother share a laugh further on in their conversation, as shown in Example (2.8). This follows a stretch where Kristy's mother was telling Kristy that Ruth was a *goose* for putting her hand under the lid of a box, slamming the lid shut, and jamming her fingers. Kristy then asks, *do goosies do that?* The rest of this conversation is presented as analysed below, with laughter at the end (labelled *deferring*, following Knight's analysis) responding to the series of moves that have come before.

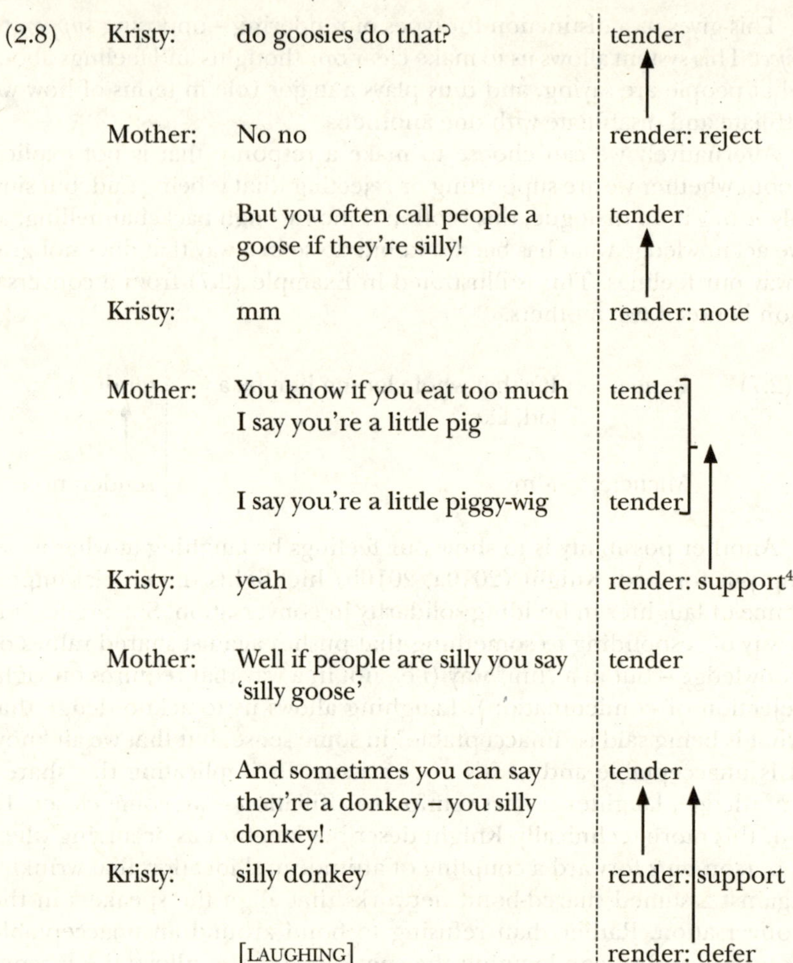

(2.8)			
	Kristy:	do goosies do that?	tender
	Mother:	No no	render: reject
		But you often call people a goose if they're silly!	tender
	Kristy:	mm	render: note
	Mother:	You know if you eat too much I say you're a little pig	tender
		I say you're a little piggy-wig	tender
	Kristy:	yeah	render: support[4]
	Mother:	Well if people are silly you say 'silly goose'	tender
		And sometimes you can say they're a donkey – you silly donkey!	tender
	Kristy:	silly donkey	render: support
		[LAUGHING]	render: defer

Here Kristy first renders her support by repeating what her mother said – *silly donkey*[5] – and then laughs off the silliness of the phrase. Based on Knight's description, Kristy defers through laughter the idea that someone is an actual donkey (or that donkeys do the same things silly humans do); in doing so, she makes clear that she is "in on the joke" and understands that although people aren't literally donkeys, they can in fact be pretty silly at times.

In more detailed work, Knight (2011) explores the sound potential of laughter in terms of its articulation, prosody, and movement. Among a number of distinctions, she shows that different types of laughter can indicate positive or negative judgment of what is being said. In our terms, this means that laughter can also indicate support or rejection, in addition to deferring meaning. In Example 2.8 (without having the phonology to hand to make this clear), it is likely that Kristy is laughing in support of her mother's joke, rather than rejecting it – that is, laughing off the idea that she and Ruth are donkeys, while at the same time admitting that they do stuff up sometimes.

By contrast, Knight (2011) gives Example (2.9), where the laughter is used to *reject* what is being said. In this example, T, a Brazilian man, is trying to clarify an observation that K, his Canadian wife, made about Brazilian men dressing in women's clothes. When T suggests they might do this while trying to pick up girls, K laughs. But in this instance, she is laughing *at* T, not with him – she is shooting T down. Here we will only analyse the laughter itself in bold (= = indicates overlapping segments).

(2.9)	K:	Yeah but you see a lot of guys in Brazil who aren't necessarily gay who like to dress like women and. . . . Because I remember being at = =
	T:	= = Oh you're talking about (festival) right
	K:	The Carnival and like a whole group of guys they were all dressed like women = =
	T:	= = Yeah but they're not men dressed like women; they're like in a costume like a little costume like you know whaddamean? You can i – they're not reading into this about women's feelings you know what I mean? They – they don't wanna know what it's about to be a woman. They – they wanna just have fun an – an – I don't know pick up girls that's the idea of the thing. Well that's how they = =

K: = = Dressed like a girl
[LAUGHS]= = render: defer/reject

T: = = Well they don't really *dress* like a girl! Alright?

In this example, in addition to deferring through laughter, K is rejecting the idea that dressing up as a girl is a way of picking up girls – so much so that T feels the need to clarify immediately and forcefully that they are not really *dressing* like girls. Knight (2011) describes the laughter phonetically as follows – the laugh begins "quiet, half-close, and pulsed through K's speech, but as the laugh continues past her own speech and through T's following utterance, the pitch moves from low to high, and the constriction moves to nearly close. The quiet, near closed and high-pitched quality of her laughter indicates negative judgement" (pp. 23–24).

In commonsense terms, the difference between Kristy's laugh and K's laugh is the difference between laughing *with* someone and laughing *at* someone. In our terms, it is the difference between deferring and supporting (laughing with) and deferring and rejecting (laughing at). Deferring while rejecting is a rich area of affiliation in its own right, underpinning the risky but enjoyable realm of teasing and gossip. Eggins and Slade's (1997/2004) work on gossip lays some groundwork in this area, but much more exploration is needed in SFL.

We can pull together the discussion so far as the set of preliminary options for rendering shown in the system network in Figure 2.1. This network outlines that when speaking, we have the option of tendering positions or rendering them. If rendering, we can *address* what has previously been said by enacting a stance of some kind, or we can simply *note* it and not give away our feelings. If we address these meanings, we can either *support* or *reject* them, and we can do this in a way that either directly *confers* this support or rejection (what Knight [2010a] calls "communing" and "condemning" affiliation) or *defers* it through laughter. These resources allow us to negotiate meanings used to enact our social relations in a nuanced way.

2.5 Building Dialogue

To this point we have looked at relatively simple cases of tendering and rendering, where different turns do one or the other. However, in dialogue, tendering and rendering are regularly realized together in

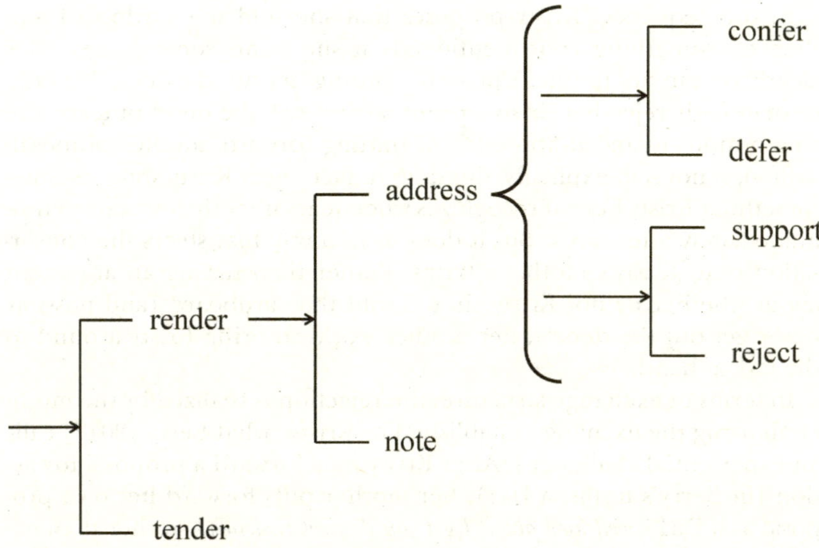

Figure 2.1 Preliminary options for rendering

the same move. Indeed this is often the preferred method in conversation as it allows the chat to flow smoothly from one turn to the next, with each move both looking backward in terms of rendering something that has been said and looking forward by tendering something to be negotiated (related to what Eggins [1990, p. 271] calls Janus moves, which relate both forward and backward in a conversation). For example, at the beginning of Kristy and her mother's chat, rather than directly rejecting Kristy's suggestion that she fold the cardboard, her mother proposes instead that she get dressed. This tenders the proposal of getting dressed and in doing so rejects Kristy's proposal of folding the cardboard.

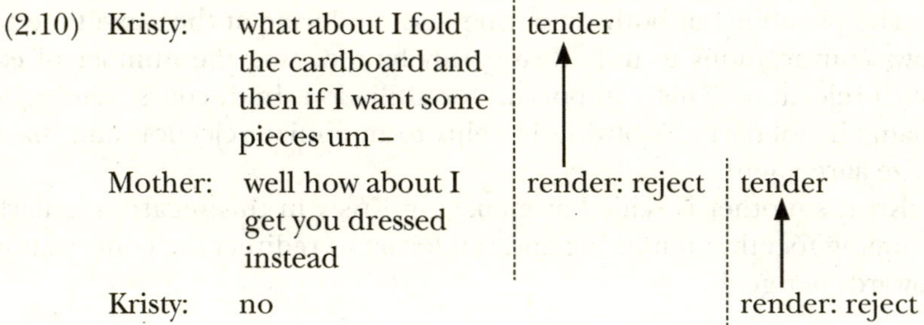

(2.10)	Kristy:	what about I fold the cardboard and then if I want some pieces um –	tender	
	Mother:	well how about I get you dressed instead	render: reject	tender
	Kristy:	no		render: reject

In this sequence, Kristy proposes that she fold the cardboard and then do something (not mentioned) if she wants some pieces. This clearly isn't in her mother's plans for getting her out the door. But rather than flatly rejecting Kristy's proposal and risk the onset of tears, she tries a more nuanced approach of putting forward another proposal. Although not said explicitly, this does in fact reject Kristy's suggestion – something Kristy herself recognizes when tears nonetheless start to flow immediately afterwards. But it does so in a way that steers the conversation onto Kristy's mother's terms. Rather than having an argument about whether or not Kristy should fold the cardboard (and possibly never get out the door!), her mother works to bring Kristy around to the task at hand.

In terms of exchange structure, the rejection is realized by the mother aborting the exchange established by Kristy (what Berry [2017] calls an experiential challenge). After Kristy puts forward a proposal for action (in Berry's terms, a Da1), her mother puts forward her own proposal as a Da1 (*well how about I get you dressed instead*) – rather than explicitly resolving Kristy's proposal itself. An exchange structure analysis could show this tension by analysing the Mother's move as a challenge (ch) and so considering it as a reaction to Kristy rather than a new proposal itself (Martin, 1992).[6] This indeterminacy between boundaries of exchanges has long been an issue for the otherwise neat multivariate analysis of exchange structure proposed by Berry (1981a) and elaborated by Martin (1992). Zappavigna and Martin (2018b), in their work on youth justice conferencing, work towards resolving this issue by proposing multiple layers of exchange, associated with what they call "regulative" and "integrative" discourse (adapting Bernstein's [1996/2000] distinction between regulative and instructional discourse for education). Although working at a stratum above, we adopt a similar multi-layered analysis here, suggesting that the mother's *well how about I get you dressed instead* functions in two ways – rendering Kristy's proposal by rejecting it, and tendering a new proposal (that Kristy subsequently also rejects).

The possibility of both rendering and tendering at the same time allows conversations to unfold smoothly by reducing the number of explicit rejections. This is important for affiliation. In discourse aiming to maintain solidarity, it obviously helps to minimize rejection and maximize agreement.

Kristy's mother is skilled at managing Kristy in this regard, regularly bringing together tendering and rendering to redirect the conversation towards her goals.

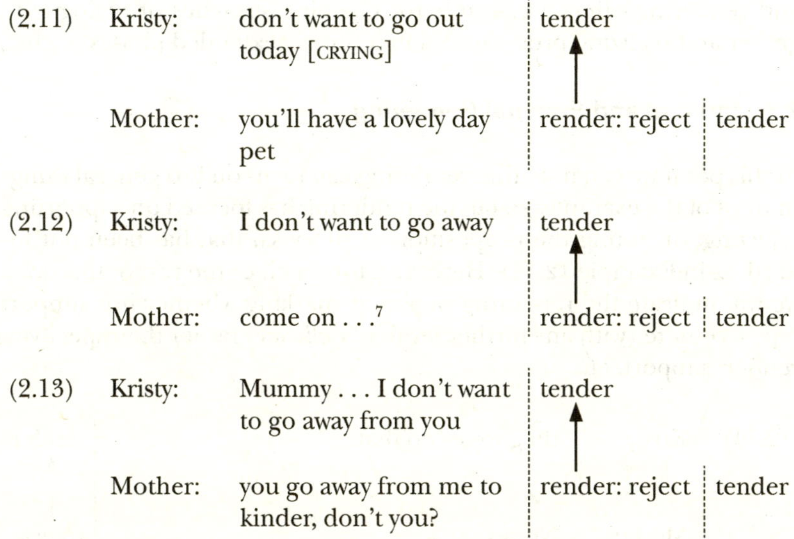

Although she regularly brings together tendering and rendering to manage Kristy's emotions, her mother of course does more than this – when Kristy's emotions peak, she turns to explicit renderings of support to bring her closer and help her calm down, and when things start to calm down, she moves more directly towards tendering to get things going again. The waxing and waning of tendering and rendering throughout the conversation allow her mother to get Kristy to do what she wants, while at the same time making it seem like they are doing it together – rather than having her mother seemingly force her purely by her own authority (i.e., making Kristy get dressed, whether or not she agrees).

From the perspective of genre, this possibility for both looking backward through rendering and looking forward through tendering offers a simple means of chaining positions together. This helps us understand the structure of conversation that continues indefinitely. Being able to render and tender at the same time offers a simple mechanism for indefinitely extending conversations (as Eggins [1990, p. 261] notes) and achieving one of the goals of the genre of chat – to "keep the conversation going" (Eggins, 1990, p. 16).

More generally, the relatively simple distinctions we have introduced so far help us deal in broad terms with two of our main concerns with regard to dialogue. First, the options in rendering offer a set of resources for negotiating feelings in dialogue, and so bring together attitude and exchange in discourse semantics. Second, the conflation of tendering and rendering offers a resource for chaining stretches of dialogue together and realizing prosodic and indefinitely extended phases of chat.

2.6 Internal and External Rendering

At this point we can note that rendering can focus on two general things. In most of the examples so far, the rendering has focused on supporting, rejecting, or noting the proposition or proposal that has been put forward, as in Example (2.14). Here, and for much of the rest of this book, we will indicate the rendering by simply marking whether it is support, reject, or note (with any further levels of delicacy) rather than specifying render: support, etc.

(2.14)	Kristy:	do goosies do that?	tender
			↑
	Mother:	No no	reject

Alternatively, we can also render a move not in terms of the meanings being tendered, but as a "speech act" in its own right. This is illustrated in Example (2.15). Here, after an interviewer asks whether an interviewee feels they have continued on someone's legacy, the interviewee renders the question itself with *Hmm good question.* Immediately following this, the interviewee additionally renders support to the proposition itself by saying that they do think they have continued on the legacy.

(2.15)	Interviewer:	Do you feel you have continued on his legacy?	tender
			↑ ↑
	Interviewee:	Hmm good question.	support: internal
		Yes, I feel I have.	support: external

Analogizing from Halliday and Hasan's (1976) distinction between external and internal conjunction, we can distinguish these as two types of rendering called external and internal rendering (see also Martin, 2024). External rendering supports, rejects, or notes the proposition or proposal being put forward, as in the *Yes, I feel I have* in Example (2.15). Internal rendering, on the other hand, renders what has been put forward as a linguistic act, as in the *Hmm good question.*

Internal and external rendering is regularly used to organisation conversations. This is illustrated by another conversation from Hasan's data (2009, HS4AB2), this time between Stephen and his mother.

Here, they are having a conversation about what Stephen had been watching on television with his father. In particular, they are chatting about the sea snakes Stephen saw, which leads to a question of whether they eat people.

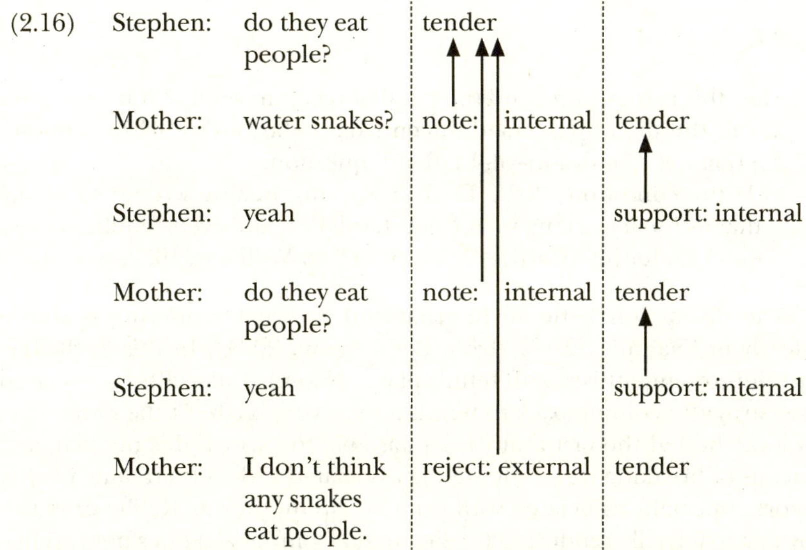

When Stephen tenders the question, *do they eat people?*, his mother is not quite sure what *they* refers to. To check what he is asking, she asks, *water snakes?* and *do they eat people?* In terms of Martin's (1992, pp. 66ff.) model of exchange structure, these are tracking moves that confirm what is being asked. As O'Donnell (1990) notes, these effectively function as complete exchanges in themselves within the larger exchange focusing on whether snakes eat people. Stephen's response in both cases is *yeah*, which renders support for what his Mother is saying. But here, Stephen's response is not answering the question of whether they eat people. Rather, his *yeah* is confirming that his mother has got the questions right. Stephen is rendering these questions not in terms of the propositions being put forward (whether or not water snakes eat people) – i.e. he is not rendering them externally –, but internally, in terms of the speech act (that is, whether or not this was the question being asked). We can see this by the fact that, once these questions have been clarified, his mother then renders externally his initial question by saying, *I don't think any snakes eat people.*

In addition to being used in dialogue, internal rendering is often used to provide a "meta" comment on language, often in service of establishing higher level periodicity (Martin & Rose, 2003/2007) and involving semiotic entities – such as *question*, *statement*, and so on (Hao, 2020). This is illustrated in Example (2.17), where cultural critic Raymond Williams renders a question by 19th-century Scottish cultural critic Thomas Carlyle as *famous*. This example also illustrates how rendering can be prospective of what is to come, rather than just retrospective.

(2.17)

> After this recognition, and the parallel recognition that it is no answer to call the discontent 'mad, incendiary, nefarious', Carlyle proposes the **famous** 'Condition–of–England' question:
>
> > 'Is the condition of the English working people wrong; so wrong that rational working men cannot, will not, and even should not rest quiet under it?' (Carlyle, 1841, p. 111, in Williams, 1958, p. 110)

The distinction between internal and external rendering is shown clearly in Example (2.18) (from Beddington, 2024). In this exchange, the author empathises with tennis player Naomi Osaka, after she shared her struggles coming back to tennis after giving birth. At the same time, she celebrated the fact that Osaka was able to express this publicly, as a means of breaking down the stigma associated with vulnerability in elite sport, especially associated with women and motherhood. She does this by first externally rendering the fact that Naomi Osaka does not feel like she's in her body as *awful* (underlined), before then internally rendering the fact that she said it as *fantastic* (in bold).

(2.18)

> My biggest issue is that I don't feel like I'm in my body," Naomi Osaka wrote this week on Instagram. A year after her daughter was born, the Grand Slam champion, who returned to the competitive circuit in January, is struggling to find her form. "I try and tell myself 'it's fine you're doing great' ... Internally I hear myself screaming 'what the hell is happening?!?!'"
>
> <u>That is awful</u>, **but how fantastic that she is talking about how she feels.**

Finally, in classrooms, it is common for student responses to be rendered internally. In Example (2.2) above, replayed here as Example (2.19), the teacher's *Good* can be read not as expressing an opinion on the fact that an electron while in a stable energy state emits no radiation, but rather as evaluating the statement as a linguistic act – as being a correct answer.

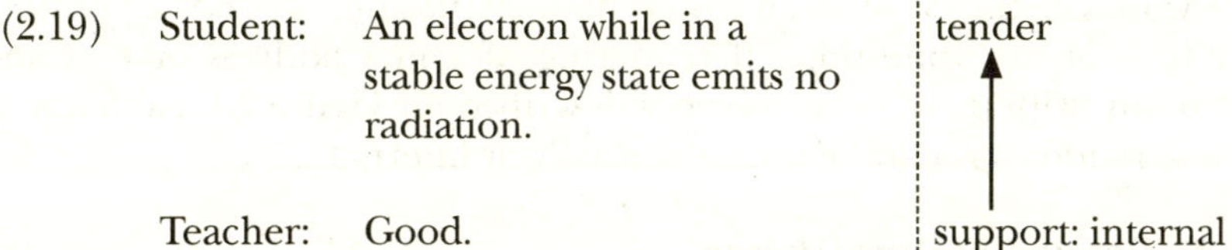

We will not explore our generalization of Halliday and Hasan's (1976) original internal-external distinction across discourse semantic systems any further here, other than to say this distinction is crucial for our discussion of what we will call *open* propositions and proposals in Chapter 3. As external rendering is the default choice, in analyses below we will leave this as the unmarked case and add a note on internal renderings only where relevant. Adding these choices into our system network gives us Figure 2.2. In this figure the joint square bracket and brace mean *and/or*. That is, one may choose to render, tender, or both. Thus this

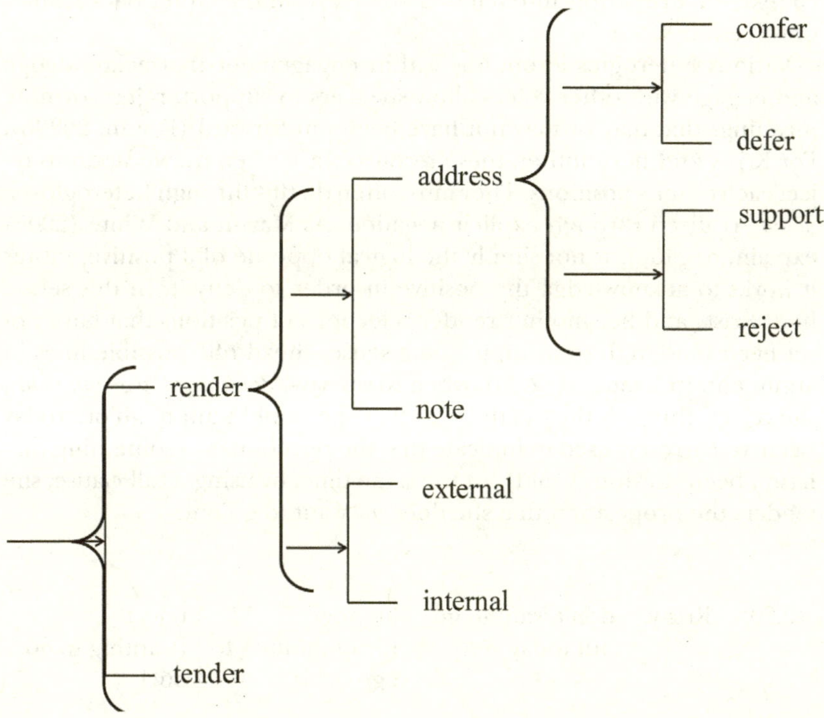

Figure 2.2 Network for rendering

network says that in tenor, one may tender a position, render a position, or both at the same time. If rendering, this may address or note the position (with the various subtypes described for Figure 2.1), and any of these renderings may be done externally or internally.

2.7 Rendering Other Voices

So far, we have focused largely on how people draw on exchange resources to render positions between turns in dialogue. However, as decades of work on interpersonal meaning have shown, speakers and writers regularly acknowledge and engage with a range of voices within their turns as well. One of the key resources for engaging with other voices is the discourse semantic system of ENGAGEMENT (Martin & White, 2005; White, 2003). In terms of tenor, ENGAGEMENT offers a wide range of resources for rendering different positions. Very often, these positions are not ones that have been explicitly tendered in preceding co-text, but are simply implicit or assumed from the larger background of voices.

Various heteroglossic options within engagement that acknowledge and engage with other voices allow speakers to support, reject, or note meanings that may or may not have been put forward (Doran, 2020b). For Kristy and her mother, these resources are often drawn upon to reject each other's positions. They most often do this through heteroglossic *denial*, realized through explicit negation. As Martin and White (2005) explain, negation is not simply the logical opposite of a positive; rather it works to acknowledge the positive in order to deny it. In this sense, both Kristy and her mother render rejections of positions that have not yet been tendered, so as to, in some sense, "head off" possible lines of argument. In Example (2.20), when Kristy says, *don't want to go out today*, she rejects through the *-n't* the idea that she would want to go out today (a curved arrow is used to indicate that the rejection is to something that hasn't been previously said). At the same time, by using a full clause, she tenders the proposition that she does *not* want to go out.

(2.20)	Kristy:	do**n't** want to go out today	tender [not wanting to go out]	reject [wanting to go out]

In Example (2.21), when her mother says, *I won't be home later either*, she rejects a possible line of argument that Kristy could take that she will be home late (and tenders this as a proposition that could be argued).

(2.21)	Mother:	I wo**n't** be home late either	tender [not being home late]	reject [being home late]

And in Example (2.22), *don't get cranky*, she pre-emptively rejects any acceptance of Kristy getting cranky.

(2.22)	Mother:	do**n't** get cranky	tender [not getting cranky]	reject [Kristy getting cranky]

As the analysis shows, in each of these cases the rejection is part of a full clause, which also tenders a (negative) proposition. The justification for this is that each of these positions can themselves be subsequently negotiated. As we will see, the use of engagement typically allows for both the rendering of a proposition while at the same time a tendering of another proposition. In the cases above, they reject an implied positive proposition and tender the negative proposition.[8]

Here we are emphasizing the similarities in tenor between rejection and support done dialogically and monologically. In terms of discourse semantics, this indicates similarities between heteroglossia, which offers resources for managing multiple voices, and negotiation (dialogica), which offers resources for managing multiple turns. Put another way, we are suggesting a parallel between Example (2.23), where the tendering and rendering are established across two turns, and Example (2.24), where the tendering and rendering occur in a single turn.[9]

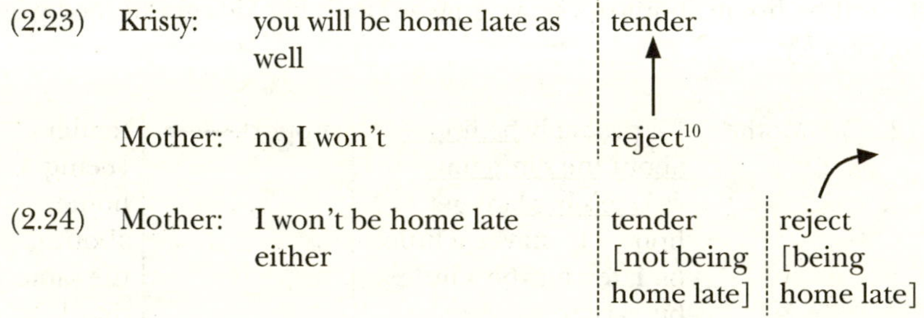

In addition to heteroglossic denial, rejections can also occur through *distancing* (Martin & White, 2005). In these cases the speaker indicates they do not align with what is being proposed (though with lower stakes; see Chapter 5). As shown in Example (2.25) (from Doran, 2020b), in these instances the proposition they are rejecting is in fact specified, so we have underlined it and drawn a horizontal arrow between the rendering and the tendering. Like the rejections above, this instance also tenders a new proposition centred on the *claim* – which itself can be negotiated. That is, there are three things going on in Example (2.25). First, the UNSW Diversity Toolkit is tendering the proposition that the word *settlement* ignores the reality of Indigenous lands being stolen; second, it is rejecting this position through the distancing of *claim*; and third, it is tendering the proposition that *The UNSW Diversity Toolkit is claiming* that the word *settlement* ignores reality.[11]

(2.25)	The UNSW Diversity Toolkit **claims** the word settlement ignores the reality of Indigenous lands being stolen	tender ["The UNSW Diversity Toolkit claims . . ."]	reject ⟶	tender ["the word settlement ignores the reality . . ."]

Support can be done through a range of heteroglossic *proclaiming* resources (Martin & White, 2005). In this case a position is endorsed, pronounced, or concurred with, as in Example (2.26), but like Example (2.25) it renders the position it tenders.[12]

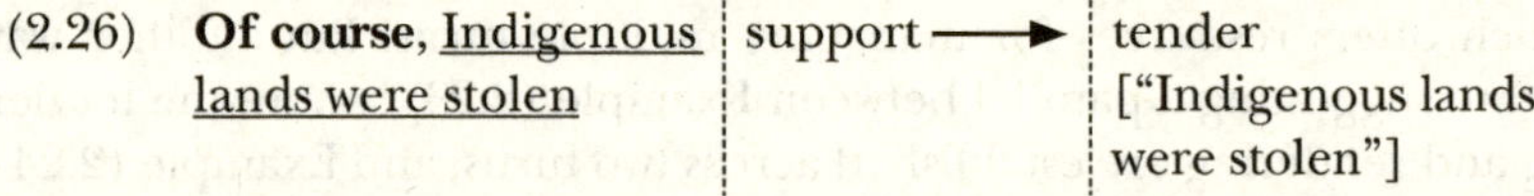

(2.26)	**Of course**, Indigenous lands were stolen	support ⟶	tender ["Indigenous lands were stolen"]

Similarly in Example (2.27), Kristy's mother supports the position that she will be home about the same time as Dee's big kids get home by using *probably*.

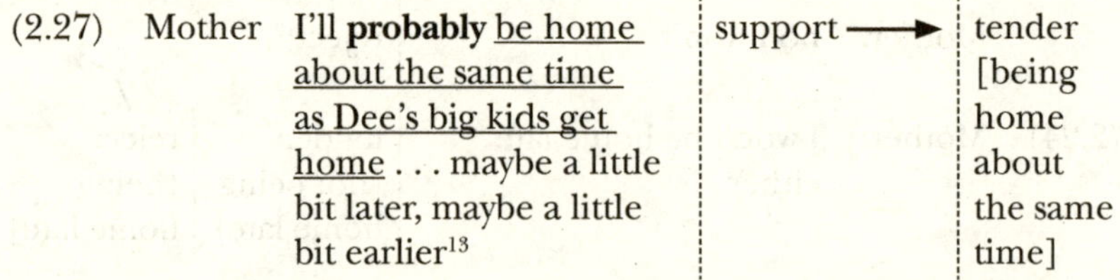

(2.27)	Mother	I'll **probably** be home about the same time as Dee's big kids get home . . . maybe a little bit later, maybe a little bit earlier[13]	support ⟶	tender [being home about the same time]

Turning to the note option, these can be enacted through the heteroglossic option for *entertain*, where there is an acknowledgment of the possibility of different voices, but no explicit stance is taken.

(2.28)	**It is possible** there was an invasion	tender ["It is possible . . ."]	note ⟶	tender ["there was an invasion"]

A noting move in this kind of example will typically occur for the low positions of modality (Halliday & Matthiessen, 2014, pp. 178–179), for example using *possible, perhaps, maybe, can, may,* and so on. Median and higher modality, such as *probably, likely, must, will, certainly,* and so on, is more likely to realize some sort of support or rejection (though see Chapter 3 for how this interacts with speaker and listener purview).

In addition to one *supporting* and the other *noting* what is being tendered, there is a second difference between Examples (2.27) and (2.28). Looking grammatically, in Example (2.28) there are two clauses being given – a ranking clause *It is possible* . . . and an embedded clause *there was an invasion.* This means that there are two possibilities for rendering. For example, one may reject that there was an invasion by saying, *No, there wasn't*; or alternatively, one may reject the *possibility* that there was an invasion by saying, *No, it isn't.* This indicates that (in the absence of a modality metaphor; Halliday & Matthiessen, 2014, pp. 686–687) there are in fact two positions being tendered here, which is shown in the analysis – one by the ranking clause *It is possible* . . . and one by the embedded clause *there was an invasion,* the latter of which is being rendered by the former. In Example (2.27), the *probably* does not tender a position separate to that of *I'll be home* (i.e., we cannot negotiate *probably* independent of the whole position without tendering something new – something like *It's not only probably, but definitely*). Thus, there is only one position being tendered. This is a distinction in Halliday's terms between what he calls explicit objective modality (e.g., *It is possible*) and implicit objective modality (e.g., *possibly*).

As these examples show, the use of engagement can produce a text that is very interpersonally nuanced – rendering a proposition that may or may not have been stated, while at the same time tendering a new proposition. This gives some insight into why humanities texts, which regularly draw heavily on engagement, can at times be such "heavy going" (i.e., why they can have such strong interpersonal *mass*; Martin, 2017) – they are responding to a range of stances in their academic community while at the same time trying to put forward a stance themselves (Doran, 2020a, 2020b; Hood, 2010, 2022).

This discussion also brings us back to the point made above – namely that attitude itself can also indicate rejection or support, as long as there is a target or trigger for the attitude (i.e., it is not what Martin [2017] calls "moody" affect or some other attitude without an explicit trigger or target, as in *She's happy and has no idea why*).

Kristy's mother relies on this throughout the conversation, sourcing support or rejections to Kristy herself (see Chapter 4), in a bid to show her that she will in fact enjoy being out of the house (we have removed the *I think* in Example [2.29] to simplify the analysis, but we will discuss it below).

(2.29)	you're **upset** because the TV wasn't working	tender ["you're upset because . . ."]	reject [that the TV wasn't working] (sourced to Kristy)

(2.30)	and you **like** going away from me sometimes	tender ["you like . . ."]	support ["going away from me"] (sourced to Kristy)

There is also one instance where Kristy's mother renders support not for a full proposition but for an item, *day*.

(2.31)	you'll have a **lovely** day pet	tender ["you'll have a lovely day"]	support ["day"]

This final example highlights that rendered meanings do not need to be whole propositions, but can in fact be of any stretch in meaning. We will return to this point in the following section.

As noted above, we removed the *I think* from Example (2.29) to simplify the analysis. This is because *I think* often marks what Halliday calls an interpersonal metaphor (or more specifically, a modality metaphor enacting *explicit subjective* modality; Halliday & Matthiessen, 2014, pp. 686–687). In Example (2.32) we have included it along with the previous line that includes *I don't think.*

(2.32)	Mother:	I do**n't** think you're really **upset** about me going	reject ⟶	tender ["you're really upset about . . ."]	reject ["me going"] (sourced to Kristy)

I think you're **upset** because the TV wasn't working	support →	tender ["you're upset because . . ."]	reject [that the TV wasn't working] (sourced to Kristy)

As noted above, both *you're really upset about me going* and *you're upset because the TV wasn't working* tender a proposition of *you're really upset* and *you're upset* that in turn source rejections to Kristy of *me going* and *the TV wasn't working.* These analyses are shown in the two columns on the right in Example (2.32).

Looking at the *I think* now, as Halliday and Matthiessen (2014, pp. 686–687) note, the *I think* here is unlikely to be providing a full proposition. We can see this by the fact that if we were to tag the clause, we would more likely tag in relation to the *you're upset* rather than the *I think.* We would more likely say, *I think you're upset because the TV wasn't working, aren't you,* as opposed to *I think you're upset because the TV wasn't working, aren't I.* Similarly, if Kristy was to support what her mother was saying, she would likely support the *you're upset* rather than the *I think* with *Yeah, I am* rather than *Yes, you do.* This is because the *I think* is not presenting a proposition about thinking, but rather being used metaphorically to mean something like *probably.* In Halliday's terms, it is an interpersonal metaphor realizing modality. In this sense, the *I think* is in fact realizing support for the idea that Kristy is upset because the TV isn't working. As we will discuss in Chapters 4 and 5, the *I think* also makes explicit that what is being tendered is a personal opinion and it lowers the stakes of the position.

The *I don't think* in the first line functions similarly to the second line, but realizes a rejection. We can see this again by the fact that it is unlikely that we will reject the "thinking" (*Yes, you do*), but also the fact that the negation can be easily transferred to the *you're upset* without significantly changing the meaning: *I think you're not really upset about me going* (Halliday & Matthiessen, 2014, p. 689). So Kristy's mother has tendered two propositions in opposition to each other in order to reject one and support the other (i.e., that Kristy is not really upset about her going but that she is upset because the TV wasn't working).

As these examples illustrate, the interaction between heteroglossia and attitude means a proposition or proposal will often both render and tender at the same time. When combined with the possibility of rendering a proposition or proposal's role in the exchange, there can be many different strands of tendering and rendering going on at once. A lot of interpersonal meaning is enacted in a short period of time. And as Kristy and her mother show, conversations offer enormous opportunities for sharing the meanings involved.

2.8 Negotiating Monologue

As Kristy and her mother's text shows, in even a short conversation, a lot of interpersonal meaning can be negotiated. Speakers can tender and render different things at the same time and establish multiple tracks of negotiation all at once. But it is not just conversational texts where this occurs. Longer monologic texts also regularly involve negotiation along these lines. This is especially the case for more interpersonally oriented genres focusing on persuasion – genres such as expositions, which argue for a point; discussions that debate two sides of an argument; and challenges that argue against a position that has been put forward (Martin & Rose, 2008). Text 2.2, for example, is a discussion written by late primary (elementary) school students, debating whether there should be printed advertisements (from Metropolitan East Disadvantaged Schools Program, 1989, p. 8). This discussion comprises four stages: an Issue stage that establishes what is to be debated (*Should we have printed advertisements?*), two Arguments stages (one arguing *for* having printed advertisements and one arguing *against* having printed advertisements), and a final Recommendation stage that gives a judgment on the issue, in this case rejecting the idea that we should have advertisements by saying, *Therefore I think we should not have printed advertisements.*

Issue	**Advertisements** There are many reasons for both sides of the question, "Should we have printed advertisements?" Many people have strong views and feel that ads are nothing more than useless junk mail, while other people feel they are an important source of information.
Arguments for	Here are some reasons why we should have advertisements in newspapers and magazines. One reason is ads give us information about what is available. Looking at ads we can find out what is on sale and what is new in the market. This is an easy way of shopping. Another reason is that advertisements promote business. When shop owners compete against each other the buyer saves money, more people come to their shops and they sell more goods.

Arguments against	On the other hand, some people argue ads should not be put in newspapers and magazines for these various reasons. Firstly, ads cost the shopkeepers a lot of money to print onto paper. Also some people don't like finding junk mail in their letter boxes. People may also find the ads not very interesting. Ads also influence people to buy items they don't need and can't really afford. Ads use up a lot of space and a lot of effort has to be made to make the ads eye-catching.
Recommendation	In summary, although ads provide people with information, their costs far outweigh their benefits. *Therefore I think we should not have printed advertisements.*

Text 2.2 A discussion – tendering two sides and supporting or rejecting them (Metropolitan East Disadvantaged Schools Program, 1989, p. 8)

In each stage, the text tenders a range of arguments, such as *ads give us information about what is available* and *ads also influence people to buy items they don't need and can't really afford.* These tendered positions are grouped with others into opposing sides (see Chapter 4). Throughout, the writer also draws on engagement to render these positions as they are being put forward. For example, in the Arguments Against stage, the writer uses negation (heteroglossic denial) to reject the tendered position that people will find ads interesting: *People may also find the ads* ***not*** *very interesting.* It is the final stage, however, which culminates the rendering. After the writer has put forward the positions for and against printed advertisements, they firmly render the question in the negative, rejecting the idea that we should have printed advertisements: *Therefore I think we should* ***not*** *have printed advertisements.* This rendering in some sense provides the ultimate goal of a discussion: to arrive to a particular rendering of the initial issue.

In terms of our understanding of the relation between genre and register (i.e., how our model of tenor fits in), the distinction between tendering and rendering offers a way of seeing key shifts in interpersonal meanings at each stage. In the Issue stage, a question is tendered about whether there should be printed advertising. In the Arguments stages, distinct positions are tendered in opposition to each other. And in the final stage, a definitive rendering occurs, where one set of tendered arguments are supported and another rejected. Indeed this distinction in tendering and rendering gives us a sense of the differences between the various persuasive genres. Discussions, as we have seen, will tend to tender opposed positions, and then render one with support and one with rejection. Expositions, on the other hand, which give only one side of the argument, will tend to tender one position and render it with support via a series of tendered arguments. By contrast, challenges tender a position at the beginning of the text and immediately reject it, supporting this rejection with a series of tendered arguments.

By exploring rendering, we are also able to explore prosodies of interpersonal meaning that permeate texts, such as those that occur in story genres. This is illustrated through the excerpts in Text 2.3, written by the Russian revolutionary Alexandra Kollontai (Kollontai, 1916/1997). These excerpts compare the experience of pregnancy in tsarist Russia by bourgeois women (illustrated by Mashenka the lady) and working-class women (illustrated through Mashenka the laundress). The first excerpt is the Interpretation stage of an exemplum (Martin & Rose, 2008), which interprets the pregnancy experience of the wife of a factory owner so as to judge the bourgeoisie in general.[14] Kollontai writes the first two paragraphs of this exemplum from the perspective of the bourgeoisie (we explore the way perspectives are established through sourcing in Chapter 4). Using this bourgeois voice, she renders support for everything associated with Mashenka the lady through positive attitude (shown here in italics), while rejecting any negative feelings or efforts that Mashenka might have through *disclaim: denial* engagement (underlined). In the final paragraph, Kollontai abruptly shifts the rendering prosody established in the previous paragraph by returning to her own voice to reject the perspective of the bourgeoisie as humbug and hypocritical (realized through negative attitude in bold). Her reflection concludes by asking a rhetorical question, which on the face of it, simply asks whether the bourgeoisie do in fact consider the mother sacred. But, by virtue of the prosody that has been established in her voice rejecting the positions of bourgeoisie, we are to read it as a firm rejection (i.e., a purely rhetorical question, used to both tender a position and render it immediately; Doran, 2024).

Mashenka the lady

. . .

The *important* thing is that Mashenka should <u>not feel worried or distressed in any</u> way. Then the baby will be born *strong* and *healthy*; the birth will be *easy* and Mashenka will *keep her bloom.* That is how they talk in the factory director's family. That is the *accepted* way of handling an expectant mother, in families where *the purses are stuffed with gold and credit notes.* They take *good* care of Mashenka the lady.

<u>Do not tire yourself</u>, Mashenka, <u>do not try and move the armchair</u>. That is what they say to Mashenka the lady.

The **humbugs** and **hypocrites** of the bourgeoisie maintain that the expectant mother is *sacred* to them. **But is that really in fact the case?**

Text 2.3a Mashenka the lady – from Kollontai (1916/1997, p. 127); support through attitude in italics, rejection through engagement underlined, and rejection through attitude in bold

In the second excerpt, Kollontai uses another exemplum to compare the bourgeois woman's experience to that of the proletarian woman's experience. She rejects all conditions that the working woman experiences through negative attitude, and she also rejects propositions that would suggest there is some sort of equality between the women. Here she speaks in her own voice, except for one brief instance where she draws on what the "ladies" like to say – so that it can be firmly rejected.

Mashenka the laundress

Early in the morning before the darkness has given way to dawn and while Mashenka the lady is still having *sweet* dreams, Mashenka the laundress gets up from her **narrow** bed and goes into the **damp**, **dark** laundry. She is greeted by the **fusty** smell of **dirty** linen; she **slips around** on the wet floor; yesterday's puddles still have not dried. It is not of her own free will that Masha **slaves** away in the laundry, she is driven by that **tireless overseer** – need. Masha's husband is a worker, and his pay packet is **so small two people could not possibly keep alive on it**. And so in silence, **gritting her teeth**, she stands over the tub until the very last possible day, right up until the birth. Do not be mistaken into thinking that Masha the laundress has "*iron health*" as the ladies like to say when they are talking about working women. Masha's legs are **heavy with swollen veins**, through standing at the tub for such long periods. She can walk **only slowly and with difficulty**. There are **bags under her eyes**, her arms are **puffed up** and she has had no *proper* sleep for a long time.

. . .

If only she could lie down for an hour . . . have some rest . . . but working women are not allowed to do such things. Such pamperings are not for them. For, after all, they are not ladies. Masha puts up with her **hard** lot in silence. The only "*sacred*" women are those expectant mothers who are not driven by that **relentless taskmaster**, need.

Text 2.3b Mashenka the laundress – from Kollontai (1916/1997, p. 128)

Table 2.1 Rendering Mashenka the Lady and Mashenka the Laundress in Kollontai (1916/1997, p. 128)

Source	Instance	Rendering	Position Being Rendered
	Mashenka the Lady (Text 2.3a)		
Factory director's family	*important thing . . .*	support	That Mashenka should not feel worried or distressed in any way
	should not feel . . .	reject	Mashenka feeling worried or distressed
	born strong and healthy	support	Baby
	easy	support	Birth
	keep her bloom	support	Mashenka
	accepted way	support	[The above positions and renderings]
Kollontai	*the purses are stuffed with gold and credit notes*	support[15]	Bourgeois families
	good	support	Care of Mashenka the lady
Factory director's family	*do not tire yourself*	reject	Tiring oneself
	do not try and move the armchair	reject	Trying to move the armchair
Kollontai	*humbugs and hypocrites*	reject	Bourgeoisie
Bourgeoisie	*sacred*	support	Mother
Kollontai	*But is that really in fact the case?*	reject	That the mother is sacred to the bourgeoisie
	Mashenka the Laundress (Text 2.3b)		
Kollontai	*having sweet dreams*	support	Mashenka the lady's dreams
	narrow	reject	Mashenka the laundress' bed
	damp, dark	reject	Laundry
	fusty	reject	Smell
	dirty	reject	Linen
	slips around	reject	Floor
	not dried	reject	Has dried
	it is not of her own . . .	reject	It is her free will that Masha slaves away in the laundry
	slaves away	reject	Working in the laundry
	tireless overseer	reject	Need
	so small that . . .	reject	Pay
	not possibly keep alive	reject	Two people could keep alive on the pay packet
Mashenka the laundress	*gritting her teeth*	reject	Standing over the tub until the last day before birth

Table 2.1 (*Continued*)

Source	Instance	Rendering	Position Being Rendered
Kollontai	*Do not be mistaken into thinking . . .*	reject	Masha the laundress has "iron health"
Ladies	*iron health*	support	Mashenka the laundress' health
Kollontai	*heavy with swollen veins*	reject	Mashenka the laundress' legs
	only slowly and with difficulty	reject	Mashenka the laundress' walking
	bags under	reject	Mashenka the laundress' eyes
	puffed up	reject	Mashenka the laundress' arms
	no	reject	Mashenka the laundress having proper sleep
	Working women are not allowed to do such things	reject	Working women lying down for an hour, having some rest
	Such pamperings are not for them	reject	Working women lying down for an hour, having some rest
	they are not ladies	reject	That working women are ladies
	hard	reject	Lot
	sacred	support	Women
	"sacred"[16]	reject	Sacred as describing women
	. . . who are not driven by . . .	reject	Sacred women include those who are driven by need
	relentless taskmaster	reject	Need

The renderings established in these texts are presented in Table 2.1, grouped by their source. The important point for us here is that despite being an extended monologue, there is extensive rendering throughout, being realized by attitude and engagement.

The effect of the rendering throughout these exempla is for Kollontai to establish clear contrastive positionings of Mashenka the lady's experiences and Mashenka the laundress' ones. This helps build sets of values that iconize bourgeois and working women in opposition to each other and contribute to larger sets of iconization associated with both class politics and feminism. Kollontai's exempla also illustrate the degree of interpersonal positioning that can be negotiated in monologic texts, despite there not being a "dialogue" (i.e., a conversation involving initiating and response moves).

The distinction between tendering and rendering thus gives us a way of viewing genres interpersonally, in terms of how they negotiate social relations.

2.9 Conclusion

To sum up this chapter, we can synthesize the options for rendering as in Table 2.2. In this table, we have included some common realizations for key options in rendering.

Rendering offers us resources for negotiating our feelings, and it is a key component in how we organize our social lives. But as the opening question of Text 2.2 shows (*Should we have printed advertisements?*), there are also many ways in which meanings can be tendered. In the next chapter, we will step through the types of tendering that can occur and how they work in different texts to achieve social goals.

Table 2.2 Rendering Options and Their Common Realizations

Rendering	Common Realizations	Examples
Support	Positive (or maintenance of) polarity Mood Adjunct	– *An electron transitioning between stable energy states emits radiation.* – ***Yes.***
	Positive attitude	*The* ***important*** *thing is that Mashenka should not feel worried or distressed in any way.*
	Replaying of attitude	– *I love it.* – ***It's amazing.***
	Proclaiming heteroglossia	***Of course****, Indigenous lands were stolen.*
	Median/high modality	*There was* ***probably*** *an invasion*
Reject	Negative (or reversal of) polarity Mood Adjunct and/ or challenges	– *An electron in stable energy states emits radiation.* – ***No.***
	Negative attitude	*The* ***humbugs*** *and* ***hypocrites*** *of the bourgeoisie*
	Reversal of attitude	– *I love it.* – ***I sucks.***
	Deny/distancing heteroglossia	– *The UNSW Diversity Toolkit* ***claims*** *the word settlement ignores the reality of Indigenous lands being stolen.*
Note	Backchannelling	– *An electron in stable energy states emits no radiation.* – ***Mm.***
	Tracking (often combined with tendering)	– *Do they eat people?* – ***Water snakes?***
	Low modality	***Perhaps*** *there was an invasion.*

3 Positioning Others: Tendering in Text

3.1 Introduction

In the previous chapter we explored how people react to various positions through rendering. We noted that people can render positions that have been previously tabled in dialogue as separate moves, or they can render implied positions that have not yet been introduced. We also saw that people can render positions at the same time as they tender them. Throughout that chapter we were concerned with the different ways people can react to positions, in terms of supporting them, rejecting them, noting them, and others, and the ways these can be realized. What we did not explore, however, was the different ways people put things forward for negotiation – the different ways people tender meanings. This is the focus of the present chapter. In particular, we will focus on how people tender meanings so as to position others to respond – to support or reject, to do something or say something, or to tender a whole new set of meanings.

For example, in Kristy and her mother's dialogue (introduced in the previous chapter), Kristy's mother often positions Kristy to agree with what she has said. In Example (3.1), she uses the tag *don't you?* to suggest that she expects Kristy will support her position.

(3.1)	Mother:	you go away from me to kinder, **don't you**?
	Kristy:	yeah but –

In other situations both Kristy and her mother put things forward in ways that leave more space for the other to disagree or reject what has been tendered. In Example (3.2), Kristy and her mother use *what about* and *how about* to soften the impact of what they are proposing, making it easier for each to reject them.

(3.2)	Kristy:	**what about** I fold the cardboard and then if I want some pieces um –
	Mother:	well **how about** I get you dressed instead?
	Kristy:	no

These examples also illustrate that what is being negotiated can vary. In Example (3.1), Kristy's mother is putting forward some information – a proposition – to be agreed with or not. In Example (3.2), Kristy and her mother are discussing possible actions (proposals) that they could do.

Negotiating meaning is a two-way affair. People can affiliate, align, gossip, attack, chat, and so on by rendering meanings, but they can also do so by tendering meaning. The way people tender meanings implicates a range of interpersonal systems – in particular those of NEGOTIATION, concerned with how people exchange meanings in dialogue (Berry, 1981a; Martin, 1992; Ventola, 1987), and ENGAGEMENT, concerned with how people manage the play of different voices (Martin & White, 2005). As we mentioned in Chapter 2, we are particularly concerned with how these two resources interact as they work together. Work by Muntigl (2009), Kim et al. (2023), and Zhang (2020a, 2020b, 2020c, 2021) in particular has highlighted how people position each other as they work towards consensus. These systems in turn implicate a wide range of interpersonal grammatical systems – including the core system of MOOD as well as systems often positioned as supporting MOOD choices, such as TAGGING and MODALITY (Halliday & Matthiessen, 2014). The way all of these systems engage with tone choices in phonology is also part of the picture (Halliday & Greaves, 2008).

In short, to understand how people organize social relations, it is not enough to just understand how people react; we also have to look carefully at how people put meaning forward – we draw on a full set of interpersonal resources in language.

3.2 Tendering Propositions and Proposals

To begin, we will return to Kristy and her mother's conversation, which focused on Kristy's mother trying to get Kristy dressed and out the door (with Kristy resisting). Here we will consider the way they shift back and forth in terms of what they are negotiating. As noted above, in broad terms, there are two main things that they tender. At the beginning, they negotiate different actions – whether Kristy will fold the cardboard or whether she will get dressed. Halliday and Matthiessen (2014) characterize exchanges of goods and services such as this as involving *proposals.*

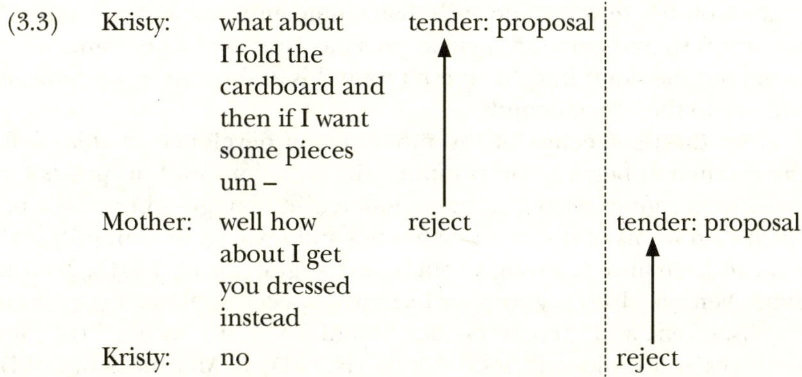

Further into the conversation, Kristy's mother changes tack and tries to reason with Kristy that she does in fact like going out sometimes. Here she turns from dealing with actions (proposals) to dealing with information – what Halliday and Matthiessen (2014, p. 135) call *propositions.*

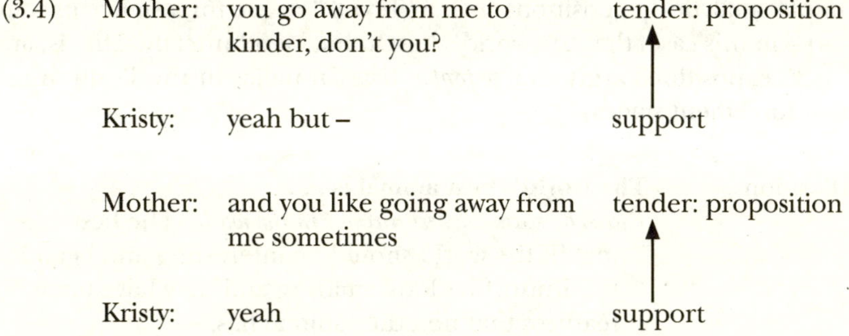

Although the ultimate goal of this conversation from Kristy's mother's perspective is getting Kristy dressed and out the door (i.e., resolving the proposal she puts forward at the beginning), in order to bring Kristy around she first needs to shift towards negotiating a series of propositions. This negotiation of propositions allows Kristy and her mother to come together and find common ground upon which they can re-negotiate whether Kristy will get dressed. This shift back and forth between proposals and propositions occurs throughout Kristy's conversation with her mother and is just as important for the flow of the conversation as the waxing and waning of tendering and rendering we discussed in Chapter 2. The shift between proposals and propositions allows Kristy's mother to manoeuvre the conversation in such a way that it unfolds on her terms, while at the same time ensuring as much positive support is shared between them as possible. Kristy's mother wants Kristy to get out the door; but she doesn't want this at the cost of a significant rupture to their social bonds.

From the perspective of the model being developed in this book, the distinction between propositions (information) and proposals (actions) determines what can be negotiated in dialogue. Looking from "below" in terms of discourse semantics and lexicogrammar, proposals tend to be realized through action exchanges (Berry, 1981b; Martin, 1992; Ventola, 1987), goods and services speech functions (i.e., commands, offers, and their responses; Halliday & Matthiessen, 2014), imperatives and options in modulation (Halliday & Matthiessen, 2014). Propositions, on the other hand, tend to be realized through knowledge exchanges (Berry, 1981b; Martin, 1992; Ventola, 1987), information speech functions (questions, statements, etc.), indicatives (declaratives and interrogatives), and options in modalization (Halliday & Matthiessen, 2014).[1]

Looking from "above," proposals and propositions also allow us to distinguish different types of genre. Looking at persuasive texts, for example, analytical expositions such as Text 3.1 argue for a stance of some sort – in this case, that the world's best animal is a butterfly. That is, analytical expositions argue for a *proposition* (in italics in the Position and Reinforcement stages).

Position	**The world's best animal is . . .** *Butterflies are the best animal in the world.* The best animal in the world should be interesting and beautiful. Butterflies look amazing and they have many features that no other animal has.
Arguments	Butterflies are beautiful. They have four wings. Every butterfly has a different pattern and colours on its wings. Some butterflies are so special that people travel to places just to see them. The Ulysses butterfly has beautiful bright patterns on its wings. People travel to Mossman Gorge near Cairns just to see a Ulysses butterfly.

	Butterflies have a special life cycle. Most animals hatch out of eggs or are born alive but caterpillars hatch from eggs, grow bigger, then change inside a chrysalis into beautiful butterflies. Some animals change as they grow, like a tadpole changes into a frog, but it doesn't change into a chrysalis first. Some insects like bees change from a pupa into a bee, but bees sting you. So they aren't as good as butterflies.
	Butterflies don't hurt anyone or anything. They help nature. When they fly from flower to flower, they take pollen from one plant to another. So they are helping the plants.
Reinforcement	Butterflies are very pretty and helpful so that is why *butterflies are the best animals in nature.*

Text 3.1 Analytical exposition – arguing about propositions (Queensland Studies Authority, 2011)

By contrast, hortatory expositions argue for action – in the case of Text 3.2 (from a Year 2 student; Humphrey & Vale, 2020, p. 80), that people should not waste water. Hortatory expositions therefore argue for a *proposal* (in italics in the Appeal and Reinforcement of Appeal stages).

Appeal	**Why water shouldn't be wasted**
	Water is a resource we need for drinking, cooking, washing and growing things. *Water should not be wasted for several reasons.*
Arguments	Firstly, people often use more water than they need, such as leaving the sprinkler on the lawn all day. If everybody uses too much water, the storage dams may run out.
	Another argument is that water costs money. If you use too much water, you have to pay a lot, and there is not enough left over to buy other important things.
	Finally, people in dry areas may feel that the city people do not care about them if they waste water.
Reinforcement of appeal	Therefore, it is important that we think about the water we use and *not waste it.* Then there will be enough water for everyone.

Text 3.2 Hortatory exposition – arguing about proposals (from Humphrey & Vale, 2020, p. 80)

Texts in the political sphere in particular often tender multiple proposals. In Chapter 2, we explored a series of exempla written by Russian revolutionary Alexandra Kollontai (1916/1997) that compared the experience of pregnancy by working-class and bourgeois women in tsarist Russia. Her ultimate goal for doing this was to set the stage for putting forward a series of proposals for women's industrial reform, shown in Text 3.3, through a genre we might call *demands.*

> The first thing that can be done and the first thing that working men and women are doing in every country is to see that *the law defends the working mother.* Since poverty and insecurity are forcing women to take up work, and since the number of women out working is increasing every year, the very least that can be done is to make sure that *hired labour does not become the "grave of maternity." The law must intervene to help women to combine work and maternity.*
>
> Men and women workers everywhere are demanding *a complete ban on night work for women and young people, an eight-hour day for all workers, and a ban on the employment of children under sixteen years of age.* They are demanding that *young girls and boys over sixteen years of age be allowed to work only half the day.* This is important, especially from the point of view of the future mother, since between the years of sixteen and eighteen the girl is growing and developing into a woman. If her strength is undermined during these years her chances of healthy motherhood are lost forever.
>
> *The law should state categorically that working conditions and the whole work situation must not threaten a woman's health; harmful methods of production should be replaced by safe methods or completely done away with; heavy work with weights or foot-propelled machines etc. should be mechanised; workrooms should be kept clean and there should be no extremes of temperature; toilets, washrooms and dining rooms should be provided,* etc. These demands can be won – they have already been encountered in the model factories – but the factory-owners do not usually like to fork out the money. All adjustments and improvements are expensive, and human life is so cheap.
>
> *A law to the effect that women should sit wherever possible is very important. It is also important that substantial and not merely nominal fines are levied against factory owners who infringe the law. The job of seeing that the law is carried out should be entrusted not only to the factory inspectors but also to representatives elected by the workers.*

Text 3.3 Demands genre – tendering a series of proposals (Kollontai, 1916/1997, p. 80; emphasis added)

Moving beyond persuasive texts, the distinction between proposition and proposal allows us to distinguish different types of factual text as well. Procedures, for example, put forward series of activities (Doran & Martin, 2021) as proposals, in order to step through how to do something. In the case of Text 3.4, in the "Method" section, these proposals are oriented towards making custard.

Stirred Custard

INGREDIENTS

1 cup milk	4 drops vanilla essence
1 egg	Nutmeg
1 tablespoon sugar	

METHOD

1. Warm milk in double saucepan or in a jug standing in saucepan of water.
2. Beat egg and sugar together until thick; add warm milk.
3. Return to double saucepan or jug.
4. Stir with a wooden spoon till the custard coats the spoon. Do not allow it to overheat or it will curdle.
5. Add vanilla. Cool.
6. Place in a serving dish or in custard glasses, with nutmeg grated on top.

Text 3.4 Procedure – presenting a sequence of proposals (NSW Public School Cookery Teachers' Association, 1970, pp. 100–101)

By contrast, explanations present activities as sets of interconnected propositions, such as the jointly constructed explanation in a senior secondary school physics classroom in Text 3.5 (from Doran, 2018, p. 29).

Teacher:	This electron by definition is accelerating. Why is it? Who can tell me? Tony?
Student:	It changes direction.
Teacher:	Right, it is continually changing direction, moving in a circular motion and circular motion is a type of acceleration. What did Maxwell say that accelerating charges do? They emit?
Student:	Emit EMR.

Teacher: They emit EMR. So this electron should be emitting radiation. And if it was emitting radiation, it is emitting energy. And if it is emitting energy, it must be losing energy, by law of conservation of energy, and if it is losing energy, sooner or later it has to slow down. And if it slows down, John, what's it going to do?

Student: Ah, crash into the nucleus?

Teacher: It'll crash.

Text 3.5 Explanation – presenting a sequence of propositions (Doran, 2018, p. 29)

This text highlights the fact that there are a number of ways that propositions can be presented. They can be presented as full statements, unfinished statements, *wh-* questions, and a range of other forms. This allows a progression of information to be developed through a text to help move towards consensus. We will explore this in the next section.

3.3 Open and Complete Propositions and Proposals

Different ways of articulating propositions underpin distinctions in questions and answers, which in turn allow us to negotiate information in different ways. For example, as Text 3.5 shows, propositions can be presented as *complete*, where enough ideational meaning is given for it to be rendered (either supported or rejected).

(3.5) Student: It changes direction. — proposition: complete

Teacher: Right — support ↑

(3.6) Student: Ah, crash into the nucleus? — proposition: complete

Teacher: It'll crash. — support ↑

Complete propositions are typically realized by discourse semantic statements (grammatically, declaratives) or by yes-no questions (grammatically, polar interrogatives).

By contrast, in this text the teacher also puts forward a series of propositions that are not complete, but rather leave some information for the students to answer. These types of propositions we will call *open propositions.* Open propositions are typically realized by elemental questions (grammatically, *wh-* interrogatives), questions that give alternative choices, or incomplete statements. Crucially, open propositions do not give enough information to be rendered – in other words, you cannot support or reject (externally speaking) the open proposition *what's it going to do?* Rather, the normal responses would be to tender another proposition.[2]

(3.7)	Teacher:	This electron by definition is accelerating.	proposition: complete
		Why is it?	proposition: **open**
	Student:	It changes direction.	proposition: complete
	Teacher:	Right	support
(3.8)	Teacher:	What did Maxwell say that accelerating charges do?	proposition: **open**
		They emit?	proposition: **open**
	Student:	Emit EMR.	proposition: complete
	Teacher:	They emit EMR.	support

To render an open proposition, you cannot render the content of the proposition as such; you rather have to support or reject the exchange itself (using an "internal" response).

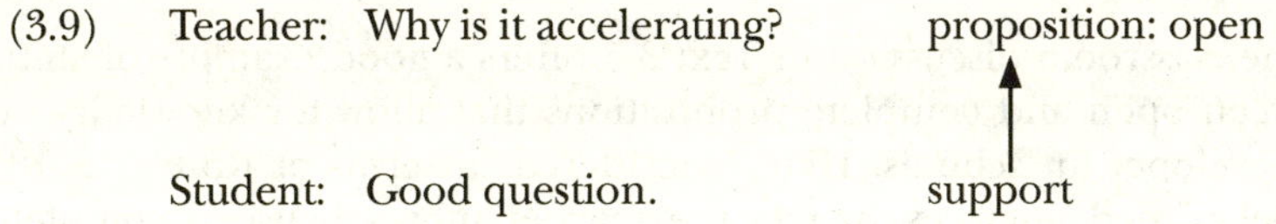

(3.10) Teacher: Why is it accelerating? proposition: open

Student: Bugger off. reject

We can view the contrast between open and complete propositions more technically in terms of the distinction between external and internal rendering. As explained in Chapter 2, external rendering involves rendering the information being given in a proposition or proposal, while internal rendering involves rendering the position as a linguistic act. From this perspective, complete propositions can be rendered both externally as in Example (3.11) and internally as in Example (3.12); but open propositions can only be rendered internally as in Example (3.13) – they cannot be rendered externally as in Example (3.14) (where the asterisk * indicates an ill-formed response):

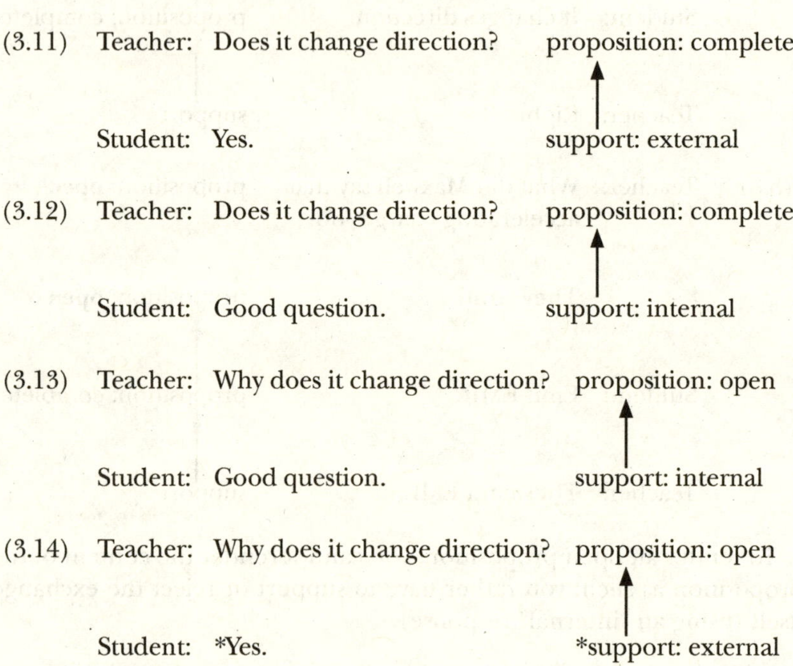

The classroom discussion in Text 3.5 offers a good example of shifts between open and complete propositions that allow for knowledge to be developed in schools. Here, considered in terms of Rose's (2018) model of pedagogic exchange, the teacher moves between complete propositions to Prepare students for the discussion that is coming, before shifting to open propositions to Focus students' attention on key points and ask them questions. For example, in line (i) of Example (3.15), the teacher tenders a complete proposition *This electron by definition is accelerating*, which Prepares the student for the question to come – by specifying the relevant knowledge needed for it. The teacher then asks a question through an open proposition (*Why is it?*), for the student to respond by tendering their own complete proposition (*It changes direction*); we will explore the intervening moves (iii) *Who can tell me?* and (iv) *Tony?* in Example (3.15). The teacher then supports this answer (Rose's Affirm) through *Right*, before giving a stretch of complete propositions that Elaborate upon the response that has been given (*it is continually changing direction, moving in a circular motion and circular motion is a type of acceleration*). This cycle is then repeated two more times, allowing the teacher to jointly construct the explanation with the students, and extend their knowledge as they go. In Example (3.15), we have aligned our tenor analysis with Rose's pedagogic exchange moves.

(3.15)

i	Teacher:	This electron by definition is accelerating.	Prepare	proposition: complete
ii		Why is it?	Focus	proposition: open ↑
iii		Who can tell me?		
iv		Tony?		
v	Student:	It changes direction.	Propose	proposition: complete ↑
vi	Teacher:	Right,	Affirm	support
vii		it is continually changing direction,	Elaborate	proposition: complete
viii		moving in a circular motion		proposition: complete
ix		and circular motion is a type of acceleration.		proposition: complete

x		What did Maxwell say that accelerating charges do?	Focus	proposition: open
xi		They emit?		proposition: open ↑
xii	Student:	Emit EMR.	Propose	proposition: complete ↑
xiii	Teacher:	They emit EMR.	Affirm	support
xiv		So this electron should be emitting radiation.	Elaborate	proposition: complete
xv		And if it was emitting radiation, it is emitting energy.		proposition: complete
xvi		And if it is emitting energy, it must be losing energy, by law of conservation of energy,		proposition: complete
xvii		and if it is losing energy, sooner or later it has to slow down.		proposition: complete
xviii		And if it slows down, John, what's it going to do?	Focus	proposition: open ↑
xix	Student:	Ah, crash into the nucleus?	Propose	proposition: complete ↑
xx	Teacher:	It'll crash.	Affirm	support

Less commonly, proposals can also be open. As with propositions, this often involves using *wh-* elements (*what, where, when,* etc.), with the typical response being to tender another proposal. At their simplest, this can involve an imperative with one element missing, such as *Go where?* This will typically occur as a clarifying response (what Martin [1992] calls a tracking move) to another proposal: *Go down to the shops for us. / Go where?*

As a means of initiating an exchange, open proposals will more commonly be realized grammatically as declaratives or interrogatives. As such, they will typically involve what we will discuss in Section 3.4 as *repositioning,* whereby multiple positions are given at the same time. This is illustrated in another of the mother-child conversations in Hasan's data (2009, GD5B3). In this conversation, Donna and her mother are jointly constructing a procedure for making glue, reviewing an activity they have done before. After agreeing that they need to include water, her mother asks what else is needed (*and we mix water with what?*); after a few prompting moves, Donna tenders *flour.*

(3.16)	Mother:	and we mix water with what? . . .
		a thing that is cream[3]
	Donna:	mm
	Mother:	and it's a bit powdery
	Donna:	mm
	Mother:	and we use it to make cakes
	Donna:	what?
	Mother:	you tell me
		and we use it to make scones
	Donna:	flour
	Mother:	right

The open proposal in this instance is the first line *and we mix water with what?* This conversation occurs in the process of making paste; so if it were a complete proposal, such as *and we mix water with flour,* a supportive rendering could be actually doing the mixing of flour with water. But without having the complete proposal, this is not possible (i.e., it cannot be rendered in this way, externally), and so it is an open proposal. However, as noted above, by virtue of it being a grammatical declarative, an alternative response is to simply treat it as a proposition that is just giving information. We will explore this in more detail in Section 3.4.

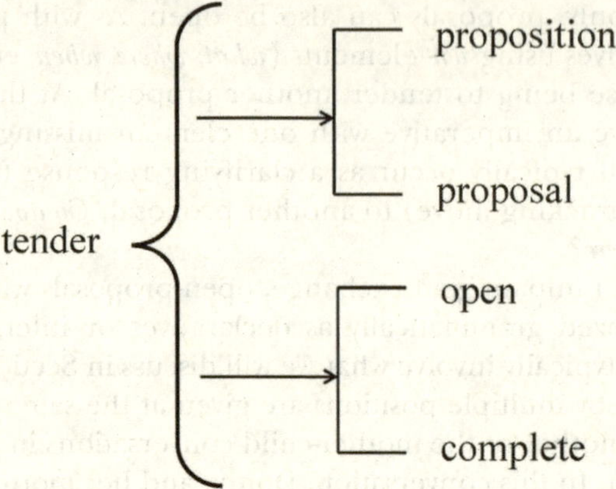

Figure 3.1 Initial network of tendering

At this point, we can present an initial network of different resources for tendering, as shown in Figure 3.1. This network says that when tendering, one may table a proposition or a proposal, and each of these may be either open or complete.

3.4 Repositioning

As we have just noted, when Donna's mother asks, *and we mix water with what?*, her move can be read as involving a proposition or a proposal. That is, it can be read as asking for the information of what we mix water with (a proposition), and it can be read as a command to mix the water with whatever is needed (a proposal). This is an instance of what we will call repositioning. Repositioning involves presenting one tenor meaning as another – in this case, repositioning a proposal as a proposition. Repositioning is a rich resource for elaborating meanings in both dialogue and monologue in ways that allow for the nuanced play of social relations that we need in many aspects of life.

We will begin to explore repositioning through what Zappavigna and Martin (2018b), drawing on Ventola (1987), call linguistic services. *Linguistic services* involve moves in dialogue that command an action, but the action requested is speech. In this sense, they look like they are both demanding action and requesting information. This is illustrated in Example (3.17), which is an example from a Youth Justice Conference (a formal legal process that aims to divert young people away from court) given in Zappavigna and Martin (2018b).

(3.17)	Convenor:	Tell me what happened when mum found out what you did. Did she cry?
	Young Person:	Lecture
	Convenor:	You got a lecture.

This example involves a Convenor, who is responsible for organizing the Youth Justice Conference, and the Young Person who has been charged with an offense. In the first line, the Convenor commands the Young Person to tell them what happened, drawing grammatically on an imperative (*Tell me what happened when mum found out what you did*). Commands and imperatives are typically used to propose actions of some sort, and so typically realize proposals in tenor. This could have been more explicitly acknowledged in the dialogue if the Young Person had begun their turn with *Yeah sure* . . . to explicitly render support for the proposal.

But what is being commanded here is that the Young Person speak – and specifically, that they give information. In other words, from the perspective of tenor, the dialogue looks more like it is negotiating an open proposition (*what happened when mum found out what you did?*). This is highlighted by the fact that once the Young Person gives their response *Lecture*, the Convenor follows up by rendering it with *You got a lecture* (i.e., they respond to the proposition), rather than rendering the action of speaking itself by saying something like *Thanks*. In terms of repositioning, the Convenor is *repositioning* a proposition as a proposal.

(3.18)

Convenor:	Tell me what happened when mum found out what you did.	proposition: open	**repositioned as**	proposal: complete

One function of such repositioning in this case is to nuance the status relations being established (Poynton, 1990a). Ideationally speaking, the Young Person is the one who has control over telling what happened at this stage of the conference. And here they have much more scope to step through the requisite activities and people involved than the Convenor (though the Convenor does in fact know in detail what happened). From the perspective of tenor, this is indicated by the Convenor through the open proposition (*what happened* . . .). But the Convenor's repositioning of this proposition as a proposal reasserts their status in interpersonal terms. It makes explicit the wider range of interpersonal choices that are available to the Convenor but are not available to the Young Person (e.g., commanding).

Analysing the full example as Example (3.19), then, the Young Person's response supports the proposal by speaking *and* completes the open proposition by specifying what happened (*Lecture*). As the Convenor followed up their initial command by asking, *Did she cry?* (a complete proposition), the Young Person's response additionally rejects this tendered proposition. As this example shows, a lot of interpersonal meaning can get negotiated in small stretches of dialogue! To indicate the repositioning, we have added a tilde (~) before the proposal analysis.

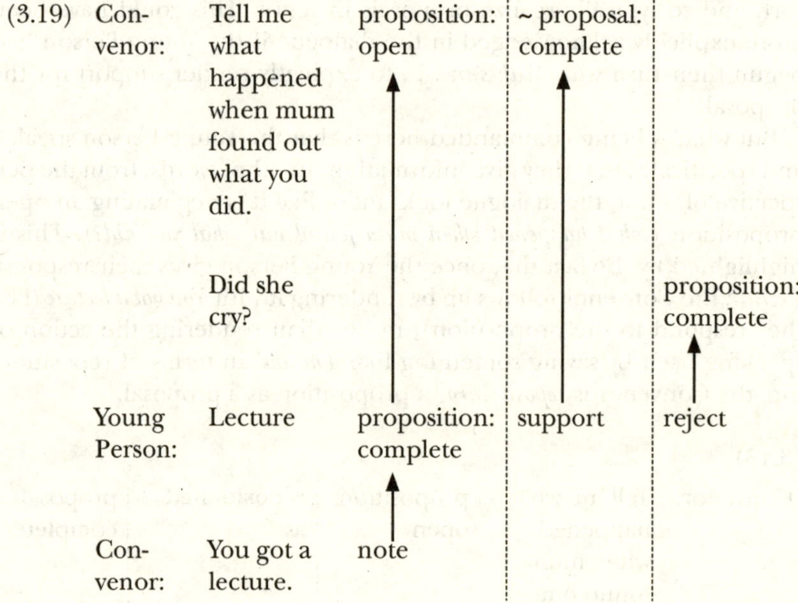

In addition to legal settings, linguistic services are common features of classroom discourse. As Zappavigna and Martin (2018b) explain, they reflect "the fact that teachers are regularly engaged in the task of managing a lesson at the same time as they are teaching a specific subject area" (p. 139). Drawing on Bernstein, such linguistic services bring to the fore that classrooms (and other arenas) involve both an "instructional discourse" associated with the "discourse of competence" regarding what is being taught, and a "regulative discourse" associated with a "discourse of social order" (Bernstein, 1990; Christie, 2002; Martin, 2021a, 2024; see also Muntigl, 2004, p. 124, for an implementation of these ideas in clinical settings).

As an example of this, when analysing the classroom discussion in Text 3.5, we left aside two positions put forward by the teacher, highlighted in grey in Example (3.20).

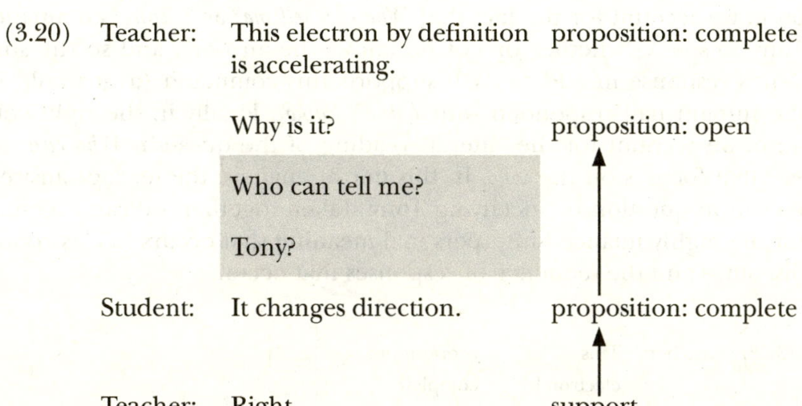

We left these aside because they also involve repositioning, though with one extra complication in comparison to the Youth Justice Conference example above. In this stretch, the *Who can tell me?* is an interrogative realizing a question, and so would typically realize an open proposition – in this case a proposition focusing on *who* can tell the teacher the answer. However, in this instance, a compliant response would not simply involve someone responding with *I can* and leaving it at that. Like in the previous example, what is being aimed at is for someone to tell the teacher why the electron is accelerating. With the Process being *tell*, we again have a linguistic service; the teacher is commanding someone to tell them the answer (i.e., this turn also realizes a proposal). But as above, the command is to speak, and so the ultimate goal is in fact to give information – that is, it is negotiating a proposition. This gives us two sets of repositionings.[4]

(3.21)

Teacher:	Who can tell me (why the electron is accelerating)?	proposition: open [asking *why*]	**repositioned as**	proposal: complete [*tell*]	**repositioned as**	proposition: open [asking *who*]

As the analysis in Example (3.22) shows, the teacher in fact answers their own question of *who* can tell him by calling on a student, *Tony.* Following the open proposition of *Why is it?* in the left column of analysis, we have analysed the dialogue for what the teacher is ultimately aiming at – to have an answer to the question *Why is it?* From this perspective, the student's *It changes direction* completes this proposition successfully, as indicated by the teacher's support through *Right.* In the middle column, we account for the fact that *Who can tell me?* and *Tony?* command Tony to speak (whether or not he knows the answer), and so the student's response in and of itself supports this command (as it would if the student had responded with *I don't know*). Finally in the right column, we account for the "literal" reading of the question *Who can tell me?* that focuses on the *who.* In this tier of analysis, the teacher answer their own question by specifying Tony. Taken together, we can account for the highly nuanced interpersonal meaning that occurs in classroom discourse and the sequence of responses that occur.

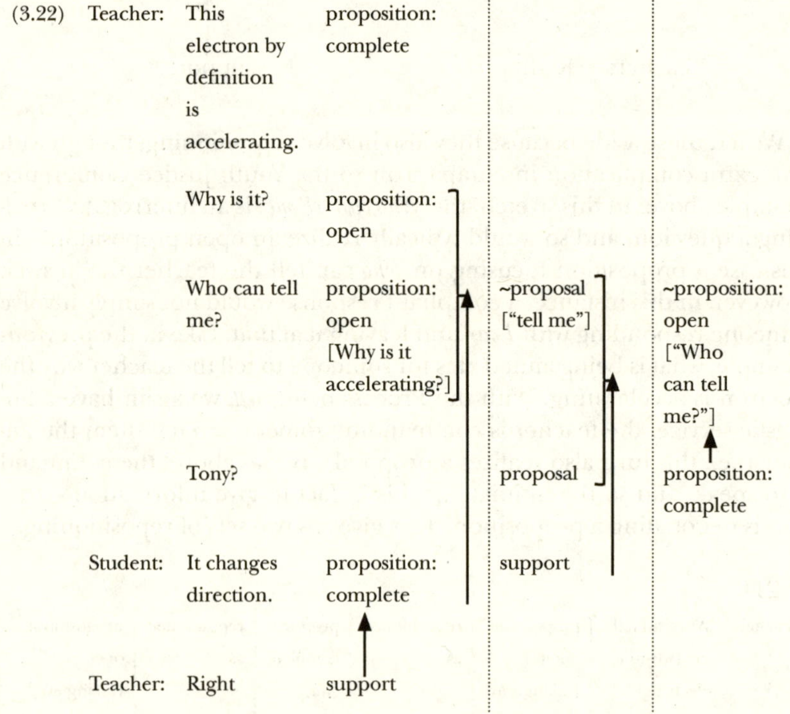

In fact it is not uncommon when responding to repositionings such as this to respond to each position in turn. This is illustrated in Example (3.23) from a job interview, focusing on the responses of *Yeah sure* and *since I've been working . . .*

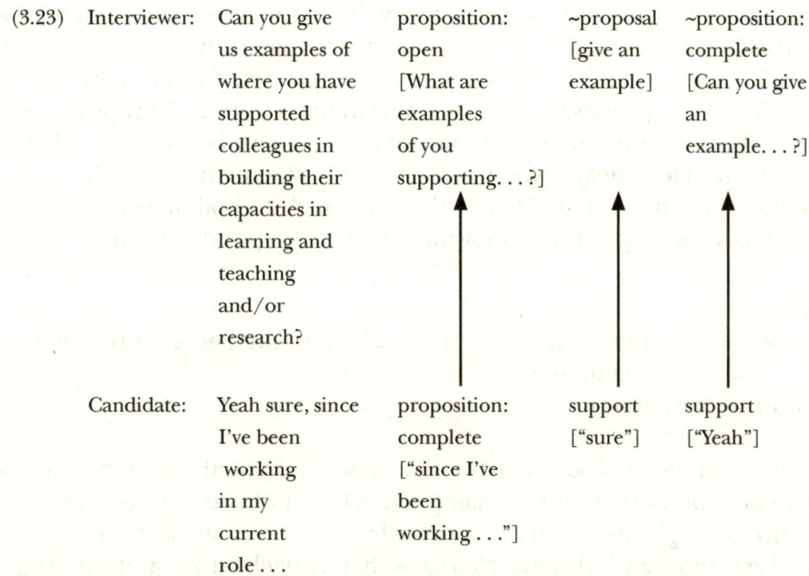

(3.23)	Interviewer:	Can you give us examples of where you have supported colleagues in building their capacities in learning and teaching and/or research?	proposition: open [What are examples of you supporting. . . ?]	~proposal [give an example]	~proposition: complete [Can you give an example. . . ?]
	Candidate:	Yeah sure, since I've been working in my current role . . .	proposition: complete ["since I've been working . . ."]	support ["sure"]	support ["Yeah"]

In this example, the interviewer's question *Can you give us examples of where* . . . involves three positions. At the literal level, it is a polar interrogative realizing a complete proposition asking whether or not you can give an answer (*Can you give* . . .), which is responded to first by the candidate as *Yeah* (in the right column). This proposition repositions a proposal that demands the candidate *give us examples* – that is, a proposal to speak (a linguistic service) – to which the candidate responds second with *sure* (middle column). But this of course repositions the main aim of the interviewer's question, which is to ask for information – *what are examples of where you have supported colleagues* – an open proposition that the candidate responds to by saying *since I've been working in my current role* . . . (left column). In doing so, the candidate is negotiating all three interpersonal tiers at once, so as to manage the significant status differential inherent in job interviews.[5]

Although repositioning is commonly involved in linguistic services, it is in fact a more general resource for re-orienting resources in tenor as other resources. It regularly involves interpersonal grammatical metaphor, in Halliday's terms.[6] This is illustrated by looking back at Kollontai's Text 3.3, which listed a series of demands to the government. In this example, we can say that proposals such as Kollontai's *The law must intervene to help women to combine work and maternity* involve repositioning. A demand such as this is a proposal by virtue of the fact that rendering support would involve the law actually doing the action demanded – intervening to help women combine work and maternity. But, lexicogrammatically speaking, it is not written as an imperative (which is the typical realization of proposals) but as a declarative (typical of propositions). If spoken at a rally, one could imagine a response by a comrade being "Yes!" or "Hear hear," which supports the statement but does not go about implementing it. That is, demands such as Kollontai's reposition proposals as propositions, allowing people to respond to both.

(3.24)

The law must intervene to help women to combine work and maternity.	proposal	**repositioned as**	proposition

Repositioned proposals such as this draw heavily on the grammatical system of MODULATION (*must* in Example [3.24]). Modulation resources mark degrees of obligation and inclination, but are only available for proposals realized through indicative clauses – that is, declaratives and interrogatives. As Halliday and Matthiessen (2014, p. 178) note, modulated clauses realize proposals, but unlike typical proposals, they regularly implicate a third person to do the action being proposed through the Subject (*the law* in this example). In addition, by virtue of involving a finite (*must* in this example), they allow for degrees of obligation to be specified.[7]

More broadly, it is common for propositions to establish action exchanges. Kristy does this when she says *don't want to go out today*. It is a declarative, grammatically speaking, and can be rendered as a proposition (e.g., through *neither do I*; *yeah, same*; or *yes, I know*). But she in fact is saying this as a proposal to not go out. Her mother recognizes this and so rejects it not in terms of the proposition of whether or not Kristy *wants* to go, but rather in terms of the proposal by characterizing what it will be like when she goes out (*you'll have a lovely day pet*). In this sense, this example also repositions a proposal as a proposition. In this instance, we can interpret this in terms of the relationship between the *want to* and the *go out* in the Process (which Halliday & Matthiessen [2014, pp. 584–587] describe in terms of projection). Rendering the move as a proposition will focus on the *want to*, while rendering it as a proposal will focus on the *go out*.

We will not explore repositioning any further here, other than to note that it offers a resource for significantly expanding interpersonal meaning, as multiple tenor resources are imposed on one another. As noted above, repositioning works with interpersonal grammatical metaphor as a resource for layering interpersonal meaning. Interpersonal grammatical metaphor does this by establishing a relation of incongruence between discourse semantics and lexicogrammar, whereas repositioning does this through an iteration of choices within tenor. As we have seen, this iteration of choices allows for more than two layers of meaning to be presented at a time, so as to engage in social regulation in some sense – whether that be in a classroom, a legal setting, or a political context. Repositioning allows proposals and propositions to come together to organize both ideas and people at the same time.

3.5 Purview: Speaker and Listener Positioning

There is one further step we need to take in order to understand how social relationships are negotiated through the system of POSITIONING. When negotiating meanings, speakers regularly nuance their messages in relation to the meanings they may share with the listener. As noted at the beginning of this chapter, speakers generally try to massage conversations towards maximizing affiliation. That is, in friendly and cooperative conversation, people will generally try to speak in a way that maximizes support and agreement; and when disagreement is a possibility, people will tend to soften the message in a way that makes the rejection less risky or impactful. As Zhang (2021, 2024) shows, extending the work of Berry (1981a) and Muntigl (2009), a major resource for doing this involves speakers indicating whether they have the knowledge being negotiated or not or responsibility for what is being negotiated or not, and at the same time positioning the addressee as either having this knowledge or responsibility or not.

Kristy's mother uses such resources to nuance her meanings effectively. This is illustrated when she attempts to bring Kristy around by illustrating that she does in fact like going away from her mother sometimes. In her first move during this stretch, she uses a tag at the end of her statement with reversed polarity (Halliday & Matthiessen, 2014), which suggests that she expects Kristy to agree.

(3.25)	Mother:	you go away from me to kinder, **don't you**?	proposition
			↑
	Kristy:	yeah but –	support

Put another way, Kristy's mother sets up her message in a way that shows she expects these meanings will likely be shared (what Hasan [1989] calls a reassuring confirmation move). This in turn positions Kristy to support them as the default, making it more socially risky for her to reject them. Whether this expectation of shared meanings is done in a "loving" way (what in Chapter 4 we call *warming*), or in a somewhat threatening way (what we call *warning*), depends on both the intonation and the voice quality of the message (van Leeuwen, 1999), plus other paralinguistic features (Ngo et al., 2022). If spoken in a higher pitch with rising tone (tone 2; Halliday & Greaves, 2008), this is likely a warming message, said with love. If said on lower pitch with falling tone (tone 1), this is likely a more threatening message as a warning ("agree or else"). Nonetheless, in both cases, the expectation is that Kristy will support what her mother says – which she of course does. The fact that she starts to come around from this point on and negotiates openly with her mother (rather than crying more or losing her temper) suggests that this was said in a warming manner.

The shared message in Example (3.26) contrasts with other messages that are simply asserted, with little indication about whether Kristy's mother expects it to be shared or not.

(3.26) Mother: you'll have a lovely day pet

Alternatively, at the beginning of the conversation, both Kristy and her mother put forward proposals, but do so in a way that suggests they are not particularly tied to them. In Example (3.27), they do this through the relatively lexicalized phrases *what about* and *how about* at the beginning of their proposals. These markers suggest that they are each relatively open to being rejected, which they are.

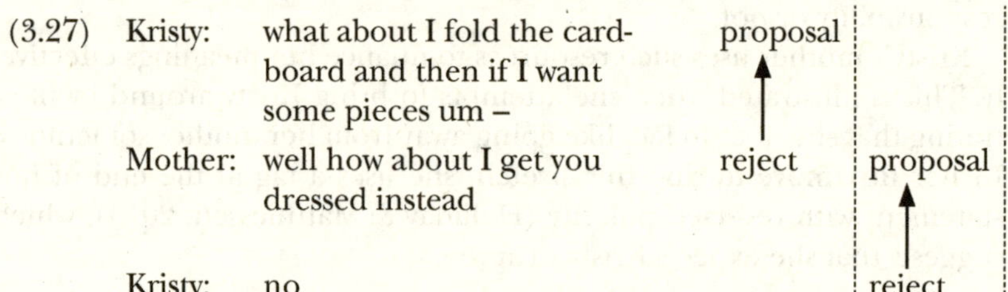

This nuancing of positions is crucial for texts to unfold smoothly. They allow meanings to be tendered in ways that increase or decrease the risk of conflict, while at the same time massaging the conversation towards support and positive affiliation (Zhang, 2020b).

To describe these nuances, we will consider them in terms of who has *purview* over the meanings being tendered. By this we refer to who (if anyone) in the conversation is interpersonally tied to the message being put forward or is wedded to its outcome. There can be speaker purview, in which case the speaker is wedded to what they are putting forward, or no speaker purview, in which case they are not. At the same time, there can be listener purview, where the speaker is handing control of the meanings over to the listener, or no listener purview, where they are not.[8]

As Example (3.28) illustrates, a speaker can maintain purview with no suggestion that the listener will already share the meanings (i.e., no listener purview). This often occurs when a speaker relatively baldly *asserts* a proposition or proposal (+ speaker purview; – listener purview).

(3.28) Mother: you'll have a lovely day pet proposition/**assert**

In this instance, Kristy's mother is stating a proposition without suggesting that Kristy necessarily has much say in the matter. For proposals, this often takes the form of a command (or an A2 in exchange structure), where the speaker proposes what the listener is to do, without any acknowledgment of whether the listener wants to or not (though we will problematize this for proposals below). This occurs when Kristy yells at Ruth after she annoys Kristy (*don't!*), and again when Kristy's mother chastises her for getting cranky (each of these instances is bolded in Example [3.29], along with an assertion of a proposition). In each of these instances, the positions are working to reject something – first Ruth's action, then Kristy's reaction, and finally the possibility of Kristy getting cranky (a prospective rendering; Zhang, 2020c).

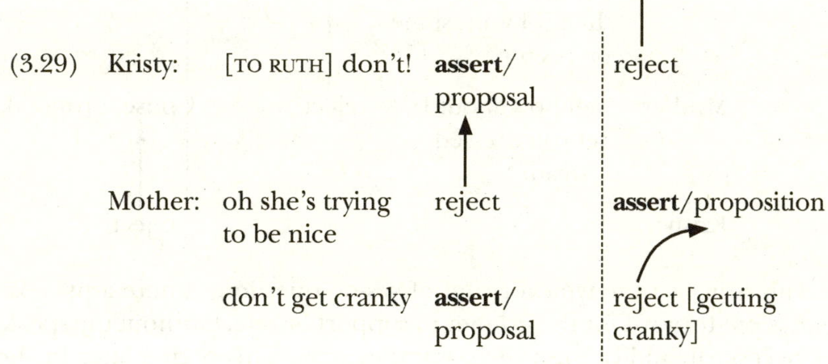

Alternatively, as we saw above, Kristy's mother can indicate that she expects meanings to be *shared* between them. In this case, both the speaker and the listener have purview over the meanings (+ speaker purview; + listener purview) – a reading reinforced by Kristy's support.

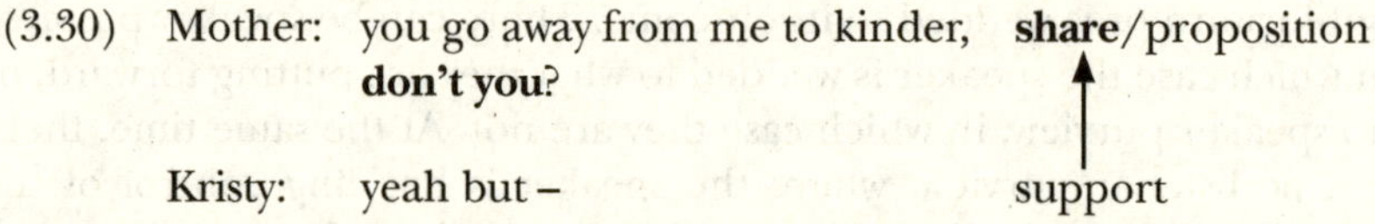

For proposals, this typically also occurs through commands (A2 moves) that include various interpersonal markers that suggest that the listener also agrees. The most common of these is tagging, perhaps reinforced by the inclusive *let's* (which Halliday & Matthiessen [2014] describe as a "suggestion – i.e., something that is at the same time both a command and an offer" [p. 166]).

(3.31) Let's go, shall we? **share**/proposal

Whereas both the sharing and asserting options maintain speaker purview, with or without listener purview, Kristy and her mother also illustrate how we may release speaker purview. We see this in Example (3.32), where both Kristy and her mother loosen control over what they are proposing and hand decision making over to the other (– speaker purview; + listener purview – though note below that we will call this *internal purview*). By *posing* a proposition or proposal in this way, they make it interpersonally easier for the other to reject what was being suggested.

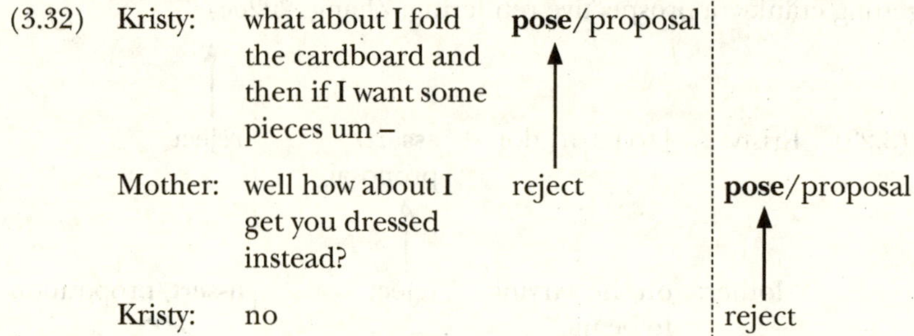

This is in fact the typical realm of yes-no questions, where a proposition is put forward for the listener to support or reject without the speaker necessarily indicating which way they lean. This occurs later in the conversation, when Kristy's mother has called Ruth a goose for squashing her hand, and Kristy asks the following:

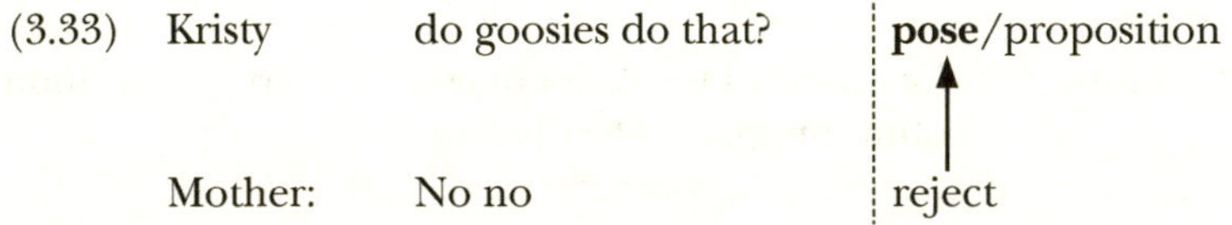

This question can be contrasted with the sharing proposition in Example (3.31). When Kristy asks, *do goosies do that?*, she is asking a genuine question (and so is relinquishing her purview to her mother); but when her mother says, *you go away from me to kinder, don't you?*, she is not in fact asking Kristy as such – she is putting forward a proposition she agrees with, and is indicating that she expects Kristy to agree. This interplay of who has purview over the meanings being tendered allows Kristy's mother to further steer the conversation in her direction. For example, she can downplay controversial proposals (like Kristy getting dressed) by giving Kristy purview to support or reject them. When Kristy does reject them, her mother can then turn to relatively uncontroversial meanings and present them in a shared way, so as to build solidarity and try again down the track. As this conversation shows, Kristy's mother is an experienced negotiator, ceding control to Kristy whenever it is needed and coaxing her into agreement when the going is good.

Finally, it is possible to indicate that neither the speaker nor the listener is expected to know the answer to something – what we will call *airing* (– speaker purview; – listener purview). This often happens with the lexicalized phrase *I don't know* (or perhaps more accurately, *dunno*). For example, once Kristy's mother has finally managed to start getting Kristy dressed, Kristy asks her why her dress is only buttoned up on one side, to which her mother attempts to give an answer, before acknowledging that she simply doesn't know.

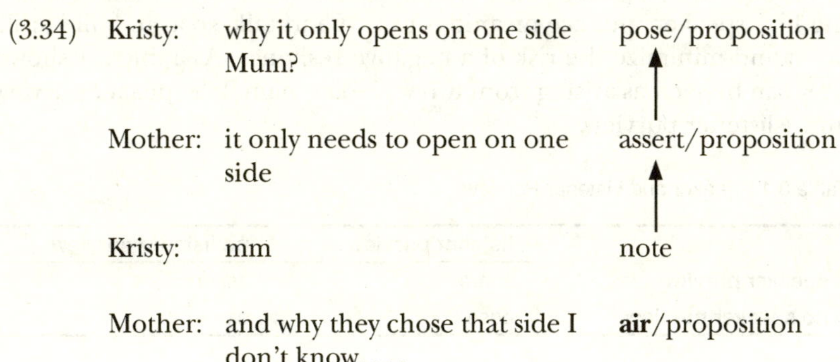

In another conversation from Hasan's data (2009, AJ6B5), a mother is reading a cookbook with her daughter and airs her exclamation about coconut cream hoppers through *I wonder.*

(3.35)	Mother:	Now, here's a whole lot of coconut things: coconut bananas, coconut fish, coconut cream hoppers	assert/proposition
		I wonder what coconut cream hoppers are!	**air**/proposition
			↑
	Janet:	[LAUGHS]	defer/support

Importantly, it is still possible to give a response in these situations; but the position can be aired without indicating that anyone should be tied to it. This occurs in a separate conversation between mothers, when one mother is describing what it's like when her child is in therapy for their disability. She suggests it might be her little break, but that she is not wedded to this at all.

(3.36)	Renee:	we're trying to have a balance	assert/proposition
		we do a lot of therapies with him	assert/proposition
		and so for me it's kinda like, I don't know if that's my little break	**air**/proposition

These four options of *assert, share, pose,* and *air* offer resources for seeing how speakers nuance meanings in text and talk, so as to build affiliation and minimize the risk of a negative response. As Table 3.1 shows, they can be seen as arising from two variables, namely ± speaker purview and ± listener purview.

Table 3.1 Speaker and Listener Purview

	listener purview	**no listener purview**
speaker purview	share	assert
no speaker purview	pose	air

The examples above all focused on complete propositions and proposals. For propositions or proposals that are open, often involving *wh-* questions, the default purview is pose (– speaker purview; + listener purview). We can see this in Example (3.37), where Kristy poses a *wh-* question to her mother.

(3.37)	Kristy:	why it only opens on one side Mum?	pose/proposition ↑
	Mother:	it only needs to open on one side	assert/proposition

Though as Example (3.35) shows, open propositions can have their purview varied – in this case, as aired through *I wonder* (replayed in Example [3.38]).

(3.38)	Mother:	I wonder what coconut cream hoppers are!	**air**/proposition ↑
	Janet:	[LAUGHS]	defer/support

A further contrast in purview for open propositions is shown in Example (3.39), from Halliday (1970, p. 22). Here a *wh-* interrogative is used with different tones – a falling tone (tone 1) in Example (3.39a) and a rising tone (tone 2) in Example (3.39b).

(3.39) a. //1 where are you **go**ing//
b. //2 where are you **go**ing//

As Halliday (1970) notes, "the first [3.39a with a falling tone] is a normal question, neither abrupt nor deferential, while the second is deferential: it is a question accompanied by a request for permission to ask 'where are you going, may I ask'" (p. 22). We can understand this by considering again the distinction between internal and external readings of these positions. Looking externally, in terms of the "information" being asked for, both simply pose a question – they have the same purview (i.e., – speaker; + listener). However viewed internally in terms of their role as speech acts initiating exchanges, on the other hand, they differ in their purview. Example (3.39a), with a falling tone, does not seek permission to ask the question; it simply asks the questions. Thus internally it can be read as an assert, with the speaker controlling the exchange (+ internal speaker purview; – internal listener purview). By contrast Example (3.39b), with a rising tone, indicates some tentativeness (Halliday & Matthiessen, 2014, p. 169) – in some sense asking permission to initiate the exchange. This example can be read internally as a pose (– internal speaker purview; + internal listener purview), handing control of the exchange over to the listener.

Similarly, in the Australian English dialect spoken by the first and third authors of this book, open propositions can be internally shared (+ internal speaker purview; + internal listener purview) by using non-lexical tags such as *ay* (/æɪ/) on a falling tone (tone 1).

(3.40) But what do we do, ay?

This example is still asking a question (externally speaking); but through the tag it is making it clear that this is a question that both interlocutors probably share.

The distinction between internal and external purview also helps us understand the interpersonal dynamics of proposals. Example (3.41), adapted from a different conversation between Kristy and her mum while they are cooking together, involves a command from Kristy for her mother to put honey and milk into a bowl. Considering it in terms of purview, there is a question as to *who* has purview: Is it Kristy as the one who commands the action (the A2/secondary actor in Berry's terms)? Or is it her mother as the one who does the action (the A1/primary actor in Berry's terms)?

(3.41) Kristy: Put honey in and milk
Mother: [PUTS HONEY AND MILK IN]

For action exchanges that involve proposals like this, the answer is in fact both. Externally, we are concerned with who has control of the action (i.e. who does the action?). Thus looking at purview externally it is the mother who has purview here, because she does the action of putting the honey and milk in the bowl (the mother here as primary actor). But viewing purview internally, we are concerned with who has control over the exchange (i.e. who does the commanding?). In this case, it is Kristy who has purview here because she does the commanding. The fact that Kristy has *internal* purview can be seen from the fact that her command can only be rendered internally: Kristy's mother can only support or abort the exchange (*Put honey in and milk / No*). By contrast, she can render the action itself externally (PUTS HONEY AND MILK IN / *Not like that!*). This analysis is illustrated in Example (3.42):

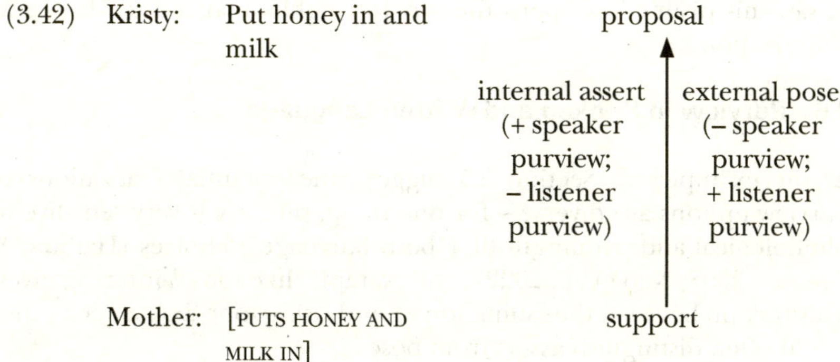

This allows us to understand in more detail the purview of offers in exchanges (exchanges with Da1^A2^A1 as their structure, in Berry's terms) – as illustrated by Example (3.43) from the same text (leaving aside the repositioning). In this example, Kristy's mother offers to fill the cup. In doing so, she gives internal purview to Kristy to decide whether the action of filling the cup will happen (internal pose), while giving herself purview over actually doing the cup filling (external assert).

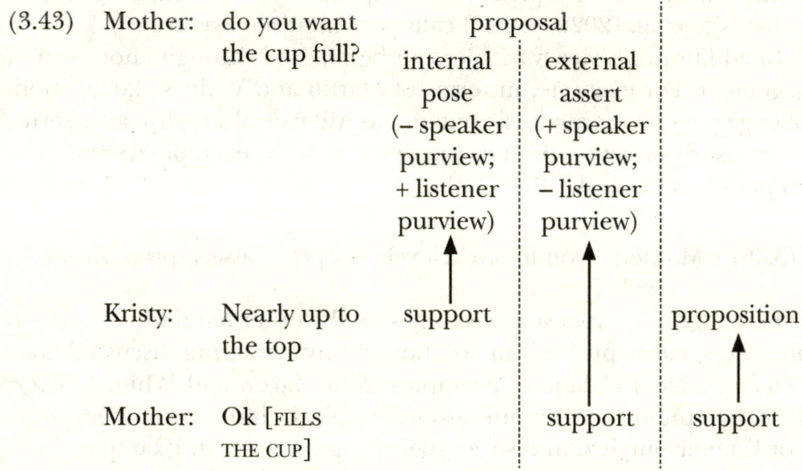

As Examples (3.39)–(3.43) illustrate, the interplay between internal and external purview allows negotiation of different aspects of semiosis to occur at the same time – the proposition or proposal being put forward *and* the use of language itself. Aside from some examples associated with engagement in Section 3.6, we will not explore in more detail the distinction between internal and external purview here. Needless to say, this distinction opens the way for highly nuanced tendering in conversation.

3.6 Purview in Spoken and Written Language

As the examples in Section 3.5 suggest, the potential realizations of purview options are diverse – for one thing, purview is very sensitive to phonological and paralinguistic ("body language") choices (Halliday & Greaves, 2008; Ngo et al., 2022). For example, like for *wh*-interrogatives, a distinction between the falling tone 1 and rising tone 2 on a declarative would often distinguish assert from pose.

(3.44)	Kristy:	//1 I don't want to go away from you //	assert/proposition
(3.45)	Mother:	//2 you don't want to go to Dee's?//	pose/proposition

Similarly, an open posture, supine hand position, and/or decentred facial features would typically lessen speaker purview paralinguistically (what Ngo et al. [2022, p. 144] calls paralinguistic expansion).

In addition, purview variables can be realized through choices in engagement. For example, in terms of Martin and White's (2005) model of engagement, monoglossic statements will typically realize an assertion (+ speaker purview; – listener purview), as in an example we saw above (replayed as Example [3.46]).

(3.46)	Mother:	you'll have a lovely day pet	assert/proposition

Heteroglossic expansion resources on the other hand will typically realize no speaker purview, in addition to any rendering discussed above (Zhang, 2020c). Adapting examples from Martin and White (2005, p. 107), heteroglossic entertain resources typically indicate neither speaker nor listener purview, and so *air* their proposition as in Examples (3.47) and (3.48).

(3.47)	The organ screen in the stables was **possibly** designed by Thomas Chippendale	air/proposition

(3.48)	Mass extinctions **could** have been caused by major changes in sea level or disruptions in the food chain.	air/proposition

When interacting with tagging resources, this – speaker purview option may also combine with + listener purview to pose a proposition, as in the constructed Example (3.49).

(3.49)	The organ screen in the stables was **possibly** designed by Thomas Chippendale, **d'you reckon?**	pose/proposition

Heteroglossia often involves instances that in fact put forward two (or more) propositions. This opens space to nuance the purview of each position at the same time. Example (3.47) could alternatively have been written as Example (3.50).

(3.50)		**air**/proposition
	It is possible the organ screen in the stables was designed by Thomas Chippendale	[organ screen was designed by ... ; external] **assert**/proposition ["It is possible"; internal]

In this instance, the proposition realized through the embedded clause *The organ screen in the stables was designed by Thomas Chippendale* indicates – speaker purview (*airing*), by virtue of the heteroglossic scoping given by *It is possible.* That is, the speaker is not committed to the proposition about whether or not the organ screen in the stables was designed by Thomas Chippendale. But the ranking clause *It is possible* . . . is baldly asserted; the speaker here is committing themselves to it being possible. In other words there are two propositions being put forward with different purview – whether or not the organ screen was designed by Thomas Chippendale is left open, but the possibility that it could have been designed by him is asserted. The distinction between Example (3.50), *It is possible that* . . ., and Example (3.47), *possibly*, is what Halliday refers to as explicit objective (*It is possible that* . . .) versus implicit objective (*possibly*) modality (Halliday & Matthiessen, 2014, p. 689). Once again we can interpret this opposition in terms of internal and external purview – the proposition of whether or not the design was by Thomas Chippendale is externally aired, but the assessment of its possibility is internally asserted.

This opens space for reconsidering examples such as Example (3.48) along the same lines, replayed here as Example (3.51). Externally speaking, considered in terms of whether or not mass extinctions were caused by changes in sea level or disruptions in the food chain, the proposition is aired – the *could* indicates that the author is not tied to whether or not this is the case. A response could render this proposition with something like *No, they weren't* – focusing on whether or not this *was* the cause, rather than any negotiation of whether it *could* be the cause. On the other hand, the possibility of them being caused this way is asserted (through the use of a declarative without any tagging). One could focus on the *could* and render the possibility of them being caused by saying something like *No, they couldn't have.* Asserting this suggests that rejecting the position along these lines would be more socially risky. But for academic discourse in particular, the play between the two purviews given through NEGOTIATION (the statement) and ENGAGEMENT (through the modality *could*) allows an author to have their cake and eat it too – to assert something baldly while not tying themselves to its actuality.

(3.51)	Mass extinctions **could** have been caused by major changes in sea level or disruptions in the food chain.	**air**/proposition [Mass extinctions *were* caused by . . .; external] **assert**/proposition ["Mass extinctions *could have been* caused by . . ."; internal]

Finally, instances that involve projection, such as Example (3.52) from a news report given in Martin and White (2005, p. 112), also establish multiple propositions with the potential for different purview (plus sourcing – see Chapter 4).

(3.52)	A bishop today **describes** the Church of England's established status as indefensible	**air**/proposition ["the Church of England's established status as indefensible"] **assert**/proposition ["A bishop today describes . . ."]

Here, the reporter does not tie themselves to whether or not the Church of England's status is indefensible (airing: – speaker purview; – listener purview), but they do assert the fact that a bishop today *described* the Church of England's established status as indefensible (+ speaker purview; – listener purview). As longstanding work in media discourse has shown (e.g. White 1998, 2022; Iedema et al. 1994, Martin & White 2005), this ability for journalists to air things while not being seen to align with them is a crucial resource for maintaining a pretence of objectivity in news reporting.[9]

As for all other resources presented in this chapter, purview is not just a resource for managing the flow of conversation; it can also nuance positions in monologic text. To exemplify this we can consider the use of purview in Text 3.6, an informational plaque about a rocky outcrop off the coast of Coogee Beach in Sydney, Australia, known as *Wedding Cake Island.* This text begins with an open proposition about the name of the island (*Why is it called Wedding Cake Island?*), which is then rejected internally as not being answerable – *No-one really seems to know for sure.* The rest of the text then plays with purview in order to put possibilities out there and leave it to the reader to decide – beginning with the proposal *so use your imagination!*

Why is it called Wedding Cake Island?

No-one really seems to know for sure – so use your imagination!

Perhaps the white spray from breaking waves over its long low shape is reminiscent of white icing on a wedding cake.

Or perhaps hundreds of seagulls frosted the cake with their whitened droppings over the edge of the rocks!

Or......... What do YOU think?

Text 3.6 Informational plaque about Wedding Cake Island, Coogee Beach, Sydney, Australia (Randwick City Council, n.d.)

After proposing that readers use their imagination, the following two sentences put forward propositions, but do so with no speaker purview (marked by *perhaps* and the two linking connectors realized by *or*): ***Perhaps*** *the white spray from breaking waves over its long low shape is reminiscent of white icing on a wedding cake.* ***Or perhaps*** *hundreds of seagulls frosted the cake with their whitened droppings over the edge of rocks!* ***Or.........***

Here, the unfinished clause complex marked by the second *or*, with its long set of ellipsis makers (.........), emphasizes that other possibilities are there and that the writer is not tied to them (or even proposing them). Together, this heavily weakens speaker purview as far as explaining the name of Wedding Cake Island is concerned. As a final step, purview is handed over to the reader through another open proposition, *What do YOU think?* – with purview highlighted through the capitalization of *YOU.*

This contrasts with the prosody of assertion in Text 3.7. By virtue of this purview, this report on different types of matter establishes the "expert" stance that is so highly valued in scientific texts:

Physicists currently view matter as being grouped into three families – quarks, leptons and bosons.

The standard model explains interactions in terms of these families, which it further classifies as follows:

1. Matter particles. These are fundamental particles (that is, they have no known smaller parts). They are the quarks and leptons.
2. Force-carrier particles. Each type of fundamental force is caused by the exchange of force-carrier particles (also called messenger or exchange particles). These are the fundamental (or gauge) bosons. They include photons and gluons.

Text 3.7 Report on types of matter (Warren, 2003, pp. 246–247)

As these texts illustrate, purview is a resource that can be drawn upon to negotiate social relations in dialogue as we manage turns in conversation. But it is also a resource we can draw on in monologue to manage the play of voices that permeate our texts. In the informational plaque, the writer is clearly aiming to engage the reader through putting forward possibilities, while at the same time making it clear that they are pure speculation. In the scientific text, the aim is to present its knowledge in an expert voice.

Purview can be more or less grammaticalized across languages. In English, as we have seen, its realization is distributed across a range of interpersonal grammatical systems. But as Bartlett (2021) notes, Scottish Gaelic makes a distinction within indicative clauses which parallels to an extent how we have described speaker purview in both monologue and dialogue. Bartlett notes that rather than having a distinction between interrogatives and declaratives, Scottish Gaelic distinguishes between [assertive] and [non-assertive] clauses – which are realized through distinct verb forms and mood clitics. The non-assertive choice "render[s] propositions open to alternatives, whether this be through questioning, attributing or entertaining other possibilities. In contrast, independent forms without mood clitics [i.e., assertive choices] realise the monogloss semantics of unmodalised K1 moves and of K2 moves eliciting specific details in an uncontested proposition" (Bartlett, 2021, p. 276). Wang (2021) describes a similar choice for Mandarin Chinese between what he calls [pose] and [tender],[10] which is simultaneous with indicative and imperative – where "[pose] indicates that we table a proposition or proposal for assessment, opening up the dialogic space; [tender] on the other hand means that we proffer the proposition or proposal as non-negotiable" (p.122–123). Similarly, the description of STANCE in Korean by Kim et al. (2023) in effect proposes that informal Korean negotiates propositions and proposals through options in a system grammaticalizing purview, in contrast to formal Korean, which negotiates through MOOD (i.e., declarative, interrogative, and imperative) options (see also Martin & Cruz [2021] on ASSESSMENT systems in Tagalog). In this regard, as we have noted throughout this chapter (see in particular note 35), it was Zhang's (2020a, 2020b, 2020c, 2021, 2024) rich description of Khorchin Mongolian in this area that was a primary influence on our work here. Work of this kind indicates that the interpersonal grammar of languages needs to be re/interpreted from a top-down perspective,

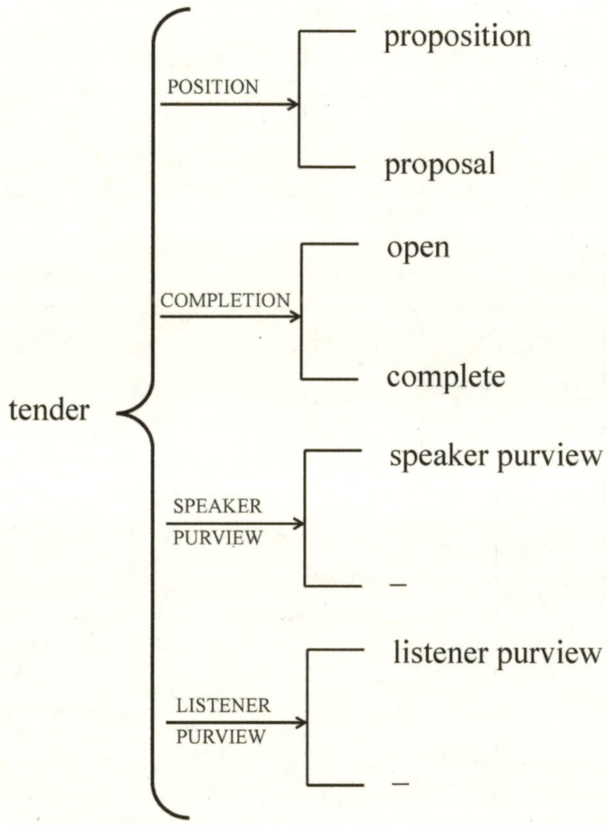

Figure 3.2 Options for tendering

beginning with something like the range of tenor options proposed in this volume. Otherwise it runs the risk of being trapped by an "Anglocentric" perspective that foregrounds declarative, interrogative, and imperative as basic interpersonal options.

With this discussion of purview, we have completed the set of options for the system of POSITIONING. Leaving aside repositioning, Figure 3.2 brings together the network of TENDERING established in this chapter. This network says that when tendering, one may tender a proposition or a proposal and that this proposition or proposal may be open or complete, may have speaker purview or not, and may have listener purview or not.

Figure 3.3 brings together the options for rendering built in Chapter 2 with those of tendering in this chapter to show the full system of POSITIONING.

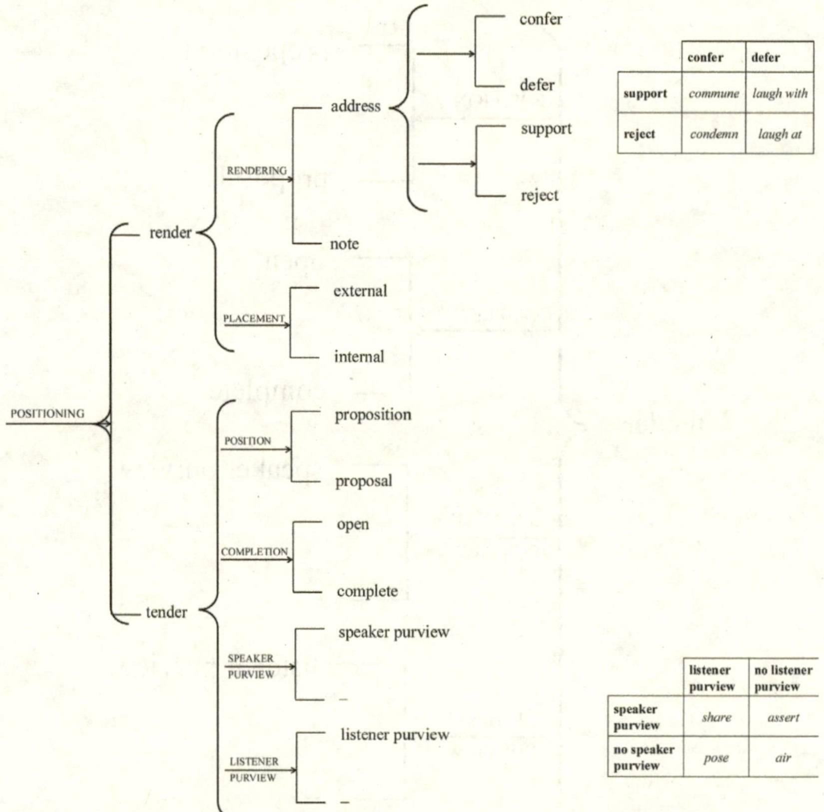

	confer	defer
support	*commune*	*laugh with*
reject	*condemn*	*laugh at*

	listener purview	no listener purview
speaker purview	*share*	*assert*
no speaker purview	*pose*	*air*

Figure 3.3 Full POSITIONING system

3.7 Conclusion

Whenever we talk to each other, we negotiate our social relations. We put forward meanings, and we react to those that have been put forward. We present meanings in a way that suggests they may or may not be shared, and we engage with them in more or less sympathetic ways. In Chapters 2 and 3, we have presented a model of resources for how we put forward and react to these meanings. We first stepped through the system of rendering to show the different ways we can engage with meanings that have been tendered or implicated in a text. Then in this chapter, we explored how people can put forward meanings in nuanced ways that acknowledge the positions of those around them. Together these resources allow for the intricate negotiation of social relations that all of us engage in everyday.

This negotiation is enabled not simply through the different ways in which we can tender and render positions, but also through the possibility of layering these meanings. In Chapter 2, we explored that people may tender and render meanings at the same time, reacting to something that has happened (or may happen) while putting something else forward to be negotiated. We saw that this was a key resource for extending conversation indefinitely, and in doing so, we offered a view on chat from the perspective of tenor. In addition, we saw that when engaging with meanings through rendering or nuancing meanings through purview, we can do so for the propositions or proposals being discussed (external negotiation), or we can alternatively do so for the speech acts themselves (internal negotiation) – in the latter case commenting on how language itself is being used. This allows for a second plane of discussion that takes the reality of text as a thing in itself, rather than just semiosis about something else. Finally, we saw all of these resources could be repositioned, with one position standing for another. This offers a third avenue through which people may negotiate their social relations along multiple lines.

Social relations are intricate – we negotiate our status and our solidarity all the time and in multiple ways at once. The system of POSITIONING we have established in Chapters 2 and 3 captures the basic set of resources we use to do this negotiation. Throughout, we have tried to capture both the *inter* of the interpersonal (in terms of how we establish turn-taking and dialogue and how we position others in relation to ourselves) and the *personal* of the interpersonal (in order to understand how we express ourselves and share our feelings). By bringing these perspectives together, we can better understand the orchestration of interpersonal meaning that unfolds through spoken and written texts.

In the next chapter, we extend our exploration of interpersonal meanings by considering how different positions can be connected to one another in dialogue and monologue. In particular, we will explore how these connections support the development of integrated sets of values – both those that are ephemeral (that are needed for only a particular situation at a particular point in time) and those that are deep and long-standing (that organize the way we see and engage with the world). By taking this step, we will gain insight not simply into how we negotiate social relations, but also into what the meanings are that underpin these social relations.

4 Building Values: Establishing Meanings to Share

4.1 Introduction

When we talk to each other, we do so upon a vast background of shared values. These may be culture-wide values that are deeply held and rarely questioned, they may be more explicit values constantly up for contestation, or they may be very personal feelings known only to a few. These values may govern the shape of our lives and lead us to take arms against a sea of troubles, or they may simply be small, liminal, and seemingly inconsequential feelings that help us sort out our day-to-day lives and commune with the people we know. Nonetheless, throughout our social life, these values guide our decisions and the ways we talk; they allow us to affiliate with people, build solidarity, and help us sort out the world as we navigate a passage through it.

When Kristy and her mother were having the chat we looked at in the previous chapters, they were not just negotiating whether to get dressed; they were also sorting out their feelings about going out. While seemingly small, by clarifying and negotiating these quotidian feelings, Kristy and her mother were able to come to an agreed solution. It also helped Kristy's mother get more of an insight into the background values that organize how Kristy sees the world – and in doing so, offered an opportunity for them to become closer.

As we have seen, when Kristy's mother suggests that she gets dressed, Kristy makes clear that she does not want to go out.

(4.1)	Kristy:	what about I fold the cardboard and then if I want some pieces um –
	Mother:	well how about I get you dressed instead?
	Kristy:	*no, don't want to go out today* [CRYING]

However, as the conversation progresses, it becomes clear that this resistance to going out is a little more complex than it initially appeared. Kristy's mother first attempts to interpret Kristy's tears by suggesting that rather than being upset about her going out today, she thinks Kristy is upset because the TV wasn't working.

(4.2) Mother: Oh dear, oh dear . . .
I don't think you're really upset about me going
I think you're upset because the TV wasn't working

But Kristy rejects this again by continuing to cry and reasserting, *I don't want to go away.* As the conversation moves on, Kristy begins to put forward a more nuanced view on what going out entails and the feelings this provokes.

(4.3) Mother: you go away from me to kinder, don't you?
Kristy: yeah but –
Mother: and you like going away from me sometimes
Kristy: yeah
but then I meet not so many kids at kinder
and there's not only a big room

Here, Kristy makes clear that although she is fine to go to kinder and be away sometimes, there are things that occur at Dee's such as meeting lots of kids and having to be in one big room that she does not like. By doing so, she makes a contrast between kinder and Dee's that her mother had not initially picked up on. Taking this as her lead, her mother then reconfigures what she takes to be Kristy's feelings and poses a question to her, to which Kristy finally agrees.

(4.4) Mother: *you mean you want to go to kinder but you don't want to go to Dee's?*
Kristy: yeah

Through this brief conversation, Kristy and her mother have developed new shared meanings. They are *new* in the sense that the opposition between wanting to go to kinder and not wanting to go to Dee's was not one that Kristy's mother had clearly appreciated, and *shared* because they arose out of a negotiation that eventually led to agreement. It is everyday sets of values and feelings such as these that underpin the social relations that tie us together with other people and larger communities, and set us apart from others who do not share our world view. In our friendships, we spend our time with those with whom we have built up large sets of shared experiences; in our work, we spend our time with those who are doing similar things and aiming towards similar goals; in activist groups, we spend our time with those who share our political outlook (or spend our time fighting those who do not share this outlook); in our sports fan life, we go to games to support our team and share our excitement or pain with thousands of other fans; at home, our relationships often thrive or wither on the mundane ways in which we negotiate our days together.

In this chapter, we will explore how sets of meanings such as this are built and arranged. In the model of tenor presented in this book, we will do so by introducing resources within a system called ORIENTING. These resources explore how positions are related to each other and oriented into coherent networks of meaning. Importantly, the networks of meaning that are explored in this chapter are not those based on ideational meaning (so we are not considering the "content" meanings of positions here) – but rather they are based on their rhetorical organization via interpersonal meanings. As we introduce these resources, we will explore how they build a "map" of meanings that underlie our talk and allow us to interpret the coherence of interpersonally oriented texts. In terms of SFL, this will involve drawing on the discourse semantic systems of ENGAGEMENT and INTERNAL CONNEXION in particular, as well as the phonological and lexicogrammatical resources that realize them. As in Chapter 3, we will also explore how these resources help realize different genres and their stages.

First, we will step through the theoretical development that underpins the resources in this chapter, focusing in particular on the interaction between SFL models of individuation and bond networks, alongside the Legitimation Code Theory conception of axiological constellations. Then we will work our way through each of the ORIENTING resources and draw on these resources to build a picture of the underlying meanings established in a series of texts.

4.2 Underlying Values

There are a number of questions that need to be asked if we are to understand the background values organizing the way we speak and write in everyday life:

- How do we orient multiple positions in relation to each other and to different people?

- How can we see the sets of shared understandings and values that organize the way we talk?
- How do these positions and values get developed and arranged through texts?

These questions directly implicate SFL's long-standing dialogue with the sociological framework of Legitimation Code Theory (LCT; Maton, 2014). LCT conceptualizes communities and social fields of practice as being organized through more or less tightly bound sets of positions called *constellations* of meaning. Constellations organize the way we see the world by offering a coherent perspective for arranging meanings. The most important type of constellation for this chapter is that which centres on emotional, aesthetic, ethical, moral, and political stances, which LCT calls *axiological constellations* (Maton, 2014).[1] Axiological constellations conceptualize how people come together not in terms of empirical or (in LCT terms) epistemic relations, but rather in terms of their social relations.

The concept of constellations in LCT thus offers a perspective on how people can be positioned in communities. As Maton (2014, p. 158) explains, tightly bound constellations in a community delimit the possible combinations of stances available to people by orienting options as necessarily associated or opposed. This means if someone aligns with one position in a constellation, it will likely be taken to mean they also align with others – regardless of whether they state this explicitly. Maton (2014) illustrates this by mapping the axiological constellation in education that opposes so-called student-centred learning environments with teacher-centred learning environments. If someone aligns themselves with student-centred learning environments, it can be presumed that they also align with *authentic* tasks, *experiential* learning, *social constructivist* models of learning, and a range of other stances, whether or not this is actually the case. By contrast, if someone is positioned as being aligned with teacher-centred approaches, it can be presumed that they are supportive of *transmission* models of teaching, *decontextualized* tasks, *reductionist* conceptualizations of knowledge, and so on, whether or not this is actually the case. In education, axiological constellations of this kind position people in the field, and in doing so, they offer a seemingly coherent view of the educational world that organizes different approaches, practices, and people into communities of shared values.

Exploring axiological constellations is thus vital for understanding how people affiliate in communities, understand the world around them, maintain solidarity, and distance themselves from "outsiders." But by their very nature, such constellations are often implicit and rarely discussed in detail. The result is that they often only surface when someone goes against the order of things – whether this be someone new to the community who does not know the way things are, someone with a different constellation that leads to a clash, or someone aiming to challenge the constellation, either through iconoclastic ruptures or through gradual progressive adjustment. As Maton (2014, p. 152) explains, this highlights that constellations are not unchanging monoliths, but are constantly being negotiated and developed. From the perspective of SFL, the construction or deconstruction of constellations draws on resources of language and related semiotic systems to organize their meaning and regularly show reflexes in texts. The challenge for a socially oriented linguistics like SFL is to understand what these resources are, how they manifest in text, how we can map these constellations in ways that make their arrangement explicit, and in addition how we can understand their dynamics, stability, and reorganization in ways that support interventions for change across contexts.

Linguistically speaking, modelling axiological constellations implicates questions of bonding, as developed by Stenglin (2004, 2022). Initially focused on how people negotiate three-dimensional space, Stenglin (2004) introduces *bonding* as "concerned with communing, that is, the way occupants of a space are positioned interpersonally to create solidarity. It is thus concerned with ways of building togetherness, inclusiveness and affiliation . . . as though [people] belong . . . to a community of like-minded people" (p. 402). Stenglin (2004) notes in particular that the process of bonding often centres on "emblems or powerfully evocative symbols of social belonging" that she calls *bonding icons* (p. 406). For example, drawing on work by Ravelli (2000), Stenglin (2004) explores a range of bonding icons associated with the Olympics, such as the Olympic Flame and the Olympic Rings, that crystallize community values – that allow people to rally around them and share their feelings. For our purposes, Stenglin's work illustrates that instances of semiosis can implicate a vast range of interpersonal meanings that are critical resources for engendering community.

This work has been extended in recent years by Martin (2010) and Carr (2023, 2025) through the concept of iconization. *Iconization* is the process by which interpersonal meanings are charged, often at the same time as ideational meanings are discharged (Martin, 2010). From this perspective, bonding icons are highly iconized meanings that are often central to larger networks of meaning. Carr (2023) highlights that bonding icons such as the Olympic Flame can be treated as iconized ideation, since they take an ideational entity or occurrence and instil interpersonal meaning. In addition, she notes how already interpersonal terms such as *respect* (i.e., an attitude) can be iconized in contexts such as sex education classes as a means of organizing the values at stake when navigating social relationships. So, complementing iconized ideation, terms such as *respect* iconize the evaluative meanings of attitude (Carr, 2025, p. 185; what Martin [2021b] calls "axicons"). This process parallels distillations of ideational meaning, whereby both ideational meanings such as *oestrogen* and attitudinal meaning such as *consent* can be technicalized (Carr, 2023; Wignell et al., 1989). This work highlights the ways in which interpersonal meaning can be "instilled" (Carr, 2023) into lexis and the centrality of this iconization process in communities of practice. In particular, it illustrates the meanings that can be encapsulated (see Section 4.3.5) as radiating individual terms.

When analysing constellations, in addition to exploring the meanings encapsulated *within* terms, it is also important to explore their outward relations with other meanings. This is highlighted in Knight's work (2010a, 2010b), where *bonds* were characterized as shared couplings of attitude and ideation (an *evaluative coupling*). In Example (4.5), Kristy's mother puts forward a coupling of positive attitude through *like* (in bold) with an ideational occurrence *going away from me sometimes* (underlined) – which is shared by Kristy, as indicated by her supporting it through *yeah.* This sharing of an evaluative coupling in Knight's model indicates that Kristy liking going away from her mother sometimes is a bond.

(4.5)	Mother:	and you **like** going away from me sometimes
	Kristy:	yeah

Knight notes that bonds do not occur in isolation, but are typically arranged into larger networks of meaning she called *bond networks.* These bond networks are conceptualized as being shared by communities as values, which are maintained and developed through conversation. For our purposes, Knight's conception of bond networks offers a linguistic perspective on axiological constellations and how they are negotiated. Knight's work also highlights the need to understand the relationships that underpin bond networks in communities, in order to grasp how they "hang together" and develop in text.

Work stemming from exploration of Japanese iconography by Tann (2010a, 2010b, 2013) offers the richest SFL model to date of relations between such values (see also Tilakaratna [2016] and Zappavigna & Martin [2018b], who develop Tann's work). In his research on national identity, Tann explores how iconography builds a communal view of the world based on "us" versus "them" through shared values and their manifestation as texts across a range of semiotic modes. Tann's model focuses attention to the range of resources that are drawn on to build this national identity. What is most important here is that the model emphasizes how a sense of community is manifested through celebrated people and semiotic artifacts (that Tann calls "Heroes" and "Heritage") and highly charged abstractions ("Isms" and "Adages"), and how these together synthesize the "unique ethos" of a community (Tann, 2010a). Tann thus offers a key insight into the types of icons and relationships between them that must be explored if we wish to understand highly interpersonally charged discourse. Significantly, Tann does not develop these types of icons and relationships in an ad hoc manner as meanings presented opportunistically; rather he shows how icons are developed in text as systematic patterns of language in unfolding texts.

Taken together, these developments of SFL theory and its description of values and shared understandings shed light on how social relations are developed in everyday life. But they also highlight the need for understanding the different types of meaning that can be shared, the relations that hold these meanings together, and the means by which they are realized in text. This is vital for making explicit meanings that organize a wide range of institutional practices. To take one institution, education, as an example, SFL research has drawn attention to the importance of values for shaping students' ways of viewing intimate relationships in sex education (Carr, 2023, 2025), for interpreting literature and poetics in relation to our view of the sociopolitical world (Jackson, 2021), for appreciating people and events in history (Coffin, 2006; Hao & Martin, 2024; Martin et al., 2010), and for understanding how second-language learning is never ideologically "neutral" (Tilakaratna, 2016).

In short, to appreciate what we know and learn over and above the "content" meanings of language (i.e., an epistemological perspective), we must understand how language builds and develops its networks of values (i.e., an axiological perspective). This chapter will explore this by extending work by Doran (2020a, 2020b, 2024) on how we can "see" axiological constellations in language. This work arose from the challenge of modelling texts such as editorials, comment pieces, and uncommonsense texts in the humanities that do not clearly unfold through discrete stages or through a logic oriented to their content meanings (field), but rather unfold through the arrangement of values and prosodies of evaluative meaning (Feez et al., 2010). Building on the model developed in previous chapters, we will see that the development of background values implicates in particular the discourse semantic systems of ENGAGEMENT and INTERNAL CONNEXION (Halliday & Hasan, 1976; Martin, 1992; Martin &

White, 2005) and leads to a fine-grained understanding of how interpersonal rhetoric unfolds. As for all resources in this book, we will illustrate how these resources are drawn on in both monologic and dialogic texts.

4.3 Orienting Positions

To explore how positions are arranged, we will introduce five resources within a system called ORIENTING:

- *sourcing* – where positions are oriented as being **from** the perspective of someone or something (as "theirs" in some sense);
- *convoking* – where positions are oriented **towards** someone or something, or someone is being brought into the position;
- *opposing* – where positions are oriented as being **opposed** to each other;
- *likening* – where positions are oriented as to some degree **similar** to each other, or on "the same side" of an opposition; and
- *encapsulating* – where sets of positions are oriented as being synthesized **within** other meanings.

These relations function to orient different meanings in relation to each other so as to build a large network of positions. As we will see, each choice can be repeated any number of times, which allows for indefinitely large networks of values to be built over time. We will explore these relations through the conversation between Kristy and her mother that we have explored in previous chapters, reproduced here as Text 4.1, as well as a primary (elementary) school discussion about whether or not there should be printed advertisements, shown in Text 4.2 (analysed for its genre stages; Metropolitan East Disadvantaged Schools Program, 1989, p. 8). In the discussion, we will see that these relations are what allow the text to hang together in terms of the rhetoric of the arguments and the different sets of positions and stances put forward. In the conversation between Kristy and her mother, we will see, as they negotiate whether or not to go out, that they orient and reorient positions in relation to each other until they jointly produce a set of positions they can agree on. In Sections 4.3.1–4.3.5, we will step through each relation in turn to show how they build the network of meanings underpinning these texts.

Kristy: what about I fold the cardboard
and then if I want some pieces um –

Mother:	well how about I get you dressed instead
Kristy:	no
	don't want to go out today [CRYING]
Mother:	you'll have a lovely day pet
	I won't be home late either
	I'll probably be home about the same time as Dee's big kids get home . . . maybe a little bit later, maybe a little bit earlier
	oh dear oh dear . . . I don't think you're really upset about me going
	[AS KRISTY CONTINUES CRYING] I think you're upset
	because the TV wasn't working
	Ruth wants to go on the potty [AS RUTH CALLS]
Kristy:	[CRYING] I don't want to go away
Mother:	come on . . . oh dear oh dear
Kristy:	Mummy . . . I don't want to go away from you
Mother:	you go away from me to kinder, don't you?
Kristy:	yeah but –
Mother:	and you like going away from me sometimes
Kristy:	yeah
	but then I meet not so many kids at kinder
	and there's not only a big room
Mother:	you mean you want to go to kinder
	but you don't want to go to Dee's?
Kristy:	yeah

Text 4.1 Kristy and Ruth being dressed by their mother (adapted from Hasan, 2009, dialogue MK6A2)

Issue	**Advertisements** There are many reasons for both sides of the question, "Should we have printed advertisements?" Many people have strong views and feel that ads are nothing more than useless junk mail, while other people feel they are an important source of information.

Arguments for	Here are some reasons why we should have advertisements in newspapers and magazines. One reason is ads give us information about what is available. Looking at ads we can find out what is on sale and what is new in the market. This is an easy way of shopping. Another reason is that advertisements promote business. When shop owners compete against each other the buyer saves money, more people come to their shops and they sell more goods.
Arguments against	On the other hand, some people argue ads should not be put in newspapers and magazines for these various reasons. Firstly, ads cost the shopkeepers a lot of money to print onto paper. Also some people don't like finding junk mail in their letter boxes. People may also find the ads not very interesting. Ads also influence people to buy items they don't need and can't really afford. Ads use up a lot of space and a lot of effort has to be made to make the ads eye-catching.
Recommendation	In summary, although ads provide people with information, their costs far outweigh their benefits. Therefore I think we should not have printed advertisements.

Text 4.2 A discussion of whether or not there should be printed advertisements (Metropolitan East Disadvantaged Schools Program, 1989, p. 8)

4.3.1 Sourcing

One of the most explicit relations in terms of marking social relations in a text is sourcing. *Sourcing* involves linking positions or items to a particular person or voice. In one sense, all texts involve sourcing as they are written with a particular voice, usually the author's. However, here we will limit our discussion to sourcing that is marked in some way – either as the author's voice or as a different voice. Sourcing is often done by explicitly attributing a position to someone through what Martin and White (2005) call attribution heteroglossia, which often involves positioned figures (Hao, 2020). Grammatically speaking, the most typical realization is through projected clauses or a circumstance of Angle (Halliday & Matthiessen, 2014). This is illustrated in the opening Issue stage of the discussion in Text 4.2, where the student links the two main sides of the issue being discussed to "many people" and "other people." We will indicate sourcing through the back slash (\).

Many people have strong views and feel that
  \ **[sourcing]**
  ads are nothing more than useless junk mail.
Other people feel
  \ **[sourcing]**
  they are an important source of information.

The student also uses this strategy to position a series of arguments against the proposition.

some people argue
  \ **[sourcing]**
  ads should not be put in newspapers and magazines
some people don't like
  \ **[sourcing]**
  finding junk mail in their letter boxes.
People may also find
  \ **[sourcing]**
  the ads not very interesting.

The student also draws on sourcing at the conclusion of the text to source the final recommendation as their personal opinion.

Therefore I think
  \ **[sourcing]**
  we should not have printed advertisements.

In the conversation between Kristy and her mother, Kristy's mother also draws on sourcing to put forward her attempts at understanding why Kristy is upset.

I don't think
  \ **[sourcing]**
  you're really upset about me going
I think
  \ **[sourcing]**

you're upset because the TV wasn't working.
You mean
\ **[sourcing]**
you want to go to kinder but you don't want to go to Dee's?

These examples involve sourcing tendered propositions or proposals. However, renderings can be sourced as well. This often occurs through affect, where both the Emoter (who is feeling the emotion) and the Trigger (what the feeling is about) of the affect are specified. In Kristy and her mother's case, this centres on sourcing Kristy's unhappiness and desires about going out through *you're upset about, you want,* and *you like.*

I don't think
\ [sourcing]
you're
\ **[sourcing]**
really upset about me going
I think
\ [sourcing]
you're
\ **[sourcing]**
upset because the TV wasn't working.
You mean
\ [sourcing] \ [sourcing]
you *but you*
\ **[sourcing]** \ **[sourcing]**
want to go to kinder *don't want to go to Dee's?*
You
\ **[sourcing]**
like going away from me sometimes

This is a repeated pattern through the text. In the above examples, each of Kristy's desires or emotions are those suggested by her mother. But Kristy also makes explicit her desires as well – by first suggesting a possible supportive rendering:

if I
\ **[sourcing]**
want some pieces

but, more commonly, making very clear what she is rejecting:

[I]
\ **[sourcing]**
don't want to go out today
I
\ **[sourcing]**
don't want to go away
I
\ **[sourcing]**
don't want to go away from you

In addition to renderings of propositions (*you're upset because the TV wasn't working*) and proposals (*I don't want to go out today*), affect can also be used to source renderings of items. This is illustrated from examples further into the conversation between Kristy and her mother, beyond Text 4.1.

Kristy: *I*
\ **[sourcing]**
want a short-sleeved cardigan – a long-sleeved one.

Kristy: *She*
\ **[sourcing]**
doesn't like me.

Kristy: *If she doesn't sit on my lap, I'll*
\ **[sourcing]**
be angry with her.

This opens the way for sourcing items through possession (e.g., through the relational possessive clause below), such as the *strong views* sourced to *many people* in the discussion.

Many people have
\ **[sourcing]**
strong views

When sourcing proposals, one significant resource is the grammar of agency (Halliday & Matthiessen, 2014). This is seen in the following examples from an advice article about how to manage "mum guilt" – the guilt that mothers feel about their parenting.[2]

"Ask a trusted friend to help you to re-frame the guilt into positive expressions"

Ask a trusted friend
\ **[sourcing]**
to help you
\ **[sourcing]**
to re-frame the guilt into positive expressions

"Let them help you to see the great things you do"
Let them
\ **[sourcing]**
help you
\ **[sourcing]**
to see the great things you do

In the first example, the main proposal is to *re-frame the guilt into positive expressions*. Responsibility for this is sourced to the reader (*you re-frame the guilt into positive expressions*). This responsibility is then extended to *a trusted friend*, who is sourced with *helping* the reader re-frame the guilt (*a trusted friend to help you to re-frame the guilt into positive expressions*). And then this is extended once more through the Process *ask*, which is sourced to the reader (although being an imperative, this is not specified as there is no Subject – *ask a trusted friend to help you to re-frame the guilt into positive expressions*).

Varied agency structures like this have often been noted for how they distribute or obscure responsibility (Trew, 1979). In our terms, these structures help distribute purview, with all the possible variations that this entails (as outlined in Chapter 3). Reading the second example above in these terms, the main proposal is for the reader *to see the great things they do*, purview for *helping you see* this is sourced to *them* (a trusted friend), and purview for *letting them help you see* this is sourced once more to the reader.

Proposals can also be sourced via indicatives with modulation. This is drawn on, for example, in the demands that we explored in Chapter 3 (from Kollontai, 1916/1997, p. 80):

The law
\ **[sourcing]**
must intervene to help women to combine work and maternity.
The law
\ **[sourcing]**

should state categorically that working conditions and the whole work situation must not threaten a woman's health; harmful methods of production should be replaced by safe methods or completely done away with; heavy work with weights or foot-propelled machines etc. should be mechanised; workrooms should be kept clean and there should be no extremes of temperature; toilets, washrooms and dining rooms should be provided, etc.

In these exhortations, the law is positioned as responsible for enacting the proposal to intervene and stating categorically that working conditions must not threaten a woman's health.

So far, the examples we have seen have involved the source being marked for each position. It is also common for sources to range across longer stretches of text, far beyond what is made explicit – which requires readers to abduce the relation across a phase of discourse (Bateman, 2007). In the following instance from the advice article, for example, the sourcing *Gold recommends* occurs only in the first sentence, suggesting it is only this position that is sourced. But the most likely reading is in fact that it extends across the following sentences that are on the face of it monoglossic:

Gold recommends
\ **[sourcing]**
being conscious of your thought patterns, and stopping them before they walk you into guilt territory. Talk to someone, and let them help you to see the great things you do, not just the things you should feel bad about. Ask a trusted friend or partner to help you to re-frame the guilt into positive expressions, to write you a list of things you do well, and keep it handy, for when you're having an attack of the guilt.

Abducing such relations also allows for retrospective readings (supported by other relations of likening and opposing that we will introduce below):

It's very hard to do, but first of all, try to be aware that you're doing it. We often don't even realise that we're beating up on ourselves, as it is such an ingrained habit. But try to recognise when you're doing it, and stop, and re-frame the story to omit the guilt
\ **[sourcing]**
emphasises Gold.

The ability to prosodically scope across units often correlates with interpersonal resources that shift the perspective (e.g., shifts in the "focalization" of attitude – Martin & White, 2005, p. 72). In the Kollontai (1916/1997) text that we explored in Chapters 2 and 3, for example, in addition to the explicit sourcing (in bold), there is a shift from statements, which are in the voice of Kollontai, to a series of commands, which are in the voice of the doctor or the family (underlined):

> Mashenka is the factory director's wife. Mashenka is expecting a baby. Although everyone in the factory director's house is a little bit anxious, there is a festive atmosphere. This is not surprising, for Mashenka is going to present her husband with an heir. There will be someone to whom he can leave all his wealth – the wealth created by the hands of working men and women. **The doctor has ordered them** to look after Mashenka very carefully. Don't let her get tired, don't let her lift anything heavy. Let her eat just what she fancies. Fruit? Give her some fruit. Caviare? Give her caviare.
>
> The important thing is that Mashenka should not feel worried or distressed in any way. Then the baby will be born strong and healthy; the birth will be easy and Mashenka will keep her bloom. **That is how they talk in the factory director's family**. That is the accepted way of handling an expectant mother, in families where the purses are stuffed with gold and credit notes. They take good care of Mashenka the lady.
>
> Do not tire yourself, Mashenka, do not try and move the armchair. **That is what they say to Mashenka the lady.**
>
> The humbugs and hypocrites of the bourgeoisie maintain that the expectant mother is sacred to them. But is that really in fact the case?

As Logi (2021; Logi & Zappavigna, 2021) explores in detail, sourcing is often realized through a wide range of prosodic features in language and paralanguage, including shifts in voice quality, head and torso position, eye contact, and transitions in movement and walking. Indeed, Logi's work has also shown that each of these features can be varied independently from one another, allowing for the negotiation of multiple positions from multiple sources at the same time (see also Ngo et al., 2022).

Looking again at the advertising discussion and Kristy and her mother's conversation, we see they both draw on sourcing to organize the positions they are putting forward. In the case of Kristy and her mother's text, the sourcing is almost entirely individual – either specifying what they personally want or think (*Mummy, I don't want to go away from you*; *I think you're upset because the TV wasn't working*) or putting forward what they think the other's positions are (*you like going away from me sometimes*; *you mean you want to go to kinder but you don't want to go to Dee's?*). This use of sourcing makes explicit the (inter)subjective nature of the conversation, as each probes the other's thoughts and feelings so as to better understand each other and affiliate.

By contrast, the advertisement discussion draws on sourcing to arrange two opposed positions, not in terms of the author's individual thoughts or feelings (aside from the last paragraph), but rather in terms of a generic and collective body of opinion (*Many people have strong views and feel that . . .* ; *while other people feel they . . .*).[3] This is used to add weight to the different arguments being put forward and is a precursor to more intricate discussions in humanities discourse, where different collective opinions and stances are often named as schools of thought or political factions. It is only in the final Recommendation stage that the author shifts to a personal sourcing (*Therefore I think we should not have printed advertisements*) and in doing so shifts from presenting an apparently more "objective" comparison of positions in the Issue and Arguments stages to a more "subjective" evaluation of these positions in the Recommendation stage.

Table 4.1 provides an overview of different realizations that can be used to source meanings.

As noted in the beginning of this section, sourcing provides one of the most explicit markings of social relations – by specifying *who* a meaning is aligned with. Its counterpart is *convoking*, which offers resources for directing meanings *to* people or communities or for bringing people into a position.

Table 4.1 Realizations of Sourcing

Realization	Example	Notes
Positioned figures	*Other people feel \ they are an important source of information*	Typically sourcing tendered propositions
Emoter of affect	*I \ want a short-sleeved cardigan* *I \ 'll be angry with her*	Sources renderings when affect has a Trigger
Possession	*Many people \ have strong views*	Typically sources items
Extended agency	*Ask a trusted friend \ to help you \ to re-frame the guilt* *The law \ must intervene to help women.*	Typically sourcing proposals
Voice quality, body paralanguage, etc.		See Logi (2021) and Ngo et al. (2022)

4.3.2 Convoking

Convoking involves bringing people or a community into a position by virtue of directing meanings towards them. Like sourcing, all texts convoke to some degree in that they have a purported audience. But once again we will limit our discussion to convoking that is marked in some way. The most explicit means of convoking involves the use of Vocatives to direct a position to someone, such as in the following examples from Kristy and her mother. We will mark convoking through the angled bracket >.

Mother: *You'll have a lovely day*
> **[convoking]**
pet

Kristy: *Mummy . . .*
> **[convoking]**
I don't want to go away from you

As Poynton (1984, 1990a) explores, Vocatives afford a wide range of naming choices that mark nuanced interpersonal meanings associated with solidarity and status. For instance, Kristy's mother uses the pet name *pet* rather than, say, *Kristy* in a way that marks her attempt at endearment in a situation where tears are already flowing. Kristy uses *Mummy* rather than *Mum* to do a similar thing. As we will explore in more detail for social media texts in Chapter 5, convoking is often the site for nuancing how meanings should be read, interpersonally speaking – as relatively warm, sympathetic, and positive or as more serious or even tinged with warning.

As for sourcing, convoking is realized through a range of grammatical resources, often working together through a phase of discourse. For example, in each of the instances above, the convoking through Vocatives (*Mummy*, *pet*) is reinforced by the use of the second person *you*, making explicit who the position is directed at. Although we do not have video recordings, presumably Kristy and her mother also draw on eye gaze and body orientation towards one another to direct their meanings (Ngo et al., 2022). Taken together these resources enact a prosody of convocation.

By contrast, the advertising discussion draws on different means for convoking, due to its audience being less well defined.[4] In particular, it draws grammatically upon Receivers in verbal clauses (Halliday & Matthiessen, 2014, p. 306), such as *us*.

ads
\ **[sourcing]**
give . . . information about what is available
> **[convoking]**
us

As this example illustrates, such realizations often also indicate a source (here via a Sayer function). A similar example is the use of a "receiver" in material or behavioural clauses, where what is being received is a semiotic entity such as the *call* in the following – *the student . . . who will get a call from the clinic.* The examples below are from an opinion piece (Donegan, 2022) reacting to the overturning of *Roe* v. *Wade* – a key judicial protection of abortion in the United States.

The real story is the student whose appointment is scheduled for tomorrow,
> **[convoking]**
who will get a call
\ **[sourcing]**
from the clinic sometime in the next hours
\ **[sourcing]**
telling
> **[convoking]**
her
that no, they
\ **[sourcing]**
are sorry
they
\ **[sourcing]**
cannot give her an abortion.

In general terms, commands will typically involve convoking. If realized by a jussive imperative, it will be the second person who is implicitly convoked (which can be made explicit via a tag – "Don't get cranky, will you!" – or an explicit Subject), as in the following from Kristy and her mother.

Kristy: yeah
> **[convoking]** [TO RUTH] don't!
Mother: oh she's trying to be nice
> **[convoking]** [TO KRISTY] don't get cranky

Such imperatives often rely on paralanguage, including eye contact and body position, to make the convoking explicit (Kress & Van Leeuwen, 2021; Ngo et al., 2022); alternatively convoking may have to be abduced from co-text and context.

The interaction between sourcing and convoking allows for multiple perspectives and characters to be organized in a text. Extending our analysis of Kollontai's text about Mashenka the lady, we can see the different voices that arise in Table 4.2. For ease of reading, we have only included one level of sourcing and convoking here – that is, when Kollontai states in her own voice to the reader, "The doctor has ordered them to look after Mashenka very carefully," we have just marked this as being sourced to Kollontai and convoking the reader (where we take the reader as the default audience who is convoked, if there is nothing explicit marked). This presentation gives us an overview of how Kollontai establishes the relations between people involved in the story.

Kollontai begins the Orientation in her own voice – introducing the characters and Mashenka's pregnancy. At the end of this stage, Kollontai explains that *the doctor has ordered them* [the family] *to look after Mashenka very carefully.* The text then shifts voices to the perspective of the doctor. Grammatically speaking, this is done by shifting the mood of the text to imperatives: *Don't let her get tired, don't let her lift anything heavy. Let her eat what she fancies.* In terms of genre, this shift in sourcing and convoking realizes a shift from the Orientation stage to the main Incident stage (where the incident to be interpreted is not Mashenka's pregnancy as such, but rather the reaction to her pregnancy by the doctor and family). Throughout the Incident stage, the text bounces between the voices of the doctor and the factory director's family (all concerned with directing how Mashenka is to be looked after) and comments by Kollontai on the Incident (e.g., *That is how they talk in the factory director's family. That is the accepted way of handling an expectant mother, in families where the purses are stuffed with gold and credit notes*). In terms of Rose's (2020) story phases, these shifts in sourcing and convoking within the Incident mark shifts from reflection phases, where the characters use their own voices to evaluate the situation, to comment phases where the narrator inserts their own evaluations. To round out the exemplum, the final comment, in Kollontai's voice, signals the final stage of the Interpretation. Here, Kollontai makes explicit her judgment of the bourgeois family's reaction that is only implied through the rest of the text: *The humbugs and hypocrites of the bourgeoisie maintain that the expectant mother is sacred to them. But is that really in fact the case?* This final open proposition marked by *but* (realizing an opposing relation, discussed in Section 4.3.3) opens the way for another exemplum that follows as a comparison – about working-class Mashenka's pregnancy.

Table 4.2 Sourcing and Convoking in Kollontai's (1916/1997) Text Marking the Exemplum Genre Stages

Stages	Source	Convoked	Exemplum
Orientation	Kollontai	Reader	Mashenka is the factory director's wife. Mashenka is expecting a baby. Although everyone in the factory director's house is a little bit anxious, there is a festive atmosphere. This is not surprising, for Mashenka is going to present her husband with an heir. There will be someone to whom he can leave all his wealth – the wealth created by the hands of working men and women. The doctor has ordered them to look after Mashenka very carefully.
Incident	The doctor	Everyone in the factory director's house	Don't let her get tired, don't let her lift anything heavy. Let her eat just what she fancies. Fruit? Give her some fruit. Caviare? Give her caviare.
	The factory director's family		The important thing is that Mashenka should not feel worried or distressed in any way. Then the baby will be born strong and healthy; the birth will be easy and Mashenka will keep her bloom.
	Kollontai	Reader	That is how they talk in the factory director's family. That is the accepted way of handling an expectant mother, in families where the purses are stuffed with gold and credit notes. They take good care of Mashenka the lady.
	The doctor	Mashenka	Do not tire yourself, Mashenka, do not try and move the armchair.
Interpretation	Kollontai	Reader	That is what they say to Mashenka the lady. The humbugs and hypocrites of the bourgeoisie maintain that the expectant mother is sacred to them. But is that really in fact the case?

This text shows that the interaction between sourcing and convoking can realize distinct shifts in relation to genre stages and phases. It allows for different perspectives to be established and related to another in ways that organize views of our social world (in conjunction with choices in rendering, as discussed in Chapter 2). Table 4.3 gives an overview of different resources used to realize convoking; as noted above, multiple resources often work together to realize convoking prosodically across different components of a text.

Table 4.3 Realizations of Convoking

Realization	Example
Vocatives	*Mummy > I don't want to go away from you*
Second person pronouns	*you > 'll have a lovely day pet*
Imperatives	*Don't!*
Receivers in verbal and behavioural clauses	*ads give > us information about what is available.*
Eye gaze, body orientation, etc.	

The sensitivity of the ORIENTING system to genre is particularly apparent for the next two relations, *likening* and *opposing*. These relations work to connect positions together – and in doing so, allow texts to elaborate their meaning rhetorically in ways that are critical for interpersonally oriented texts such as persuasive genres and the various genres used in conversation. We will begin with opposing and then explore likening.

4.3.3 Opposing

Persuasive texts involve orienting different positions in relation to each other. From the perspective of LCT, this typically involves building or drawing upon axiological constellations that arrange meanings in terms of emotional, aesthetic, or ethical stances (Maton, 2014). Such axiological constellations are often binary, in that they arrange positions into two distinct positions.

In terms of tenor, one of the main resources for building such constellations is what we will call *opposing*. Opposing resources involve establishing an opposition, and in doing so explicitly indicating that there are competing ideas (Doran, 2020b). The primary school discussion makes use of this resource to arrange its two opposing Arguments. It draws on internal connexion (Halliday & Hasan, 1976; Martin, 1992) to do so – more specifically, the signal of difference *on the other hand*. We will mark this opposition using ||.

> *Here are some reasons why we should have advertisements in newspapers and magazines. One reason is ads give us information about what is available. Looking at ads we can find out what is on sale and what is new in the market. This is an easy way of shopping. Another reason is that advertisements promote business. When shop owners compete against each other the buyer saves money, more people come to their shops and they sell more goods.*
> || **[opposing]**

> ***On the other hand,*** *some people argue ads should not be put in newspapers and magazines for these various reasons. Firstly, ads cost the shopkeepers a lot of money to print onto paper. Also some people don't like finding junk mail in their letter boxes. People may also find the ads not very interesting. Ads also influence people to buy items they don't need and can't really afford. Ads use up a lot of space and a lot of effort has to be made to make the ads eye-catching.*

It is not just between stages that this text presents its oppositions. It also does so within both the opening Issue and closing Recommendation stages. These oppositions are used to synthesize the larger opposition established through the Arguments – first to preview these positions:

> *Many people have strong views and feel that ads are nothing more than useless junk mail,*
> || **[opposing]**
> *while other people feel they are an important source of information.*

and then, at the end, to review the opposition:

> *although ads provide people with information,*
> || **[opposing]**
> *their costs far outweigh their benefits.*

The importance of these oppositions to this text is symbolized in its opening sentence by the semiotic entity (Hao, 2020, p. 85) *both sides of the question* (in *There are many reasons for both sides of the question, "Should we have printed advertisements?"*).

To begin to see how these positions fit together, we can arrange them as in Table 4.4 with the opposed positions organized horizontally. In this table we have also included the symbols for sourcing (\) and convoking (>) to illustrate how these also get arranged. As we introduce other relations, we will progressively build this table to illustrate the constellation of meaning this student develops through their text.

Table 4.4 illustrates the two broad sides that the student establishes in their discussion. One side focuses on ads as a useful source of information. Following the initial presentation of this side (*Other people feel that they are an important source of information*), the author presents a series of unsourced statements associated with their utility and their positive effect on the economy (e.g., *ads give us information about what is available; Looking at ads we can find out what is on sale and what is new in the market*). By contrast, for the other side that focuses on reasons why we

Table 4.4 Some Oppositions in a Primary School Discussion

Many people \ have, feel strong views ads are nothing more than useless junk mail	Other people \ feel ads are an important source of information
Some people \ argue ads should not be put in newspapers and magazines for these various reasons. Firstly, ads cost the shopkeepers a lot of money to print onto paper. Also some people \ don't like finding junk mail in their letter boxes. People \ may also find the ads not very interesting. Ads also influence people to buy items they don't need and can't really afford. Ads use up a lot of space and a lot of effort has to be made to make the ads eye-catching.	Here are some reasons why we should have advertisements in newspapers and magazines. One reason is ads \ give information about what is available. > us Looking at ads we can find out what is on sale and what is new in the market. This is an easy way of shopping. Another reason is that advertisements promote business. When shop owners compete against each other the buyer saves money, more people come to their shops and they sell more goods.
ads' costs far outweigh their benefits	ads provide people with information

shouldn't have ads, the author largely sources each of their arguments to the generic *some people* or *people* (*some people argue ads should not be put in newspapers and magazines; some people don't like finding junk mail in their letter boxes; People may also find the ads not very interesting*).

In addition, for the side arguing against ads, the author focuses on the negative aspects of ads (rather than, say, the positive aspects of an ad-free world). In doing so, they rely heavily on negation (*disclaim: denial*, in terms of engagement; Martin & White, 2005), as in *some people* ***don't*** *like junk mail in their letter box* or *people may also find ads* ***not*** *very interesting*.

This establishes a second set of oppositions that reject possible positions associated with ads (as discussed in Chapter 2). Whereas in the oppositions discussed above, the two sides are explicitly stated and then opposed to each other, positions rejected using negation resources have often not been explicitly presented earlier in the text, but involve rejecting unstated assumptions (Martin & White, 2005).[5] To indicate this, the rejected implied positions are greyed out:

ads are nothing more than useless junk mail
|| **[opposing]**
ads are more than useless junk mail

ads should not be put in newspapers and magazines
|| **[opposing]**
ads should be put in newspapers and magazines

some people don't like finding junk mail in their letter boxes
|| **[opposing]**
some people like finding junk mail in their letter boxes

people may also find the ads not very interesting
|| **[opposing]**
people may also find the ads very interesting

ads also influence people to buy items they don't need and can't really afford
|| **[opposing]**
ads also influence people to buy items they need and can afford

I think we should not have printed advertisements
|| **[opposing]**
I think we should have printed advertisements

Adding these into the previous table leads to Table 4.5. In the left-hand column, these smaller oppositions are arranged horizontally, and those rejected are greyed out to their right.

Table 4.5 outlines in synoptic form the strategy this student draws on to write their discussion. To organize the different sides of the debate, they build one large set of oppositions between positions for ads (associated with *advertisements give information*) and positions against ads (associated with *ads are nothing more than useless junk mail*). For the position against ads, rather than focusing on the positive aspects of an ad-free world, the student focuses on the negative aspects of ads, and so sets up a smaller set of oppositions used to reject unstated positions (e.g., that ads are interesting, people like junk mail, and ads influence people to buy things they can afford). The arguments against are reinforced through the generic sourcing of these positions to *people* and *some people,* which potentially suggests wider backing for these positions (which we will describe in Chapter 5 as expanding their scope). This acts as a precursor to more elaborate sourcing and citation patterns that will be drawn on through secondary and tertiary education (Swales, 1986).

The negotiation between Kristy and her mother also draws heavily on oppositions. In terms of the realizations we have discussed so far, we can see this by comparing the distinct positions of *going out* and *not going out* through negation.

Table 4.5 Oppositions in a Primary School Discussion

Many people \ have, feel strong views ads are nothing more than useless junk mail	ads are more than useless junk mail	Other people \ feel ads are an important source of information
Some people \ argue ads should not be put in newspapers and magazines for these various reasons.	ads should be put in newspapers and magazines for these various reasons.	Here are some reasons why we should have advertisements in newspapers and magazines. One reason is ads \ give information about what is available. > us
Firstly, ads cost the shopkeepers a lot of money to print onto paper.		
Also some people \ don't like finding junk mail in their letter boxes.	like finding junk mail in their letter boxes.	Looking at ads we can find out what is on sale and what is new in the market. This is an easy way of shopping. Another reason is that advertisements promote business. When shop owners compete against each other the buyer saves money, more people come to their shops and they sell more goods.
People \ may also find the ads not very interesting.	the ads very interesting.	
Ads also influence people to buy items they don't need and can't really afford.	Ads also influence people to buy items they need and can afford.	
Ads use up a lot of space and a lot of effort has to be made to make the ads eye-catching.		
Ads' costs far outweigh their benefits		Ads provide people with information

Kristy: *don't want to go out today*
|| **[opposing]**
want to go out today

Kristy: *I don't want to go away*
|| **[opposing]**
I want to go away

Kristy: *Mummy, I don't want to go away from you*
|| **[opposing]**
Mummy, I want to go away from you

Being in a dialogue, Kristy and her mother also forward opposing positions by simply stating them in contrast to each other.

Kristy: *what about I fold the cardboard and then if I want some pieces um –*
|| **[opposing]**
Mother: *well how about I get you dressed instead?*
|| **[opposing]**
Kristy: *no, don't want to go out today [*CRYING*]*
|| **[opposing]**
Mother: *you'll have a lovely day pet*

In Chapter 2 we discussed these instances in terms of their role in rendering positions and in particular rejecting the other positions put forward. There, we described this in terms of their pattern in an exchange – when Kristy says *what about I fold the cardboard . . .*, a compliant response would be to support her proposal (e.g., through *Sure!*); but by putting forward her own proposal (*well how about I get you dressed instead?*), Kristy's mother both rejects Kristy's proposal and puts forward her own. This analysis, however, did not account for the relations between the two positions, namely that they are also *opposed*. So here we are accounting for the difference between *what about I fold the cardboard? / No* and *what about I fold the cardboard? / well how about I get you dressed instead?* The first is simply a rejection of the proposal; the second is a rejection plus an opposition.

This opposition is established through resources in exchange structure. Following the initial action being proposed (A2) *what about I fold the cardboard and . . .*, Kristy's mother's response can be read as either a challenge in this initial exchange or an A2 in a new exchange (Berry, 1981b; Martin, 1992; Zappavigna & Martin, 2018a). Though quite marked in this situation, we can make these oppositions explicit by including explicit connexions (contrast, alternation, or concessive).

Kristy: *what about I fold the cardboard and then if I want some pieces um –*
|| **[opposing]**

Mother: *well [**alternatively**] how about I get you dressed instead?*

|| **[opposing]**

Kristy: *no, don't want to go out today* [***but***][6] *[*CRYING*]*

|| **[opposing]**

Mother: *you'll have a lovely day,* [***though,***] *pet*

When viewed in this way, Kristy's mother's *well* at the beginning of her turn in a sense predicts the opposition. As Halliday and Hasan (1976) comment, "*Well* serves to indicate what follows IS [original emphasis] in fact a response to what has preceded: in other words, it slips in quietly the respondent's claim to be answering the question (*sometimes with a show of reluctance* [our emphasis])" (p. 269). In other words, the *well* here does not itself mark the opposition but rather indicates some doubt about the consensus (Martin, 1992, p. 218) and provides a kind of warning about a potential interpersonal shift (as in the opposition here).

Such oppositions also occur within turns. Kristy's mother draws on this when she first puts forward her thoughts about why Kristy is upset.

Mother: *I don't think you're really upset about me going*

|| **[opposing]**

I think you're upset because the TV wasn't working.

This contrast here relies on implicit connexion (Martin, 1992) and can again be made explicit by inserting a cohesive conjunction.

Mother: *I don't think you're really upset about me going*

|| **[opposing]**

[***Rather,***] *I think you're upset because the TV wasn't working.*

This example provides another resource through which conversations can be indefinitely extended – a concern we explored in Chapter 2. In addition to resources for both rendering and tendering positions at the same time, an indefinite number of positions can be linked by oppositions (and likening, as we will see next in Section 4.3.4), whether this is marked explicitly or is implicit.

This type of opposition, realized through implicit connexion, is in fact a more general resource for organizing text. Looking again at Kollontai's text, the exemplum of Mashenka the lady is immediately contrasted with that of Mashenka the laundress in order to highlight the different attitudes towards, and effects of, pregnancy depending on one's class. But this contrast is implicit (realized through implicit contrastive connexion, which could be made explicit by a conjunction such as *in contrast*). In this instance, the opposition realizes specific relations between genres in the genre complex (Martin & Rose, 2008).

Mashenka the factory director's wife

Mashenka is the factory director's wife. Mashenka is expecting a baby. Although everyone in the factory director's house is a little bit anxious, there is a festive atmosphere. This is not surprising, for Mashenka is going to present her husband with an heir. There will be someone to whom he can leave all his wealth – the wealth created by the hands of working men and women. The doctor has ordered them to look after Mashenka very carefully. Don't let her get tired, don't let her lift anything heavy. Let her eat just what she fancies. Fruit? Give her some fruit. Caviare? Give her caviare.

The important thing is that Mashenka should not feel worried or distressed in any way. Then the baby will be born strong and healthy; the birth will be easy and Mashenka will keep her bloom. That is how they talk in the factory director's family. That is the accepted way of handling an expectant mother, in families where the purses are stuffed with gold and credit notes. They take good care of Mashenka the lady.

Do not tire yourself, Mashenka, do not try and move the armchair. That is what they say to Mashenka the lady.

The humbugs and hypocrites of the bourgeoisie maintain that the expectant mother is sacred to them. But is that really in fact the case?

|| **[opposing]**

Mashenka the laundress

In the same house as the factory director's wife, but in the back part in a corner behind a printed calico curtain, huddles another Mashenka. She does the laundry and the housework. Mashenka is eight months pregnant. But she would open her eyes wide in surprise if they said to her, "Mashenka, you must not: carry heavy things, you must look after yourself, for your own sake, for the child's sake and for the sake of humanity. You are expecting a baby and that means your condition is, in the eyes of society 'sacred'." Masha would take this either as uncalled-for interference or as a cruel joke. Where have you seen a woman of the working class given special treatment because she is pregnant? Masha and the hundreds of thousands of other women of the propertyless classes who are forced to sell their working hands know that the owners have no mercy when they see women in need; and they have no other alternative, however exhausted they may be, but to go out to work.

Looking back at Kristy and her mother's text, there is one final resource they draw on to establish their oppositions. This is the use of the concessive connexion *but* – which in terms of engagement is a *disclaim: countering* resource (Martin & White, 2005).

Mother:	*you go away from me to kinder, don't you?*
Kristy:	*yeah* ***but*** *–*
Mother:	*and you like going away from me sometimes*
Kristy:	*yeah*
	ll **[opposing]**
	but *then I meet not so many kids at kinder*
	and there's not only a big room
Mother:	*you mean you want to go to kinder*
	ll **[opposing]**
	but *you don't want to go to Dee's?*
Kristy:	*yeah*

Like the other connexion resources, this establishes an opposition between the positions that are specified.

you go away from me to kinder . . . and you like going away from me sometimes
ll **[opposing]**
but then I meet not so many kids at kinder and there's not only a big room

you want to go to kinder
ll **[opposing]**
but you don't want to go to Dee's?

However, the use of *but* here does more than this, . arising from the fact that *but* is a concessive connexion that establishes a counter-expectancy (Martin, 1992, pp. 199–200). In the first example above, the fact that Kristy goes away from her mother to kinder and likes going away from her sometimes establishes an expectancy that Kristy will be Ok to go away from her today. However, Kristy's *but* disrupts this expectancy and flags that she holds a different position to what her mother presumes.

For the purposes of our analysis, this means that there is another opposition established (in bold) between what was expected and what was said.

Kristy goes away from her mother to kinder and likes going away from her sometimes ***so she will like going away from her today.***
|| **[opposing]**
Kristy goes away from her mother to kinder and likes going away from her sometimes ***because there she meets not so many kids and there's not only a big room.***

As with the examples with negation above, Kristy's use of counter-expectancy recognizes that there is an assumed background constellation of meanings that she is not going to follow. It functions to both acknowledge and modify the shared set of assumptions that underpin her familial relationships.

Although we have described this in terms of concessive connexion (from the logical discourse semantic system of CONNEXION), the main realizational resource for these types of oppositions is in fact the interpersonal choice of disclaim: counter within engagement. This can be seen by the fact that in addition to concessive connexions, the opposition can be marked by resources including Comment Adjuncts and Conjunctive Adjuncts that indicate counter-expectancy – for example, "I'm keen to go to kinder. **Surprisingly**, she isn't" – and continuity markers such as *just, only, still,* and so on (Martin & White, 2005, p. 121). Some of these resources are illustrated in the advice article we looked at above.

Let them help you to see the great things you do, not ***just*** *the things you should feel bad about.*
Write yourself a list of things you feel guilty about. Now look again at the list and cross off everything you are **actually** *guilty of and which make you a bad person.*
When you **actually** *stop to think about each item, you will realise that your guilt is* ***just*** *a bad habit, not a reality.*

Hood and Forey (2008, p. 402) discuss the interpersonal effect of these resources from the perspective of appraisal by arguing that, in our terms, these resources function like other concessive conjunctions such as *but* and *however* to establish an opposition. However, whereas *but, however,* and conjunctions like them tend to flip any prosody of evaluative meaning (from, say, supporting to rejecting something), resources such as *just, already,* and *actually* tend not to flip the rendering. Rather, they function to "limit or contract" the rendering (p. 403) by softening or adjusting it (what in Chapter 5 we will describe in terms of TUNING).

Taking *just* as an example, this lowers the stakes or the scope of what is being said (see Chapter 5). For example, in *your guilt is* ***just*** *a bad habit, not a reality,* the *just* counters the idea that *your guilt* is something other than a bad habit (i.e., *a reality*); in doing so, it establishes an opposition between *guilt as a bad habit* and *guilt as something else* (specified explicit immediately afterwards as a *reality*). So rather than using *just* to suggest that guilt is in fact good (i.e., rather than flipping from rejecting to supporting rendering), it maintains it as bad (i.e., rejecting) but softens it and lowers its stakes. In this sense, these concessive continuity markers offer a complementary strategy to concessive conjunctions for nuancing the interpersonal relations between positions, by allowing for their meanings to be adjusted rather than just negated.

Table 4.6 Some Realizations for Opposing

Realization	Example	Notes
Internal connexion	*When shop owners compete against each other the buyer saves money, more people come to their shops and they sell more goods.* ‖ ***On the other hand,*** *some people argue ads should not be put in newspapers and magazines for these various reasons.*	Typically difference, concessive, or alternation connexion; both implicit and explicit
Disclaim: denial heteroglossia	*ads should* ***not*** *be put in newspapers and magazines* ‖ *ads should be put in newspapers and magazines*	Used to realize an implied opposition and a rejection of the implied position
Disclaim: counter heteroglossia	*I'm keen to go to kinder.* ***Surprisingly,*** *she isn't.*	Used to oppose an unstated expectancy
Counter-expectant continuity	*Let them help you to see the great things you do, not* ***just*** *the things you should feel bad about.*	Used to adjust the stakes or scope of the opposition
Challenges in exchange that also tender a position	Kristy: *what about I fold the cardboard and then if I want some pieces um –* ‖ **[opposing]** Mother: *well how about I get you dressed instead?*	Used dialogically to both reject and put forward an opposition to a position

The survey in this section illustrates the range of ways that oppositions can be enacted in text, and it gives some indication of how extensively they are used. They form a key resource for building text across genres, and both acknowledging and establishing constellations of values. Table 4.6 gives an overview of realizational resources for opposing.

4.3.4 Likening

The counterpart to opposing is *likening*. Likening involves grouping things as the same or similar. This similarity is not necessarily in terms of any ideational similarity but in terms of how they are positioned rhetorically within a set of oppositions. Like opposing, likening is a regular resource for building constellations and extending text, and it offers resources for organizing sets of apparently different things, ideationally speaking, as "the same." These things may be propositions or proposals, they may be items in field (see Doran, 2024), or they may be longer stretches of text that encompass a range of meanings.

The primary school discussion draws on likening within each of its arguments to link together distinct points. For example, in the Arguments For having ads, the student links together two main reasons – with likening marked by =.

> *One reason is ads give us information about what is available. Looking at ads, we can find out what is on sale and what is new in the market.*
> = **[likening]**
> *Another reason is that advertisements promote business. When the shop owners compete against each other the buyer saves money, more people come to their shops and they sell more goods.*

Likening here is realized through implicit internal connexion – in particular comparative connexions of similarity (Martin, 1992). We can make this explicit by using *By the same token.*[7]

> *One reason is ads give us information about what is available. Looking at ads, we can find out what is on sale and what is new in the market.*
> = **[likening]**
> **[*By the same token,*]** *Another reason is that advertisements promote business. When the shop owners compete against each other the buyer saves money, more people come to their shops and they sell more goods.*

Within each of these reasons, the student also puts forward a series of positions that illustrate and reformulate the more general positions. We can also consider these as likenings because the positions are put together as "the same" argument, rhetorically speaking. In this sense, they present layers of positions, likened together. In these examples, we have once again inserted explicit connexions to make clear the relation:

One reason is ads give us information about what is available.
= **[likening]**
[That is,] Looking at ads, we can find out what is on sale
= **[likening]**
and [likewise] what is new in the market. This is an easy way of shopping.
= **[likening]**
[By the same token,] another reason is that advertisements promote business.
= **[likening]**
[I.e.,] When the shop owners compete against each other the buyer saves money,
= **[likening]**
[also] more people come to their shops
= **[likening]**
and [also] they sell more goods.

The student uses the same strategy for the Arguments Against. In this case, the student draws at times on the internal additive connexion *also* as well as implicit connexion to realize the likenings:

Firstly, ads cost the shopkeeper a lot of money to print onto paper.
= **[likening]**
Also some people don't like finding junk mail in their letter boxes.
= **[likening]**
People may also find the ads not very interesting.
= **[likening]**
Ads also influence people to buy items they don't need
= **[likening]**
and [similarly] can't really afford.
= **[likening]**
[By the same token,] Ads use up a lot of space
= **[likening]**
and [also] a lot of effort has to be made to make the ads eye-catching.

Adding likening into Table 4.7 illustrates how it works to hold the positions within the text together. Where positions are likened together within larger sets of positions, they have been indented.

Table 4.7 Arguments for and Against Advertisements, Including Likening

<table>
<tr><td colspan="2">Many people
\ have, feel
strong views</td><td rowspan="2">Other people
\ feel
ads are an important source of information</td></tr>
<tr><td>ads are nothing more than useless junk mail</td><td>ads are more than useless junk mail</td></tr>
<tr><td colspan="2">Some people
\ argue</td><td rowspan="9">Here are some reasons why we should have advertisements in newspapers and magazines.
One reason is ads
\ give
information about what is available.
>
us
=
Looking at ads we can find out what is on sale
=
and what is new in the market. This is an easy way of shopping.
=
Another reason is that advertisements promote business.
=
When shop owners compete against each other the buyer saves money,
=
more people come to their shops
=
and they sell more goods.</td></tr>
<tr><td>ads should not be put in newspapers and magazines for these various reasons.</td><td>ads should be put in newspapers and magazines for these various reasons.</td></tr>
<tr><td colspan="2">Firstly, ads cost the shopkeepers a lot of money to print onto paper.
=
Also some people
\</td></tr>
<tr><td>don't like finding junk mail in their letter boxes.</td><td>like finding junk mail in their letter boxes.</td></tr>
<tr><td colspan="2">=
People
\ may also find</td></tr>
<tr><td>the ads not very interesting.</td><td>the ads very interesting.</td></tr>
<tr><td>=
Ads also influence people to buy items they don't need
=
and can't really afford.</td><td>Ads also influence people to buy items they need and can afford.</td></tr>
<tr><td colspan="2">=
Ads use up a lot of space and a lot of effort has to be made to make the ads eye-catching.</td></tr>
<tr><td colspan="2"></td></tr>
<tr><td colspan="2">Ads' costs far outweigh their benefits</td><td>Ads provide people with information</td></tr>
</table>

Kristy and her mother also draw on likening to hold together their positions. As in the advertisement discussion, where opposing is primarily used to contrast their distinct arguments, likening is used to join series of positions together as a single argument. Kristy's mother initially uses this to link together positions when trying to convince Kristy that she should go out.

Kristy: *no, don't want to go out today* [CRYING]

|| **[opposing]**

Mother: *you'll have a lovely day pet*

= **[likening]**

I won't be home late either

= **[likening]**

I'll probably be home about the same time as Dee's big kids get home . . . maybe a little bit later, maybe a little bit earlier.

Kristy's mother uses this tactic once more later in the conversation to try to get Kristy onside, likening her two propositions of *you go away from me to kinder* and *you like going away from me sometimes* – to both of which Kristy agrees. But as we saw above, Kristy then opposes going away to kinder to going away to Dee's. She justifies this by presenting two positions about kinder that she likens to each other: *then I meet not so many kids at kinder* and *there's not only a big room.*

Mother: *you go away from me to kinder, don't you?*

Kristy: *yeah but –*

= **[likening]**

Mother: *and you like going away from me sometimes*

Kristy: *yeah*

|| [opposing]

but then I meet not so many kids at kinder

= **[likening]**

and there's not only a big room

By drawing on likening and opposing, Kristy and her mother are able to bring positions together to establish a developing constellation of meaning that they can share and to extend the conversation. The roles of likening and opposing to extend conversations can be further illustrated through the following conversation from Eggins and Slade (1997/2004, pp. 170–171). In this conversation (leaving aside POSITIONING and other relations), many of the turns are linked by offering either a similar position that reinforces what the other has said (i.e., likening) or a contradictory position (i.e., opposing). There are of course other relations holding this text together, both those discussed elsewhere in this book and others associated with field and mode; but the tenor relations of likening and opposing allow the conversation to slide between ideational foci while maintaining cohesion.

In particular, likening and opposing work to hold together stretches of rendering, where multiple people either support or reject some aspect of various people. To illustrate this, in Table 4.8 we have chunked up the text in terms of the overarching rendering of each stretch. In the right-hand

Table 4.8 Likening and Opposing in a Conversation

i	David		This conversation needs Allenby.		Support for David Allenby
ii	Fay	Oh,	he's in London so what can we do?[8]		
			|| [opposing]		
iii	Nick		We don't want – we don't need Allenby in this bloody conversation. Cause all you'd get is him bloody raving on.	[On the contrary]	Rejection of David Allenby
iv	Fay [to Liz]		He's a bridge player		
			= [likening]		
v			A naughty bridge player.	[that is]	
			= [likening]		
vi			He gets banned from everywhere because of his antisocial or drunken behaviour.	[that is]	
			= [likening]		
vii	Nick		And he just yap yap yaps all the time.	And	
viii	David		S'pose he gives you a hard time Nick?		
			|| [opposing]		
ix	Nick	Oh,	I like David a lot.	[On the contrary]	Support for David Allenby
			|| [opposing]		
x			Still but	but	Rejection of David Allenby
			= [likening]		
xi	Fay		He has a very short fuse with alcohol[9]	[indeed]	
			[Pause 10 seconds]		

(Continued)

Table 4.8 (*Continued*)

xii	Fay		You met his sister that night we were doing the cutting and pasting up. D'you remember?[10]		Support for proposition of Liz meeting Jill
			= [likening]		
xiii	Nick	Oh yea,	you met Jill.	[indeed]	
xiv	David	Oh yea			
			= [likening]		
xv	Fay		That's David's sister	[to clarify]	
xvi	Liz	Oh right			
			= [likening]	[i.e.]	
xvii	Fay		Jill		
			‖ [opposing]		
xviii	David		Jill's very bright actually	actually	Support for Jill
			= [likening]		
xix	Fay		She's extremely bright	[in fact]	
			= [likening]		
xx	David		Academ – academically she's probably brighter than David	[in fact]	Support for David Allenby
			= [likening]		
xxi			David's always precocious with his . . .[11]	[that is]	
			= [likening]		
xxii			The only sixteen-year-old superstar arrives in Sydney to and straight into the mandies.	[e.g.]	
xxiii	Nick		Straight into the what?		
xxiv	Fay		Mandies		
			= [likening]		
xxv	David		He was a good boy	[that is]	
			‖ [opposing]		
xxvi			but just no tolerance for the alcohol.	but just	Rejection of David Allenby
			= [likening]		
xxvii			I've pulled him out of so many fights, it's ridiculous.	[e.g.]	

column, we have included the connexion used (without brackets) or possible connexions that could be inserted (in brackets) to make explicit the likening or opposing, and we have separated out any explicit markings of the rendering that begin a turn in their own column on the left.

This text illustrates one means through which chat unfolds through the use of likening and opposing in conjunction with rendering. The use of likening, which at the same time renders support, is particularly prominent – a kind of conversational analogue of an improv artist's "yes, and" strategy.[12] There are ideational shifts throughout. But looking at the text globally, we can see that likening and opposing in this conversation are largely oriented towards organizing the flow of renderings through the text. Following the initial opposition to having Allenby in the conversation, justified through rejections of Allenby by Nick (*we don't want – we don't need Allenby . . . all you'd get is him bloody raving on*), the likened positions put forward by Fay and Nick are all oriented to continuing the rejection of certain aspects of Allenby's behaviour: *a naughty bridge player, gets banned from everywhere, his antisocial or drunken behaviour, just yap yap yaps all the time.* This is briefly interrupted in line viii, when David suggests to Nick, *I suppose he gives you a hard time Nick?*, and Nick rejects this using an opposition *I like David a lot.* But he very quickly opposes this once more with *still but*, with Fay following up by putting forward another rejection of Allenby's behaviour (*he has a very short fuse with alcohol*).

After a pause, Fay tells Liz that she has met Allenby's sister (line xii). The following stretch involves each of the members of the conversation supporting this (*oh yea*) and repeatedly clarifying who his sister is, once more drawing on likening to hold the chat together (*you met his sister that night, you met Jill, that's David's sister, Jill*). Once this stretch is completed, David renders support for Jill by suggesting she is very bright (*Jill's very bright actually*), using *actually* to oppose the expectation that she may not be a great person, established by the fact that they have been gossiping about her brother's alcohol issues. The next series of propositions are likened together to reinforce Jill's brightness, culminating in a comparison between Jill and David and support for David's intellect (*She's extremely bright, she's probably brighter than David, David's always precocious, the only sixteen-year-old superstar, he was a good boy*) – before they shift back to the opposed position, rejecting David's behaviour when drinking (*but just no tolerance for alcohol, I've pulled him out of so many fights*).

In Chapter 2, we raised the question of how conversation keeps going indefinitely. This challenge arose due to the fact that discourse semantic tools developed in SFL (e.g., through Berry, 1981a; Halliday, 1985; Martin, 1992; Ventola, 1987) have tended to model conversation in terms of discrete exchanges or speech functions. But, as Eggins (1990) points out and models through both interpersonal and logical reticula, chat in fact unfolds serially, sliding between topics as it goes but still being perfectly coherent in context. In Chapter 2 we offered one mechanism for how these two perspectives can be reconciled through the possibility of both rendering a previous position and tendering a new one at the same time. This allows strings of positions to be put forward indefinitely, which can help construct chat. In this chapter we propose that likening and opposing offer other mechanisms for serial expansion, as distinct positions can be linked together to either "say the same thing," rhetorically speaking, or be used as "points of difference."

4.3.5 Encapsulating

To round out our discussion of ORIENTING resources, we introduce the relation *encapsulating*. Encapsulating involves orienting sets of positions as being synthesized "within" other positions.[13] This often occurs in higher level periodicity (Martin & Rose, 2007), where general positions are put forward before or after more specific points are given. This is in fact how the primary school discussion draws on encapsulating. In the opening paragraph that gives the Issue stage, the text puts forward two opposed positions as its Macrotheme.

> *Many people have strong views and feel that ads are nothing more than useless junk mail*
> *While other people feel they are an important source of information.*

These positions in the Macrotheme of the text encapsulate the positions put forward in the Hyperthemes of each argument.

> *Here are some reasons why we should have advertisements in newspapers and magazines.*
> ...
> *On the other hand, some people argue ads should not be put in newspapers and magazines for these various reasons.*[14]

These Hyperthemes in turn work to encapsulate a range of points that have been likened together as more specific Arguments, before each being encapsulated once again into more general positions in the final Recommendation stage. To mark the encapsulation relation, we will use = =.

> Here are the Arguments Against:
> *Many people have strong views and feel that ads are nothing more than useless junk mail*

= = **[encapsulating]**

some people argue ads should not be put in newspapers and magazines for these various reasons.

= = **[encapsulating]**

Firstly, ads cost the shopkeeper a lot of money to print onto paper.

= **[likening]**

Also some people don't like finding junk mail in their letter boxes.

= **[likening]**

People may also find the ads not very interesting.

= **[likening]**

Ads also influence people to buy items they don't need

= **[likening]**

and [similarly] can't really afford.

= **[likening]**

[Similarly] Ads use up a lot of space

= **[likening]**

and [also] a lot of effort has to be made to make the ads eye-catching.

= = **[encapsulating]**

Their costs far outweigh their benefits.

Here are the Arguments For:

While other people feel they are an important source of information.

= = **[encapsulating]**

Here are some reasons why we should have advertisements in newspapers and magazines.

= = **[encapsulating]**

One reason is ads give us information about what is available.

= **[likening]**

[that is] Looking at ads, we can find out what is on sale

= **[likening]**

and [likewise] what is new in the market. This is an easy way of shopping.

= **[likening]**

[Similarly,] Another reason is that advertisements promote business.

= **[likening]**

[That is] When the shop owners compete against each other, the buyer saves money,

= **[likening]**

[similarly] more people come to their shops

= **[likening]**

and [likewise] they sell more goods.

= = **[encapsulating]**

In summary . . . ads provide people with information

At the very end of the text, the student specifies their own position, rendering support for the Arguments Against by stating that *we should not have printed advertisements.* Placing these all together in Table 4.9 allows us to see how the range of positions put forward by the student hold together as a coherent constellation.

Table 4.9 The Constellation Underpinning the Arguments for and Against Advertisements

Issue	Many people \ have, feel strong views ads are nothing more than useless junk mail	ads are more than useless junk mail	Other people \ feel ads are an important source of information
Arguments	= = Some people \ argue ads should not be put in newspapers and magazines for these various reasons.	ads should be put in newspapers and magazines for these various reasons.	= = Here are some reasons why we should have advertisements in newspapers and magazines. = = One reason is ads \ give information about what is available. > us
	= = Firstly, ads cost the shopkeepers a lot of money to print onto paper. = Also some people \ don't like finding junk mail in their letter boxes.	like finding junk mail in their letter boxes.	= Looking at ads we can find out what is on sale = and what is new in the market. This is an easy way of shopping.
	= People \ may also find the ads not very interesting.	the ads very interesting.	= Another reason is that advertisements promote business.
	= Ads also influence people to buy items they don't need = and can't really afford.	Ads also influence people to buy items they need and can afford.	= When shop owners compete against each other the buyer saves money, = more people come to their shops = and they sell more goods.
	= Ads use up a lot of space and a lot of effort has to be made to make the ads eye-catching.		

(Continued)

Table 4.9 (*Continued)*

Recom-mendation	= = ads' costs far outweigh their benefits	= = ads provide people with information
	= = I think \	
	we should not have printed advertisements	we should have printed advertisements

This constellation synthesizes the meanings put forward by the student for discussing whether or not there should be advertisements. By drawing on relations from the ORIENTING system, they are able to arrange distinct propositions into a coherent set of arguments before giving support to one of them. The ORIENTING system thus gives us a view of how sets of meanings hang together in terms of not their ideational relations, but their rhetorical and axiological relations.

Although Kristy and her mother do not draw on encapsulating, by drawing on the relations we have looked at so far, we are able to look at how the various positions they put forward unfold. As discussed previously, the two begin at loggerheads, with opposed proposals that they each reject (Table 4.10).

Table 4.10 Kristy and Her Mother's Developing Constellation, 1

Kristy's Positions	**Kristy's Mother's Positions**
what about I fold the cardboard and then if I want some pieces um – **[Mother rejects]**	how about I get you dressed instead? **[Kristy rejects]**

Kristy then reiterates her opposition by exclaiming that she doesn't want to go out today. Once more, however, her mother tries to convince her to go out, this time by setting up a series of likened positions that explain why she might in fact want to go out (Table 4.11).

When this doesn't get Kristy on side, her mother makes an attempt to understand what Kristy's issues are. Here she first rejects that Kristy is upset about her going, and puts forward an opposing suggestion that she is in fact upset because the TV isn't working. Despite this, Kristy rejects her mother's interpretation by restating, *I don't want to go away* (Table 4.12).

Table 4.11 Kristy and Her Mother's Developing Constellation, 2

Kristy's Positions		**Kristy's Mother's Positions**
(Kristy) don't want \ to go out today	(Kristy) want \ to go out today	
		You'll have a lovely day > pet = I won't be home late either = I'll probably be home about the same time as Dee's big kids get home . . . maybe a little bit later, maybe a little bit earlier.

Table 4.12 Kristy and Her Mother's Developing Constellation, 3

Kristy's Positions	**Kristy's Mother's Positions**	
	I don't think \ you're really upset \ about me going	I think \ you're upset because \ the TV wasn't working
I don't want to go away	**[Kristy rejects]**	

With this rejection, her mother tries again by listing the times that Kristy does in fact like going away, such as to kinder. But this time, Kristy retorts by putting forward why kinder is different to where she is going today (Dee's) (Table 4.13).

Table 4.13 Kristy and Her Mother's Developing Constellation, 4

Kristy's Positions		**Kristy's Mother's Positions**
		you go away from me to kinder **[Kristy supports]** = you like \ going away from me sometimes **[Kristy supports]**
But then I meet not so many kids at kinder = and there's not only a big room	I meet as many kids at kinder = there's only a big room	

At this point, Kristy's mother understands and is able to conceptualize why Kristy is reacting the way she is – namely that it is not about going out per se, but that Kristy is distinguishing between liking going to kinder and not liking going to Dee's. To this, Kristy makes the supporting move *yeah* (Table 4.14).

Table 4.14 Kristy and Her Mother's Developing Constellation, 5

Kristy's Positions	**Kristy's Mother's Positions**	
	you mean \ \	
	you want \\ to go to kinder	you don't want \\ to go to Dee's
	[Kristy supports with yeah]	

The map we developed for the student discussion gave a synoptic view of the constellation put forward by the student. For Kristy and her mother, the maps provide an overview of the development and change of this constellation as it gets negotiated over time. In this sense, resources in the system of ORIENTING interact with resources within POSITIONING (resources for tendering and rendering) to negotiate and build meaning over time.

Figure 4.1 outlines the system for ORIENTING, which includes the resource of repositioning described in Chapter 3 that reorients one position as another – for example, a proposal repositioned as a proposition in *you should go out today.* Like the rest of the ORIENTING system, repositioning focuses on how different positions are related to each other.

The network in Figure 4.1 says that in the system of ORIENTING, one can choose to orient two positions together [orienting] or not (indicated by –). The superscript ^{n} indicates that any number of positions can be oriented together. If relating two positions together, this may be done

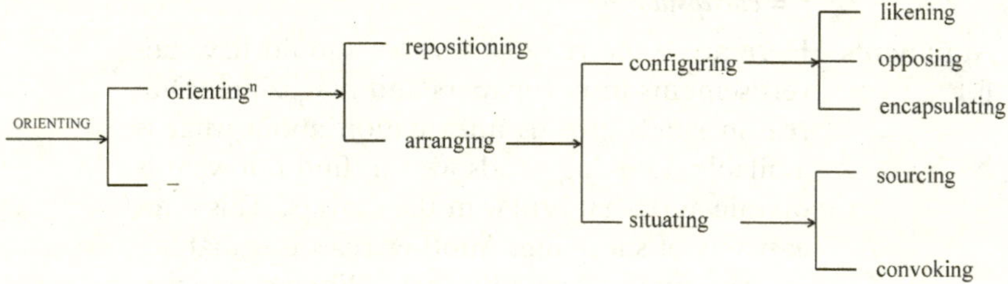

Figure 4.1 System of ORIENTING

through [repositioning] (discussed in Chapter 3) or through the resources we have described in this chapter, grouped together as [arranging] resources. Meanings can be arranged either by [configuring] them together, which includes [likening], [opposing], and [encapsulating], or by [situating] them in relation to another through either [sourcing] or [convoking]. This system is simultaneous with the system of POSITIONING described in Chapters 2 and 3, which means that any choice in POSITIONING can occur with any choice in this system of ORIENTING.

4.4 Orienting and Genre

Resources for orienting are fundamental for realizing a range of genres. As we've seen throughout this and previous chapters, this is particularly the case for persuasive genres that aim to organize different positions into arguments where they regularly work in conjunction with choices in both tendering and rendering.

The primary school text about advertisements illustrates the fact that discussions are globally organized around an opposition – in this case, between Arguments For and Arguments Against advertisements. At the beginning of the discussion, the Issue stage tenders positions that encapsulate those given in the Arguments, and at the end, the Recommendation stage renders each side. In the case of Text 4.3, the rendering involves supporting the position that we should not have printed advertisements, and rejecting the position that we should.

Issue	**Advertisements** There are many reasons for both sides of the question, "Should we have printed advertisements?" Many people have strong views and feel that ads are nothing more than useless junk mail, while other people feel they are an important source of information. = = ***encapsulating***
Arguments for	Here are some reasons why we should have advertisements in newspapers and magazines. One reason is ads give us information about what is available. Looking at ads we can find out what is on sale and what is new in the market. This is an easy way of shopping. Another reason is that advertisements promote business. When shop owners compete against each other the buyer saves money, more people come to their shops and they sell more goods.

	ll ***opposition***	
Arguments against	On the other hand, some people argue ads should not be put in newspapers and magazines for these various reasons. Firstly, ads cost the shopkeepers a lot of money to print onto paper. Also some people don't like finding junk mail in their letter boxes. People may also find the ads not very interesting. Ads also influence people to buy items they don't need and can't really afford. Ads use up a lot of space and a lot of effort has to be made to make the ads eye-catching.	
	= = ***encapsulating***	
Recommendation	In summary, although ads provide people with information, their costs far outweigh their benefits. Therefore I think *we should not have printed advertisements.*	reject *support*

Text 4.3 A discussion – tendering two sides and supporting or rejecting them

By contrast, expositions will generally tender one position, support it through a series of arguments that are likened to each other, and finally encapsulate these into a reiterated position at the end. As we saw in Chapter 3, analytical expositions do this for a proposition – in Text 4.4, the proposition that *Butterflies are the best animal in the world.*

Position	**The world's best animal is . . .** *Butterflies are the best animal in the world.* The best animal in the world should be interesting and beautiful. Butterflies look amazing and they have many features that no other animal has.	*tendered proposition*
	= = ***encapsulating***	
Arguments	Butterflies are beautiful. They have four wings. Every butterfly has a different pattern and colours on its wings. Some butterflies are so special that people travel to places just to see them. The Ulysses butterfly has beautiful bright patterns on its wings. People travel to Mossman Gorge near Cairns just to see a Ulysses butterfly.	
	= ***likening***	

	Butterflies have a special life cycle. Most animals hatch out of eggs or are born alive but caterpillars hatch from eggs, grow bigger, then change inside a chrysalis into beautiful butterflies. Some animals change as they grow, like a tadpole changes into a frog, but it doesn't change into [a] chrysalis first. Some insects like bees change from a pupa into a bee, but bees sting you. So they aren't as good as butterflies.	
	= ***likening***	
	Butterflies don't hurt anyone or anything. They help nature. When they fly from flower to flower, they take pollen from one plant to another. So they are helping the plants.	
	= = ***encapsulating***	
Reinforcement	Butterflies are very pretty and helpful so that is why *butterflies are the best animals in nature.*	*support/ tendered proposition*

Text 4.4 Analytical exposition (Queensland Studies Authority, 2011)

Hortatory expositions do the same, but focus on proposals:

Appeal	**Why water shouldn't be wasted** Water is a resource we need for drinking, cooking, washing and growing things. *Water should not be wasted for several reasons.*	*tendered proposal*
	= = ***encapsulating***	
Arguments	Firstly, people often use more water than they need, such as leaving the sprinkler on the lawn all day. If everybody uses too much water, the storage dams may run out.	
	= ***likening***	
	Another argument is that water costs money. If you use too much water, you have to pay a lot, and there is not enough left over to buy other important things.	
	= ***likening***	

	Finally, people in dry areas may feel that the city people do not care about them if they waste water. = = ***encapsulating***	
Reinforcement of appeal	Therefore, it is important that we think about the water we use and *not waste it.* Then there will be enough water for everyone.	*support/ tendered proposal*

Text 4.5 Hortatory exposition (from Humphrey & Vale, 2020, p. 80)

Kollontai's "demands" text that we saw in Chapter 3 illustrates a particular case where a very long list of proposals are likened together within the general proposal of *the law must defend the working mother.* In Text 4.6, there is less emphasis on arguments for this proposal, but rather emphasis on sets of proposals that are encapsulated into it.

Position	The first thing that can be done and the first thing that working men and women are doing in every country is to see that *the law defends the working mother.* == ***encapsulating***
Demands	Since poverty and insecurity are forcing women to take up work, and since the number of women out working is increasing every year, the very least that can be done is to make sure that *hired labour does not become the "grave of maternity."* = ***likening*** *The law must intervene to help women to combine work and maternity.* = ***likening*** Men and women workers everywhere are demanding *a complete ban on night work for women and young people,* = ***likening*** *an eight-hour day for all workers,* = ***likening*** *and a ban on the employment of children under sixteen years of age.* = ***likening*** They are demanding that *young girls and boys over sixteen years of age be allowed to work only half the day.* This is important, especially from the point of view of the future mother, since

between the years of sixteen and eighteen the girl is growing and developing into a woman. If her strength is undermined during these years her chances of healthy motherhood are lost forever.
= ***likening***
The law should state categorically that working conditions and the whole work situation must not threaten a woman's health;
= ***likening***
harmful methods of production should be replaced by safe methods or completely done away with;
= ***likening***
heavy work with weights or foot-propelled machines etc. should be mechanised;
= ***likening***
workrooms should be kept clean and there should be no extremes of temperature;
= ***likening***
toilets, washrooms and dining rooms should be provided, etc. These demands can be won – they have already been encountered in the model factories – but the factory-owners do not usually like to fork out the money. All adjustments and improvements are expensive, and human life is so cheap.
= ***likening***
A law to the effect that women should sit wherever possible is very important.
= ***likening***
It is also important that substantial and not merely nominal fines are levied against factory owners who infringe the law.
= ***likening***
The job of seeing that the law is carried out should be entrusted not only to the factory inspectors but also to representatives elected by the workers.

Text 4.6 Demands genre – likening a series of proposals (from Kollontai, 1916/1997, p. 80)

Challenges, on the other hand, put forward a position so as to reject and oppose it, with the arguments given being likened to this opposed position (see Text 4.7).

Position challenged	**The image of the convict women** Government officials, ministers of religion and wealthy landowners created an image of convict women that last a long time. They described convict women as being the worst types of people. They said that the women had no morals and were mostly prostitutes (people who offer sex in exchange for money or gifts) and hardened criminals.
	Rejecting + opposing ||
Rebuttal argument 1	However only one in five had been involved in prostitution before being transferred. Of the convicts sent to Australia, 11,083 convict women were sent to New South Wales and 12,595 to Van Diemen's Land (Tasmania). Prostitution, like theft, was usually the result of poverty. On the convict ships, many more were probably forced into prostitution to get small necessities or luxuries from the ships' officers and crews. In the colonies women were outnumbered six to one by male convicts and that situation must also have encouraged prostitution.
	= likening
Rebuttal argument 2	In Australia most convict women were assigned to free settlers and officers as servants. In many cases they were forced into sex by these masters. They could complain to a magistrate, but magistrates were part of the class of wealthy free settlers and officers. Magistrates were more likely to blame the victim than to accept the word of a convict.
	= likening
Rebuttal argument 3	Few convict women committed crimes in Australia. There were more opportunities here for success without crime than in Britain. As well, most convict women formed stable relationships. The 1814 muster (a kind of survey of the colonial population) found that most were married or living with a man. Many did not marry because of the high price of a marriage licence and for those who were Catholics, there were few priests to conduct ceremonies.

Text 4.7 Challenge genre – opposing a position (cited in Metropolitan East Disadvantaged Schools Program, 1996, p. 124, adapted from Darlington & Hospodaryk, 1993, p. 94)

4.5 Conclusion

This concludes our discussion of ORIENTING resources. As we have seen, they are fundamental to organizing sets of positions into coherent frameworks, and function to realize a number of more interpersonally oriented genres. In the next chapter, we will propose our final set of resources for enacting tenor. These resources occur within a system we call TUNING. They offer means to nuance meanings – to raise or lower the stakes of what is being said, to broaden or narrow the scope of who it relates to, and to shift the spirit in which the meanings are being put forward. Together with the resources of POSITIONING and ORIENTING, the resources of TUNING help us enact our social relations by acknowledging the nature of the feelings and the range of people involved in any instance of text and crafting our positions in relation to this.

5 Tuning: Adjusting the Meanings We Share

5.1 Introduction

Following on from our exploration of POSITIONING and ORIENTING, this chapter explores another significant dimension in relation to how interpersonal meanings are negotiated – which we will refer to as TUNING. TUNING offers additional ways to adjust meanings that are being put forward – to raise or lower the *stakes* of what is being said, to broaden or narrow the *scope* of who it relates to, and to shift the *spirit* in which the meanings are being put forward. In this chapter we will introduce three main resources within the TUNING system:

- *scope* – whereby the ambit of a position is either broadened or narrowed in terms of the personae and communities it may concern (*How inclusive or encompassing is the meaning?*)
- *stakes* – whereby positions are calibrated in terms of interpersonal risk (*How concerning or significant is the meaning? How tenuous is its standing?*)
- *spirit* – whereby a position is adjusted to be read more or less favourably (*What's the vibe of the meaning? What's its tone?*)

Returning to the exchange that we have considered throughout the book, as Kristy's mother is attempting to get her dressed, we have seen that an interpersonal juggling act characterizes the interaction. In this chapter we will add the dimension of TUNING to our consideration of the interpersonal dynamics of this exchange. In this negotiation the mother moves Kristy towards compliance with her request, at the same time as getting Ruth to stop pushing her sister – avoiding, as she does so, potential interpersonal meltdowns that might delay her end goal of getting out the door on time. The skill with which she manages this interaction is apparent in the ways she adjusts the levels of risk in her proposals, as she guides her less than optimally compliant children towards departure. Throughout she adjusts the vibe of the negotiation, all the while attending to the needs of the individuals present in the exchange. Not only is it important for everyone to feel like they are heard, but also it is important that everyone knows that the instructions, even though often cast indirectly, are to be interpreted as directed to the two children present in the exchange.

If we look at the language in this unfolding phase, we can see its interpersonal dynamics play out as distinct choices in TUNING. Rather than directly commanding Kristy to get dressed, an option likely to put her mother at loggerheads with her small and obstinate interlocutor, the mother leverages the persuasive power of interpersonal metaphor by adopting an interrogative clause structure. In addition to shifting purview, the indirectness of *how about* softens the impact of the proposal by casting it as tentative. In terms of TUNING, it lowers the stakes – most likely with the hope of avoiding the explosion of emotion that does unfortunately eventuate. Kristy's blunt refusal (*no*) raises the stakes of her rejection of the mother's proposal, though as Kristy tries to manoeuvre her way out of going, she strategically lowers the stakes of her rejection. This is realized through the indirectness of interpersonal metaphor (*don't want to go* for "don't make me go"). Nonetheless, her crying largely overrides this by significantly raising the stakes of her refusal.

(5.1)	Mother:	well how about [↓ stakes] I get you dressed instead?
	Kristy:	no [↑ stakes]
		don't want to go out today [↓ stakes]
		[CRYING] [↑ stakes]

At the same time, the mother's repetition of reasons for Kristy to get dressed, combined with her use of modality (*probably, maybe*) and lowering force (*a little bit*), can be interpreted via graduation (Martin & White, 2005) as lowering the stakes of Kristy leaving.

(5.2)	Mother:	you'll have a lovely day pet
		I won't be home late either [↓ stakes]
		I'll probably be home about the same time as Dee's big kids get home . . . maybe a little bit later, maybe a little bit earlier [↓ stakes]

Kristy's mother also lowers the stakes of her initial suggestion for why Kristy doesn't want to go out through modality metaphor, using *I think* and *I don't think* to indicate the tentativeness of her suggestions.

(5.3)	Mother:	I don't think [↓ stakes] you're really upset about me going
		I think [↓ stakes] you're upset because the TV wasn't working.

Kristy and her mother's use of grammatical metaphor earlier in the conversation contrasts with the more direct kinds of rejecting used later on, such as *don't!* by Kristy to Ruth and *don't get cranky* by Kristy's mother in response, where stakes are raised through their frankness. In this case, Kristy tries to assert her status over her younger sister by combining both asserting purview and high stakes (also suggested by the exclamation mark, suggesting a loud, sharp voice quality); but her mother trumps her by using the same strategy to protect Ruth.

(5.4)	Kristy:	[TO RUTH] don't! [↑ stakes]
	Mother:	oh she's trying to be nice
		don't get cranky [↑ stakes]

At the same time that Kristy and her mother are adjusting stakes, differing levels of "friendliness" are also involved. In terms of TUNING, we refer to this as SPIRIT – a scale whereby propositions and proposals are cast as more convivial [warming] or more threatening [warning]. For example, the mother employs Vocatives of endearment such as *pet* and *sweetie* to warm her proposals (Poynton, 1984, 1990a). Similarly, Kristy's use of a warming Vocative *Mummy* in *Mummy . . . I don't want to go away from you* can be interpreted as the child capitalizing on the opportunity afforded by the momentary lowering of stakes that occurs when the mother reflects on the challenging time they are having together (*oh dear oh dear*). We do not know from the transcript what exactly was happening at this time; but one might imagine that while they are talking, Kristy's mother may have given her a hug, and both may speak in a higher pitch and smoother voice quality to emphasize this warmth (Ngo et al., 2022; Van Leeuwen, 1999). This moment in the exchange is interrupted by Kristy's sister Ruth pushing her leg, possibly out of jealousy at all the attention being given to Kristy in this delicate negotiation. The mother's choice to address the child as *Ruth* when she attempts to stop this act of minor violence is sterner than her other vocation choices in this exchange. It is a warning, even though it is tempered via the interpersonal metaphor that tends to pervade the mother's talk (*she doesn't want her leg pushed, Ruth* for "Don't push her leg, Ruth"). Nonetheless, despite these nuances, Kristy's crying establishes a prosody of negative spirit combined with raised stakes that colours the entire conversation.

In addition to the various ways that the positions in this exchange are put at risk and the extent to which they are cast in more or less threatening terms, we also need to consider the personae and communities for whom they are positioned as relevant. Even though shared background values about motherhood are leveraged at points in this interaction (as we have seen in Chapters 3 and 4), the mother-child dyad remains the primary locus for establishing the relevance of the meanings construed. In other words, in terms of what we refer to as SCOPE, the negotiation is mainly individualizing rather than collectivizing. As we saw when considering vocatives, the proposals in the exchange are directly targeted at the interlocutor – making their ambit very clear and giving the children little wiggle room in which to get out of doing what the mother wants them to do. Also relevant to how scope is regulated is the way in which the source of feelings is directly ascribed to the children by the mother, rather than making general statements about pushing legs or going out (e.g., *she doesn't want her leg pushed; you'll have a lovely day*). There are some instances of collectivizing, for instance the *we* in *we'll get Kristy dressed*; but these are bounded by the limited scope of the mother-child dyad. As this example shows, the scope, stakes, and spirit are constantly being nuanced, all at the same time, and often through the same language resources (such as Vocatives – *Mummy, pet, Ruth,* etc.) as Kristy, her mother, and Ruth all try to get what they want.

5.2 Multilogue Communication

Up until this point, we have largely been concerned with how social relations are negotiated in monologue and dialogue. But in contemporary society, there are many ways in which we enact these relations without necessarily interacting directly with other people – via broadcast and digital media. Multilogue communication has become an important feature of contemporary social life due to the expansion of "semiotic technologies" (technologies for making meaning; Zhao et al., 2014) affording one-to-many and many-to-many communication. This kind of communication has engendered "status updating" and various kinds of comment genres whereby people share their experiences and opinions with others in real time on social media. The expanded communicative affordances offered by such digital platforms have augmented the ways in which people can interact, in terms of both increasing the range of connection possible and reducing the extent to which direct interaction is required for tenor to be negotiated (Zappavigna, 2018; Zappavigna & Martin, 2018a). At the same time, social media platforms operate by the essential logic inherent in digital platform economies – namely that of aiming to profit financially from the ways in which people connect with one another.[1] They thus advance a capitalist agenda that has pervaded the last few centuries towards what is perhaps its maximal endgame – in other words, our very social relations are now being mined for profit.

As we saw in Chapter 4 when dealing with monologue, direct interaction is not a prerequisite for "communion of feeling" (Firth, 1964, p. 112). Dialogic exchanges are possible on social media platforms, although "the unfolding is more often a 'multilogue' of simultaneous voices that, at times, can seem more of a cacophony than a conversation" (Zappavigna, 2018, p. 44). Early research into computer-mediated communication focused on exploring the differences between synchronous and asynchronous communication. However, a more pertinent variable from the perspective of tenor is whether the interaction is dialogic or multilogic (many to many) and whether it also affords ambient affiliation. In other words, an important dimension is whether direct exchanges between participants are a prerequisite for interactive social bonding or whether communion can occur through other means. These include the coordination possibilities afforded by features of digital environments that support different ways of creating connection, on both localized and aggregated levels. Concepts that have been used to study how such groupings are formed discursively online include online affinity spaces (Gee, 2005) and conviviality (Varis & Blommaert, 2015), as well as the kind of ambient affiliation we will consider in this chapter.

Although not our direct focus here, it should also be noted that social media communication is multimodal in nature, with visual media such as static images, GIFs, and digital stickers regularly functioning as moves within the type of exchange structure allowed by the particular digital platform (Jovanovic & Van Leeuwen, 2018). Processes of reposting material across platforms also comprise an important form of meaning making (Adami, 2014), and this type of re-articulation complicates what is meant by dialogue and exchange. Social media communication also tends to be highly multilingual and multicultural (Bouvier, 2015), another dimension beyond the scope of the present work and that is deserving of attention given the great potential for translanguaging (Zhao & Flewitt, 2020) and cross-cultural affiliation in "superdiverse" multiplatform environments (Leppänen et al., 2018).

5.3 Guilt and Motherhood on Social Media

Our exploration of tuning in this chapter will continue the thread we have traced throughout this book regarding discourses of motherhood, here focusing on stances, identities, and communities related to digital motherhood. Also termed *motherhood online,* this is a field of interdisciplinary work that "brings together two critical social research agendas concerning, on the one hand, the evolution of maternal identities, communities and practices in post-industrial societies; and on the other, the role of digital and social media in shaping such contemporary identities, communities and social practices" (Mackenzie & Zhao, 2021, p. 1). Drawing on a specialized corpus of tweets, we will explore a key concern within such communities, namely negotiating complex meanings about what has become popularly known as *mum/mom guilt* – the feelings of shame and frustration that many mothers experience during parenting due to the societal pressures that are placed upon them to be "good" mothers, which we also saw in the advice article in Chapter 4.

As mentioned above, the expanded affordances of digital platforms and social media have in turn expanded semiotic resources for forging and coordinating connection and have enabled various kinds of "multiloguing." This chapter, building on previous work by Zappavigna (2015, 2018) and Zappavigna and Martin (2018a) on ambient affiliation in social media discourse, explores the role of TUNING in the kind of communing affiliation possible in social media. This kind of communing draws on the affordances of semiotic technologies that support the formation of social alignments without necessarily relying on or presupposing direct interaction. For example, hashtags (**bold underline** in Example [5.5]) support various kinds of communing around shared values because they enable large-scale multiloguing about various kinds of things, such as experiences, events, issues, and emotions.

Example (5.5) is a tweet containing multiple hashtags sampled from the corpus that we will explore in this chapter, a specialized corpus of tweets containing the hashtag *#momguilt,*[2] hereon the *corpus.* It is an example of the kinds of thoughts and feelings that are recurrently shared on social media platforms about the challenging aspects of everyday experiences of motherhood.

(5.5) 3 soccer games 5+ hrs, sunburned. It wasn't enough. Now I have 1/2 the boys on our block here. **#Momguilt #MilKids #dadsdeployed #momsdone**

As we have seen in previous chapters of this book, guilt is a very significant part of contemporary discourses of motherhood. Social media platforms are spaces in which such quotidian experiences are regularly shared (Zappavigna, 2014a), particularly through configurations of text and visual images in practices somewhat problematically referred to as "mommy blogging" (Zappavigna, 2016; Zappavigna & Zhao, 2017). Social bonds that have been identified as frequent in online communities of mothers (Zappavigna, 2014b) include:

- A collective "frazzle bond," featuring expression of shared exhaustion
- A "self-deprecation bond," expressing the flawed reality and challenges of motherhood
- An "addiction bond," articulating the panacea that apparent vices such as wine and coffee consumption offer as a potential salve for the difficulties of mothering children

All of these bonds are also associated with social media expressions of guilt by mothers and were observed in our corpus. For example, by way of contextualizing the analyses of tuning in this chapter in terms of these bonds, we observed expressions of fatigue (underlined) together with guilt about neglecting children (bold), enacting a frazzle bond that routinely renders aspects of a mother's own parenting by rejecting it.

(5.6) I know this is probably selfish of me but I'm so tired of pumping. 😞 I'm contemplating weaning. **#momguilt**

(5.7) I didn't want to mom today- new blog post. Learning to give myself a break. [URL] #teamcartwright **#momguilt** #tiredmom

(5.8) One day, the **#momguilt** was too much. I returned home with crying child & called in sick. Exhausted, decided to nap on couch. Not more than 20 minutes later, she said "I'm bored" & wanted to play with daycare friends.

There was also sharing of feelings of guilt and inadequacy at being a bad mum (**bold**), in the face of rising to the challenge of motherhood (self-deprecation bond).

(5.9) Mom guilt is the worst kind if **guilt**. **#momguilt #badmom** #schoollunch **#imsorry** #kids #family #school #momlife **#badparenting** [image featuring the text "$%#*! I got stuck at work and missed parent lunch at school. I think it's safe to say this **mom guilt** will easily last the next 5 years. $%#*! *TiredNotDead*"]

(5.10) Is it a <u>**bad mom**</u> move to stop by the dairy bar on the way to pick up you kids?? Asking for a friend . . . . **#momguilt**
(5.11) At work . . . missing my boys . . . feeling like a **bad mom** today, or if not **bad**, an **absent** one. **#MomGuilt** #WorkingMom

In addition, there were posts expressing guilt (**bold**) about consuming too much wine, coffee, chocolate, or other "naughty" food, beverage, or substance (underlined) in order to cope with the challenges of motherhood (addiction bond).

(5.12) My youngest daughter got me this cup for my birthday. These days <u>I live off the coffee</u> it holds. I <u>chain smoke</u> and **cry over** the fact that my oldest won't speak to me. I wish I knew why. **#heartbroken** #momlife **#momguilt #anxiety #depression**
(5.13) Kid: "Eew Yuck!" When you lie to your kid & tell them the <u>chocolate</u> you are eating tastes like coffee **#momguilt** #lifewithtoddlers
(5.14) Why do I **feel like** if I have a glass of <u>wine</u> **I'm a bad mom**? **#momguilt**

In each of these examples, the hashtags function as foregrounded tuning resources because they adjust how we interpret the meanings in the rest of the post. As we will see later in the chapter, they interact with other kinds of tuning resources that occur within the body of the posts themselves.

A corpus-based cartography of the most frequent meanings shared in #momguilt tweets is not the primary focus of this chapter. Instead, we will explore the different kinds of linguistic features that can act as tuning resources in order to explain tuning in detail. Nevertheless, the most frequent hashtags in our corpus are interesting in terms of illuminating some of the key meanings that are at stake. The 20 most frequent hashtags co-occurring with *#momguilt* are shown in Table 5.1 to give the reader a sense of the domains of meaning covered in the corpus. Some tags specify the persona experiencing the guilt – for example, *mum, mommy, dad, wife, workingmom,* and *teacher,* giving us some sense of the [people entities] likely involved in sourcing meanings about what might constitute good mothering.

While the examples explored in this section have clear relevance to communities of mothers, the reader may have noticed that the frazzle, self-deprecation, and addiction bonds introduced above are also central to other kinds of communities proliferating en masse through social media streams. The particularities of these bonds may differ depending on

Table 5.1 The 20 Most Frequent Hashtags in the Corpus (Co-Occurring with #Momguilt)

#	Hashtag	Freq.	#	Hashtag	Freq.
1	#momlife	234	11	#kids	17
2	#parenting	101	12	#breastfeeding	16
3	#motherhood	85	13	#momfail	13
4	#workingmom	74	14	#baby	10
5	#moms	40	15	#sahm	9
6	#selfcare	33	16	#newmom	9
7	#mom	33	17	#mommyblogger	9
8	#guilt	24	18	#momblog	9
9	#mumguilt	23	19	#anxiety	8
10	#workingmoms	22	20	#thestruggleisreal	7

what a certain community (e.g., academics) conceives as transgressive behaviour of which one should be mindful (e.g., being uncollegial), or where activity should be focused (e.g., writing lots of papers) and what methods might be used to cope (e.g., consuming wine). We now turn to what this has to do with social relations, ambient affiliation, and tuning.

5.4 Tuning Positions: Scoping, Staking, and Spiriting #momguilt

Tuning is the region of interpersonal meaning concerned with how a position is pitched as more or less loaded, as more or less friendly, and as more or less relevant to particular personae or communities. In this section we will consider resources for modifying the tendered and rendered meanings being put forward in a text in terms of:

- SCOPE: [individualized] ↔ [collectivized]
- STAKES: [higher] ↔ [lower]
- SPIRIT: [warming] ↔ [warning]

We begin with SCOPE, which is concerned with the extent of a position's ambit. A key dimension is how broad or narrow the group is that is being sourced or convoked. SCOPE is a clined system ranging from narrower [individualized] to broader [collectivized] options. This kind of distinction can be realized linguistically through number (e.g., *we all* vs. *I*) and more broadly through quantification of people within the discourse semantic system of GRADUATION (Martin & White, 2005), as well as through various membership categorization devices (Schegloff, 2007) that function to flag group association. Paralinguistically, it can be realized through shifts in loudness from a whisper (individualizing) to a yell (collectivizing), body orientation and eye gaze to an individual or a collective, and the breadth or narrowness of deictic pointing – using, say, the pinky finger to point (individualizing) or the whole hand (collectivizing) (Kress & Van Leeuwen, 2021; Ngo et al., 2022; Van Leeuwen, 1999).

In work on identity and iconization, Tann (2010a, 2010b, 2013) draws on membership categorization devices to specify three kinds of association that construe belonging relevant to SCOPING:

- *Categorization* – classifying by type; for example, Western, Muslim, and middle-class
- *Collectivization* – generating oppositions between groups; for example, us versus them, stay-at-home mothers versus working mothers, conservatives versus liberals, and Australians versus refugees
- *Spatialization* – classifying via place; for example, Aussies, Kiwis, and Yankees

Consider Example (5.15), which convokes an ambient community of mothers through the vocative *moms* and the collective deictic *Our*, together with the various collectivizing hashtags (underlined).

(5.15) <u>Moms</u>, we **don't need to** carry guilt. <u>Our</u> purses are **heavy enough**. <u>#momguilt #momlife #Moms</u> #thefilterfreem1 #filterfree #godcan #guilt **#letitgo** [image with the quote: "What are you feeling guilt about today? **Stop giving life to negative feelings. Bring it to God. Release it. Move forward. Be free.**"]

Mustering a community around a bond requires some way of gathering that community into the negotiation, for example via Vocatives, which include phenomena such as calls, addresses, and exclamations (Zwicky, 1974; in Poynton, 1984). Vocation is an optional system within clause grammar that is important in how power, solidarity, status, role relationships, and in/formality are interpersonally construed (Poynton, 1984). SCOPING is thus realized in this text through resources such as Vocatives, which convoke and source an ambient community of mothers – such as the Vocative *Moms* at the beginning of the tweet. The use of the plural pronoun *we* also collectivizes these mothers as the relevant identity, together with the hashtags *#momguilt*, *#momlife*, and *#Moms*. Collectivization thus runs as a prosody through the tweet, realized opportunistically throughout. Through the hashtag positively judging god (*#godcan*), together with other meanings about god in the embedded image, suggesting that the particular community is not all moms but specifically Christian ones, this tweet convokes a very particular community.

Another system in tuning, STAKES, is about raising or lowering the degree of risk imbuing a meaning. For example, within a particular community we might consider how much of an issue it is if someone rejects a particular tendered meaning. Returning to Example (5.15), it would be a controversial and high-stakes position to reject the post's tender that moms don't need to carry guilt or that they don't need to follow the commands in the image (*Stop giving life to negative feelings. Bring it to God. Release it. Move forward. Be free.*). In addition to implicit staking that relies on the background of already positioned values about motherhood guilt that this community likely holds, the post raises the STAKES of the tender through various resources (**bold**). For instance, the semiotic risk is intensified via disclaiming engagement: (e.g., *don't need to*), the commands in the image and the hashtag (e.g., *#letitgo*), and the upscaled graduation (e.g., *heavy enough*).

Our third system, SPIRIT, concerns whether the message is tabled positively [warming] or negatively [warning]. Another way of thinking about this dimension is whether the message provokes bonding that moves people closer together, or whether it is oriented to something potentially disruptive and disuniting. For instance, Vocatives, in addition to acting as scoping resources, can evoke positive and negative stances about those being addressed that adjust the SPIRIT of a message. For instance, in Example (5.15) the Vocative *Moms* calls together mothers in a relatively positive way, as opposed to for instance *breeders*, which invokes negative connotations – mothers as mere biological reproducers. Example (6.16) invokes a negative stance with the Vocative *Handmaids*, most likely a reference to the handmaids in the film adaptation of Margaret Atwood's novel *The Handmaid's Tale*, which explores the oppression and subjugation of women:

(5.16) **Handmaids**, you have your orders.

These choices in vocation have potential impact across a text: "once a speaker addresses another as Your Honour for example the dominance/deference dyad has been effectively revealed" (Martin, 1992, p. 258). In a similar way, spirit can be sensitive to variations in voice quality and to the way that (Hyper/Macro-) thematized attitude is established in longer texts. As we will see later, additional paralinguistic resources such as emoji can be used to adjust the spirit of a post.

Sections 5.4.1–5.4.3 explore in more detail the variety of resources in our corpus that can be used to enact scoping, staking, and spiriting in multilogue. Our aim is not an exhaustive catalogue of options (since this would be impossible given the intricacy of interpersonal meaning) but rather to give the reader a sense of the relevant regions of meaning for each system. We will conclude the chapter with some consideration of tuning resources in interactive exchanges.

5.4.1 Scoping Resources

Tuning may be adjusted by expanding or restricting the range of individual personae or groups to whom a particular meaning is applicable. In the case of our corpus, we have, to a certain extent, built scoping into our selection criteria for constructing the corpus since the #momguilt hashtag broadly concerns mothers. Scoping can involve both expansion and contraction in terms of the group or personae relevant to the meaning in play. For instance, embracing a whole community through choices in pronominal grammar is a choice to enlarge scope.

(5.17) **We all** have it. And it's never easy #momguilt [link to an article about mom guilt] #parenting #momlife #guilt

(5.18) Moms, if this isn't **all of us** on some level I don't know what is. **We** try to do it all because the #momguilt tells us we have to . . . but God didn't make **us** to live like that. It takes a village! Walk along side **each other** and lift **each other** up!

At the same time, various resources for identifying participants can reduce the scope to the level of individuals.

(5.19) Telling **my four babies** goodbye yesterday. Enjoying some **me** time, but **I** miss them when **I**'m away. #momguilt

Scope can also be narrowed down to particular kinds of groups. For instance, in Example (5.20) the clients who experience guilt are subspecified as mothers in particular.

(5.20) #Guilt is such a common emotion from my anxiety clients, **particularly moms**. #momguilt

While the distinction between whole communities and individuals is the most obvious case, social relations are very complex. Within communities there will be different arrays of subgroups, and there will be groups that span multiple communities. There are different ways of "dog whistling" with reference to these groups without naming them or addressing them directly.

Since the corpus consisted of posts about experiences of guilt, the people and groups experiencing guilt or judging others as guilty are pertinent to tuning. The choice of the source tends to operate in the service of scoping in the corpus. For example, as we have seen, mothers reject themselves through negative self-judgment throughout the corpus (e.g., *moms* in Example [5.21]), with the most common source of such negative self-judgment being the author themselves (e.g., *I* in Example [5.22]).

(5.21) Do any other **#moms** feel guilty about just vegging and watching tv while their kid naps? #momguilt #momlife #motherhood #shouldibedoingsomethingproductive

(5.22) **I** feel like the worst parent in the world listening to my kid sniff with snot in their nose. #momguilt #momlife #sickbaby

As mentioned earlier, the most frequent hashtags co-occurring with #momguilt provide an overview of the kinds of groups that are explicitly convoked or sourced in the corpus, for instance *working moms* in posts such as Example (5.23).

(5.23) Can we talk about #momguilt? Especially that particular bind **#workingmoms** put themselves in: guilty for not being with their kids AND guilty for not devoting enough energy to work . . .

In this post the hashtag *#workingmoms* enacts scoping because it collectivizes this group as the target of negative judgment, reinforcing the *particular bind* for which this post casts them as responsible. Background meanings about the so-called mommy wars (Abetz & Moore, 2018), which set stay-at-home mothers (SAHM) against working mothers, are relevant to this scoping. An example of a hashtag used to convoke this opposing group is #SAHM in Example (5.24).

(5.24) I'm only REALLY happy when my husband is home. The second he leaves I feel like I will never be happy again. I hate this. #MomGuilt **#SAHM**

We can imagine that a high-stakes reply to this post would be to suggest that the mother find employment, because of the way that it leverages previously scoped and arranged bonds from the shared cultural context.

As mentioned in Section 5.4, membership categorization tends to be a scoping resource since in order to point out to whom a meaning is relevant, a person or group needs to be identified or at least implicated through some meaning that activates relevant associations. Less explicit collectivizing can also occur through resources that invoke putative others. For instance, *we* and *us* were quite frequent in the corpus, and this choice can be seen to invoke an implicit *them.*

(5.25) #Momguilt is real, but **we** deserve a break too. Be sure to take it #momlife [URL to blog post titled "Resetting"]

The collectivization device *we* in Example (5.25), in conjunction with *too,* implies that there is another group of non-mothers who are getting the break that these mothers deserve. Collectivization was also used in construing the shared complaint that mothers and not others are undertaking too much emotional labour, and so is involved in the policing of scoping.

(5.26) Lets talk #selfcare and #momguilt for a minute. It is all too often **we** lose sight of ourselves as Moms. **We** take on the role of boo-boo kisser, butt wiper, laundry queen, maker of meals you . . . . [link to an Instagram post]

Spatialization was much less common in the corpus, most likely due to the ambient nature of the communication rendering geographical co-location as less of a shared variable. The US spelling of *mom* in the #momguilt hashtag probably meant that the data tended to be produced by people residing in the United States, as Example (5.27) suggests.

(5.27) **American** moms: let's stop feeling guilty and start getting mad [URL to article in *The Guardian* with the same title] #MothersDay #motherhood #momguilt #workersrights #paygap #femalelabor #equalpay

Some spatialization resources acted to introduce a political inflection to the variety of #momguilt at stake, both sourcing and convoking to a specified collective community.

(5.28) Thanks to @motherwellmag for re-posting this piece. We need to take care of ourselves and **our country** at the same time. #momguilt [embedded post: We are already made to feel guilty, as mothers, about so many things, we musn't add political activism to the list. {URL}]

(5.29) A lot of horrible stuff exists in the world.. In **this country** thankfully not the case (islamophobic attacks against kids ✓). AND there is no oppressing a 4 year old - because if she wants a sparkly clip or a sparkly headscarf.. that 4 year old is getting it - #momguilt

With respect to some of the novel features of social media multilogue, as a form of social metadata hashtags have the general capacity to bridge between individual and collective experience with implications for scoping. In Example (5.30), individual feelings are linked to broader experiences across the social network.

(5.30) I feel like a bad mom but I totally brought C into bed with me last night . . . I was just so tired and I know he sleeps better and falls back to sleep faster next to me. It was only for 4hrs but I still feel the mom guilt. **#secretsmomskeep #momguilt**

In this post the source of the rendering is the author of the post, individualized as *I*, but this experience is collectivized through the hashtag *#secretsmomskeep*. This allows the mother to turn her specific experience into a generalizable truth that can be shared more widely. In addition to targeting the preceding verbiage as an evaluative metacomment, the hashtag links the particular secrets shared in the body of the post to other potential posts sharing the same hashtag. We can also interpret this as having a convoking function, calling together other mothers who have secrets to share using the same tag.

5.4.2 Staking Resources

Staking describes the resources that adjust the relative risk of a proposition or proposal, making it more or less consequential. The risk is relative in the sense that it works in concert with the constellations of values that are always in play within the discourse of any particular community and that may shift abruptly or evolve over time. The tendering of a proposition or proposal will be more or less disruptive to these constellations. For example, if within the SFL community, one was to reject Halliday's work, it would be tantamount to rejecting the SFL community itself. On the other hand, if one were to reject the work of one of the authors of this book, it would not necessarily have the same effect (though it would have a larger or smaller effect, depending on which author you are rejecting). In the constellation surrounding SFL, Halliday is very high stakes.

In the case of motherhood guilt, a lot of staking work is undertaken against a background of oriented and positioned meanings about what it is to be a "good" mother. Example (5.31) likens, through a token-value relation, self-care to the state of being a good mom.

(5.31) I **always** forget that self care **DOES** equate to being a good mom. #momguilt #iForget #poor[Name] **#moremomguilt**

The all-caps font (*DOES*) raises the stakes of the proposition by acting both as a form of emphasis and as a paralinguistic shouting token. The move to raise the stakes also suggests a direct challenge (rejection and opposition) to an implicated perspective – that is, that a bad mother takes care of their own needs. The linguistic intensification (*always*) also raises the stakes of the user's confession (*I always forget* . . .). Both instances of escalating stakes function in conjunction with the string of hashtags that explicitly mark the relevant values under scrutiny – the guilt or not of mothers and whether or not they remember their place in the order of things.

By way of probing staking further, we might ask how much of an issue it might be if a tendered meaning were rejected. In the case of Example (5.31), this involves considering how controversial it would be for another user to reply that in fact mothers tending to their own needs are committing a selfish act worthy of shame. This would be a high-stakes rendering within online communities of mothers, but potentially relatively low stakes in other communities such as the "manoverse" of toxic masculinity, where denigrating women is a shared exercise. Since answering the question involves fine-tuning levels of attitude, graduation is a resource that is frequently implicated in staking both tendered and rendered meanings. For instance, Example (5.32) deploys graduation resources (bold) to emphasize the magnitude of emotion that the mother expresses about leaving her child and thus raise the stakes.

(5.32) Having **major** mom guilt today . . . Leaving my little to go away for the weekend is **killing** me. #momguilt

Intensification via resources such as the Modal Adjuncts was frequently used in the corpus to raise the stakes of the users' attitudes towards the proposition or situation being described, in terms of possibility, probability, necessity, or obligation. For example, *always* in Examples (5.33)–(5.35) raises the stakes of the meaning by presenting the situations described as intractable and ongoing.

(5.33) You guys moms guilt is so real.. No matter what I do I **always** question whether or not I made the right decisions.

(5.34) Im SURE it's not just me but as a mom I **ALWAYS** feel like I should be doing more or that I didn't do enough before I went to work. #momguilt

(5.35) I **always** feel guilty going to the #spa when my family is free to hang. #momguilt #lifestyle

In these examples the intensification also raises the stakes by stressing that the users are engaging in a behaviour that contravenes a set of assumed values about good motherhood. These examples also illustrate that, like scoping, stakes often runs as a prosody through texts and is realized through an array of different language resources – in Example (5.33), for instance, it is realized through ***so*** *real,* ***No matter*** *what I do,* and *I* ***always*** *question.*

Unsurprisingly, given #momguilt was part of the corpus selection criteria, self-targeted upscaled rejection was one of the most common patterns implicated in raising stakes about the extent to which the users felt that they were good mothers. However, this rendering pattern was highly sensitive to other dimensions in the posts, most significantly the use of humour, and could be used in both raising and lowering the interpersonal stakes of the meaning put at risk. A simple example in the corpus is intensification of self-directed rejection regarding the user's self-perceived capacity to act as a good caregiver, which they express in terms of affect.

(5.36) [Name] stopped sleeping well recently & I got super upset with her because of it & after our visit to the ER Monday, had our follow up today to find out she has a double ear infection. & I **feel like the worst person alive** 🙁. #MomGuilt

(5.37) Legit **feel like the worst mom in the world** when I have to wake my daughter up to take her to my MIL so I can go to work #momguilt

(5.38) Summer: when you **feel like the worst parent ever** cause all your kid wants to do it play with you & you decided to have a career #momguilt

These kinds of admissions and negative self-assessments were part of an ongoing motif in the corpus of confession, whereby mothers admit the various ways in which they have failed to be a "good mom." Framing their sharing of everyday observations about the activity of motherhood as a confession raises the stakes – the confessional is after all an inherently consequential genre where for some "believers" the fate of an immortal soul hangs in the balance. Example (5.39) shows multiple resources working together to explicitly raise stakes, including a Macrotheme that directly categorizes the post as a confession.

(5.39) Confession: The #momguilt is 💯 REAL! Should I be working, teaching, cooking, cleaning, talking, listening, or encouraging? #MommyhoodChat [GIF from *Game of Thrones*]

This Macrotheme indicates that the speaker is about to make an admission about something related to being a mother, and that what follows is an elaboration or explanation of their offences. In other words, the colon serves as a thematic pivot, linking the speech function of "confession" to the subsequent clause complex, which elaborates the speaker's experience of #momguilt. The consequential nature of the confession genre that the Macrotheme invokes casts this elaboration as more profound. The post also contains other resources that work together to raise stakes, such as the "Hundred Points" emoji 💯 used to upscale the appreciation of #momguilt together with the exclamation mark. In addition, the listing of activities *working, teaching, cooking, cleaning, talking, listening, or encouraging* serves to intensify the significance of the work mothers are required to do, responding to putative meanings in the context that belittle the contribution of mothers to social life.

Perhaps the strongest staking resource in Example (5.39) is a GIF. This GIF is a snippet from an episode at the conclusion of the fifth season of the TV series *Game of Thrones* in which Cersei, the queen mother of the realm, is subjected to a humiliating punishment due to her numerous transgressions (which included engaging in an adulterous relationship with her twin brother). The penalty for this behaviour involved the removal of her hair and a naked walk through the streets, where she is forced to confront her subjects who taunt her with jeers, shouting, "Shame!" These cries are visibly rendered in the GIF through the overlayed text. Behind her is a woman ringing a bell and chanting the same words. The perpetual looping that is inherent in GIFs and animated stickers appears to amplify their interpersonal significance and require their recipients to interpret and respond to them in ways that are nuanced and contextually sensitive. In Example (5.39) the GIF serves as a kind of visual interpersonal theme, which emphasizes the shame at the heart of the confession genre that is leveraged in the body of the post to raise the stakes of the everyday experiences of motherhood expressed by the user.

Another graphicon resource regularly used for staking in the corpus is emoji. These tended to converge with both negative affect and judgment. They also often involved repetition, for instance as a cluster of emoji raising the stakes at the end of the body of a post.

(5.40) Leaving for vacation in a week and I'm **anxious as fuck** to leave my babyyyyy 😱😱😱😱 #MomGuilt

(5.41) When [Name] says she's **sad** I couldn't be group mom for dance this year. . . . 😭😭😭😭 #momguilt

(5.42) So, we experienced our first night without the boob to go to sleep & I **felt so damn sad** hearing her **cry** 😭💔 #momguilt

(5.43) #momguilt is **crushing my soul** tonight. I love my little man so much, I hope he isn't **mad** at me for yelling 😭😭😫💔

The strings of multiple emoji in Examples (5.40)–(5.43) resonate with the rejection (bold) in the verbiage as well as targeting or being triggered by the entire situation, described as a stakes-raising evaluative metacomment that concentrates the accumulated negative self-assessment. This is particularly apparent in the cluster of Loudly Crying Face 😭 emoji, Tired Face 😫 emoji, and Broken Heart 💔 emoji at the end of Example (5.43). A similar stake-raising effect was achieved through multiple hashtags negatively assessing mothers or linking mothers to negative feelings. For instance, the *#badmom*(s) hashtag co-occurred with such tags.

(5.44) I didn't kiss my son goodbye this morning because I was upset that he didn't eat his breakfast 🥞😥 **#momfail #momguilt** #momlife **#badmoms**

(5.45) Mom guilt is the worst kind if guilt. #momguilt **#badmom** #schoollunch **#imsorry** #kids #family #school #momlife

Another way that meanings about "bad moms" raise the stakes was through swearing. In these cases, the expletives construe an underspecified outburst of affect, usually in the environment of negative judgment targeted at the self.

(5.46) I had to use my mom voice tonight and I feel like **fucking shit**. #momlife #momguilt

(5.47) Got it. I'm a **shitty** mom with a short temper who curses too much. **Fuck**. #motherhood #momguilt

(5.48) I think I need to supplement with formula. Why does this make my heartbreak and me feel like such a **fucking** failure. #momguilt

(5.49) Anytime I allow myself to sit still and enjoy some downtime, I feel discombobulated and ashamed. #singlemom #workingmom #momguilt **#bullshit**

(5.50) I can't get frustrated with my kid without **fucking** hating myself for it . . . What is that??? #momguilt

In contrast, lowering stakes involves tamping down the level of controversy or significance of a meaning. Due to the nature of the corpus, which tended to feature outpourings of complaints attracting the #momguilt hashtag, such tempering of stakes was not a common pattern. Generally, it occurred in posts that moderate a meaning that might be interpreted as too scandalous for the context, for example admitting that you don't love your children.

(5.51) I've got a confession . . . there are **some** times I don't love being a mother. It's not that I don't love my kids, I **just** don't love some of the things that motherhood has brought into my life. [link to a blog post with the title "Hey, Mama. It's All Going to Be OK"] @ User #selflove #lonliness #momguilt

Example (5.51) contains a range of resources lowering the stakes of the *confession.* The quantifier *some* reduces the scope of possible times the user doesn't *love being a mother.* The user then rejects the implicated position that this might mean that she does not love her kids. In another move mitigating this putative high-stakes position, the user tempers the stakes, downplaying the stakes of her confession via the focusing adverb *just,* which further specifies its limited extent. The title of the linked post is another example of reducing stakes: the address *Hey, Mama* [warms] the proposition to follow that *It's All Going to Be OK.* It invokes the persona of someone who offers comfort and consolation in response to the vulnerability invoked by the high-stakes confession.

As the examples so far have shown, graduation is a key resource for realizing shifts in stakes. However, it is not the only resource. Humour was also used throughout the corpus to lower the stakes of confessed violations of implicated positions regarding good mothering – combining this lowering of stakes with deferring of the meanings being tendered. For example, a frequent choice was to use laughter tokens to "laugh off" positions that do not accord with shared values. These represent semiotic "wrinkles" (Knight, 2010b, p. 329) that are potentially disruptive to social relations and need to be tempered. In Example (5.52) the Face with Tears of Joy 😂 emoji targets the meaning in the post, directing evaluation towards the situation described. While it could be interpreted as "laughing at" the proposition, the hashtag provides additional evidence that the meaning clashes with some other value (and hence engenders *guilt*), making "laughing off" a more logical interpretation. In this case what is being laughed off is the notion that it is ever Ok to feed your child canned goods.

(5.52) When you buy "organic" to make yourself feel better about feeding your child dinner out of a can. #momguilt 😂

This is stakes-lowering because it is a way of stating something controversial without directly violating a shared ethical parameter or metric. The intertextuality of the proposition itself is also stakes-lowering – it is structured as a kind of point-of-view meme "When you do X" aimed at sharing an amusing observation about a particular situation. Other examples of stakes-lowering use of laughter token emoji include Examples (5.53)–(5.55).

(5.53) @user I'm not going to lie . . . the thought crossed my mind. And then the crushing #momguilt caught up with me. [response to a post about a "kid-free" flight]

(5.54) I had #momguilt, so here we are again with #2. Not that I minded eating more ice cream. . . .

(5.55) What a good idea- #momguilt is real I know and everyone feeds their kids cornflakes off the floor sometimes But keep this handy for when you have a moment of inspiration..[images of food with the overlaid caption "5 Homemade Alternatives to the Worst Processed Snacks for Kids"]

These posts lower the stakes of potentially community norm–violating activities – flying without your kids, eating too much ice cream, and letting your children eat breakfast cereal off the floor.

Modality and interpersonal grammatical metaphor are also often used to adjust the stakes. In Kollontai's demands text (Text 5.1), for example, she raises the stakes of her demands by bouncing between median (*should*) and high (*must*) modality (in bold), in addition to sharpening focus (italics) and raising force (underlined) in graduation:

> The law **must** intervene to help women to combine work and maternity. Men and women workers everywhere are <u>demanding</u> a *complete* ban on night work for women and young people, an eight-hour day for all workers, and a ban on the employment of children under sixteen years of age.
>
> They are <u>demanding</u> that young girls and boys over sixteen years of age be allowed to work only half the day. This is important, *especially* from the point of view of the future mother, since between the years of sixteen and eighteen the girl is growing and developing into a woman. If her strength is undermined during these years her chances of healthy motherhood are lost <u>forever</u>. The law **should** state *categorically* that working conditions and the *whole* work situation must not threaten a woman's health; harmful methods of production **should** be replaced by safe methods or *completely* done away with; heavy work with weights or foot-propelled machines etc. **should** be mechanised; workrooms **should** be kept clean and there **should** be no

extremes of temperature; toilets, washrooms and dining rooms **should** be provided, etc.

Text 5.1 Stakes of demands (from Kollontai, 1916/1997, p. 80)

Modality metaphor can also be used to lower the stakes of a proposition in terms of its certainty:

(5.56) **I guess** that's me off the hook for the kids dinner 🍕 #NationalPizzaDay #MomGuilt

This occurs during Kristy and her mother's discussion, where her mother tentatively puts forward an initial suggestion of why Kristy is upset, using *I don't think* and *I think*:

(5.57) **I don't think** you're really upset about me going, **I think** you're upset because the TV wasn't working.

Kristy and her mother's conversation is filled with lowered stakes in this regard. In the following stretch from later in the conversation, for instance, Kristy wants to give her baby sister Ruth a cuddle. To do this, Kristy draws on interpersonal grammatical metaphor (specifically mood metaphor) to lower the stakes of her requests, using *can I* questions to realize proposals (in bold). Despite this, however, her mother rejects her requests. But she does this rejection while also lowering the stakes – first by tendering another position rather than outright rejection and second through the modality metaphor *I think* (in italics), in addition to other resources underlined. Nonetheless, her mother's rejection sends Kristy back into her high-stakes crying.

(5.58) Kristy: **can I** give her a cuddle?
Mother: *I don't think* she wants her cuddle just now.
Kristy: She doesn't like me [CRIES]
Mother: No come on, sometimes you don't want to be cuddled either.
Kristy: . . . **could you** umm put her on my lap like a little possum?
Mother: [TO RUTH] Do you want to sit on Kristy's lap? [RUTH REFUSES]
No?
[TO KRISTY] *I think* she'd like to stay here for the moment
Kristy: No [CRIES]

Interpersonal metaphors are regular resources for lowering the stakes, but they can also raise the stakes of a proposition.

(5.59) It's raining so **I'm sure** he won't go outside. Still #momguilt. -[name]

5.4.3 Spiriting Resources

Tuning may also be adjusted through SPIRITING, that is, resources that shift the tone with which a meaning is put forward – for instance, by positioning it to be read in a positive way (e.g., as pleasant and friendly) or a negative one (e.g., as aggressive or defensive). Again, a wide range of resources can be deployed from Vocatives to emoji. For example, the Red Heart ❤ and Face Blowing a Kiss 😘 emoji in Example (5.60) resonate with the positive tone of the thanks (*Thx*) aimed at another user.

(5.60) @User That's a hard thing to remember these days, the #momguilt is real! Thx for saying so! ❤😘

This establishes a warm feeling being presented to the reader – that they should read it with positive vibes. Note that this is distinct from rendering – the ❤ and 😘 do not support anything in particular in terms of a target. Rather they colour the position overall in positive feelings.

Similarly, the cluster of emoji and the use of the exclamation mark in Example (5.61) enmesh with meanings made in the positive affirmations in the post body, the endearment vocative (*momma*), and the hashtag positively assessing mothers (*#momknowsbest*).

(5.61) @User Heck yeah,right on,momma! Way to go! 😊❤👏 #MomGuilt #momknowsbest #VoteBlueToSaveAmerica [GIF of a woman high-fiving a cat]

The coordination of these resources suggests that they are responding to a post about someone else's feelings of guilt rather than using the *#MomGuilt* tag as a reflection on their own experiences. The coordination with the political hashtag *#VoteBlueToSaveAmerica* also suggests a scope beyond the individual user. A contrasting example in terms of the polarity of spiriting is Example (5.62), where the Middle Finger 🖕 emoji converges with the offensive hashtags *#eatabagofdicks* and *#dicks* to caution the imagined voices in the culture who are pressuring the user to apologize for their parenting choices.

(5.62) No apologies for the way I'm raising my daughter. None. So just stop with the #momguilt #eatabagofdicks #dicks

In this example the emoji, the hashtags, and the command to *just stop* warn any potentially resistant reader that might be critical of the user's parenting that their opinions are not welcome.

In addition to clear positive or negative spiriting, more nuanced possibilities were present in the corpus. Humour and sarcasm were used throughout to combat prevailing cultural positions about mothers. In Example (5.63) the user employs parody to play the voice of a critical other, positioned as telling the user to pay attention to the fleeting pleasures of mothering despite the grind of daily routine.

(5.63) 2 more weeks of #summer. Today I'm letting the #Xbox babysit. I know: treasure every moment. #boymom #badmom #momguilt #SorryNotSorry

The Face with Rolling Eyes emoji together with the *#SorryNotSorry* reveal the underlying position of the user, and their combative defensive tone invokes the presence of far-reaching or ongoing criticism that needs to be dispelled or quashed.

In spoken language, voice quality and facial paralanguage are key carriers of spirit. A relatively high-pitched, loud voice with a smile will tend to indicate warmth, no matter what is being said, while a relatively low and soft voice with a narrow range of pitch and a frown will tend to indicate warning (or negative spirit in general) (Ariztimuño et al., 2022; Ngo et al., 2022). In written language these voice quality features are often replaced by other paralinguistic features, including emoji as shown above. Punctuation is also a key resource in this regard, though this seems to vary by generation. For a millennial such as the first author, for example, the following three text messages from a parent have very different spirit.

(5.64) Ok!
(5.65) Ok
(5.66) Ok.

The first is said, as it were, with a smile – the exclamation mark indicating a warm, happy response. The second, without any punctuation, is relatively neutral. The third with a full stop indicates something is wrong – whatever was said previously means they are now in trouble (whether or not the parent intends this!).

As we have seen above, another regular resource for spirit involves naming. When Kristy tries to explain to her mother that she doesn't want to go out, she uses the Vocative *Mummy* – which, when contrasted with *Mum* or the markedly formal *Mother,* makes clear that although she is rejecting her mother's attempts at getting her to leave the house, she is saying these rejections with love (Poynton, 1990a).

(5.67) Kristy: **Mummy** . . . I don't want to go away from you

As Poynton notes, naming in this regard offers a highly nuanced set of gradations of warming and warning. Crudely speaking, this means we can order names of people in terms of the degree to which they show warmth – from full names to shortened personal names to nicknames to nicknames with iterated suffixes. To return to Chapter 1 and take the names of the first author that his mother uses for him as an example, we can arrange the names from least warmth to most: *Yaegan John Doran, Yaegan John, Yaegan, Yaeg, Yaegy, Yaegy J, Yaegy JJ, Yaegy JJJ, Yaegy JJJJJ.*

Looking multimodally, spirit is also the realm of colour in images and sound quality in film (Painter et al., 2013; Van Leeuwen, 1999). These resources work to tinge the scenes being presented in ways that make them eery and dark or happy and cheerful and form a crucial resource for setting the mood and ambience of a text. Exploring this takes us further than we can go in this book, but it indicates that a major area of work in terms of our understanding of tenor resources will be to flesh out how these feelings are built across modalities.

5.5 Tuning in Dialogue

While this chapter has focused on social media multilogue and the ways tuning can be used to adjust meanings within and beyond posts shared with ambient audiences, tuning is also commonly used in social media interactions. These intersperse unfolding social streams, in our case interactions during the mass unfolding of expressions of #momguilt. In these examples, there is a regular interaction between tuning and rendering. Rendering involves putting forward opinions in ways that can at times be socially risky, and so tuning allows for people to adjust their meanings to make clear how this should be read.

For instance, the two sequenced posts Examples (5.68) and (5.69) can be interpreted as an example of the very frequent social practice of complaining about some aspect of daily life to anyone who will listen. In this example, User 1 rejects aspects of themselves and their life, as indicated in bold.

Exchange (1)
User 1:
(5.68) Looking at day care for a couple afternoons a week because taking care of a baby alone all day is <u>really</u> **hard**. (1/2)
(5.69) Admitting that <u>really</u> makes me **feel like a shitty mom**. (2/2) #Mom**Guilt** #**ICry**AsMuchAsSheDoes

User 2:
(5.70) Not shitty <u>at all</u>, <u>very</u> **normal** and **human**. Take care of her <u>AND</u> you. 💞

User 2 responds to User 1's lament with a message of reassurance. The tuning resources in Example (5.70) parallel but reverse in polarity those of User 1's posts, in order to reject the "bad mom" bond and support them. User 2 renders User 1's position, reconstruing their negative self-assessment as normality (*normal and human*) and thereby lowering the stakes by positioning the mother's confession as unremarkable. In addition, the Revolving Hearts 💞 emoji is used for spiriting and warms the message, both resonating with the positive evaluation in the post and acting as a token of solidarity with User 1. The capitalized font in *Take care of her AND you* emphasizes the importance of looking after both mothers and children, increasing the interpersonal significance of the comparison. In other words, it raises the stakes of the likening – and the parallelism in both clauses also aids this rhetorical re-coupling.

Another example that uses this kind of rhetorical flipping of appraisal polarity is Exchange (2). In this instance, rather than a bad mom bond, Example (5.71) tables a "bad society" bond, and the interactant attempts to console User 1 at first with a commiseration (*sorry*) and then via positive assessments of their capacity.

Exchange (2)
(5.71) **User 1:** I really hate how I've been shown multiple times in the past two weeks that being a mom and academic is not supported by society. #momguilt
(5.72) **User 2:** so sorry you've been experiencing that. . . . you're a total beast!!! you can do this! 💪
(5.73) **User 1:** ❤ thank you.

In this example the Flexed Biceps 💪 emoji resonates with the positive judgment (*beast!!!*) and the encouragement (*you can do this!*) as well as acting as a token of solidarity in terms of involvement. Through the lens of tuning, it would seem to concentrate warming in terms of spiriting through coordination with positive appraisal and involvement and raising in terms of stakes by coordinating with the upscaled graduation throughout the post.[3]

Exchange (3) is another example where tuning plays a pivotal role in how a "good/bad mom" bond is negotiated through adjustments in tuning. In this example the users negotiate meanings about the propriety of taking a tired child out to dinner. This exchange exemplifies the act of offering support to a mother who has directly confessed to violating a social norm, a pattern that pervades the corpus:

Exchange (3)

(5.74) **User 1:** I felt a little [↓ **stakes**] #momguilt bringing this guy out to dinner when he was so tired [↑ **stakes**], but I was really craving [↑ **stakes**] [@RamenBrand] dammit! 😂 **[warm]** [picture of a child yawning at a table with a menu in front of him]

(5.75) **User 2:** I just dragged [↑ **stakes**] my little guy out tonight for dumplings 😊 **[warm]**

(5.76) **User 3:** Lol!!!! [↑ **stakes**]

(5.77) **User 4:** Done that many a times! Haha! [↑ **stakes/warm**]

(5.78) **User 5:** Haha **[warm]**, I've been totally [↑ **stakes**] guilty of that before and I'd tell them to take a quick [↓ **stakes**] nap before the udon came out 😬. Indulging a little [↓ **stakes**] for a quick bowl of noodles 🍜 is 👌💕

(5.79) **User 1:** @User5 😂😂 okay I feel better now! **[warm]**

In this example each user renders support for "taking the kid out," with most moves also likening their own behaviour to that of the mother. In terms of stakes, rather than raising the stakes of User 1's initial rejection of guilt, the interactants raise the stakes of their own transgressions. This largely occurs through graduation resources that intensify the expressed transgression (e.g., *dragged* [rather than took] in Example [5.75], *Indulging* [rather than eating] in Example [5.78], repeated exclamation marks in Examples [5.76] and [5.77], *many* in Example [5.77], *totally* in Example [5.78], etc.). While graduation locally amplifies the transgressions described by these users, the function is to show support rather than to target judgment at the self. At the same time, the spirit of the messages is adjusted to fuel this support. In Example (5.75), the Smiling Face with Smiling Eyes 😊 after the expressed violation (*dragged my little guy out*) warms the move, inviting User 1 to interpret it as an expression of solidarity, in a similar manner to the Two Hearts 💕 emoji at the end of Example (5.78). In the final move of the exchange, the repeated Face with Tears of Joy 😂 emoji suggests that User 1 has dismissed with a laugh (laughs off) her initial expression of guilt in Example (5.74) (*I felt a little #momguilt . . .*) and has embraced the support of the interactants. The exclamation at the end of this move parallels the raising of stakes throughout the exchange, which can be read as raising the stakes of the support. All of this raising of stakes and warming of spirit occur within an individualized scope, whereby it is the individuals in question who are positioned as the relevant sources for determining the acceptability or not of the behaviours articulated and to whom the values that are negotiated matter. In other words, the choice is to cast experience as subjective rather than to appeal to norms (e.g., "As mothers we should do X").

5.6 Conclusion

This chapter has introduced the role of tuning in the orchestration of interpersonal meaning. We have explored some of the key meanings made in a corpus of #momguilt tweets within which mothers vent their frustrations over contravening community expectations about the behaviour and temperament of "good moms." As we have seen, whether the vibe is convivial or conflictual, the meanings tendered in social media

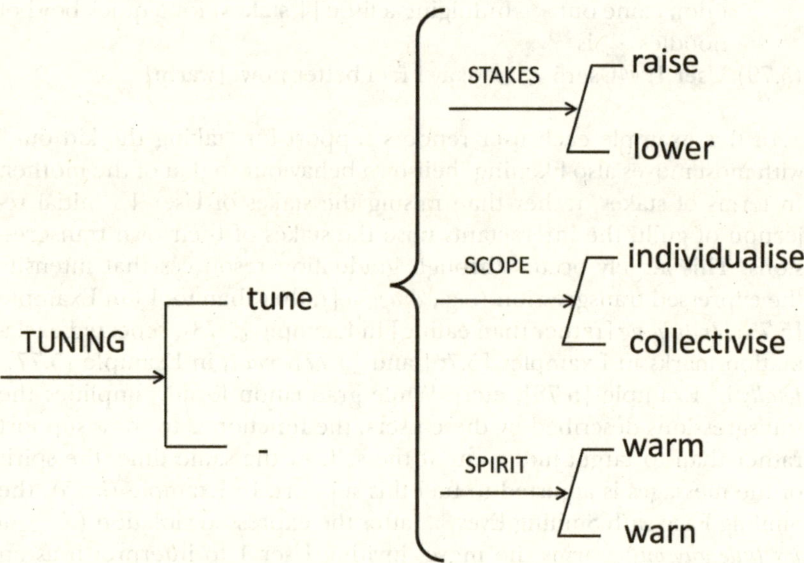

Figure 5.1 The TUNING system

posts may be adjusted via the TUNING system by modifying their relation to other meanings already tendered in a previous post or with broader background values positioned by a particular community. This might involve adjusting the amount of risk or controversy they engender (STAKES), the breadth of the voices they include or assume (SCOPE), or the level of approachability or reproach they enact (SPIRIT). These distinctions in meaning are encapsulated as the TUNING system (Figure 5.1).

6 Resources for Negotiating Social Relations

6.1 Tenor and Systemic Functional Linguistics

We are constantly negotiating our social relations. We may be doing this to reinforce the relations we already have – with our family, our friends, our community; we may be trying to build new relations – with someone we just met, with someone we want to be closer to, or with a new community we want to form; or we may be doing so to break off those relations – to let someone down, to break up with them, to make clear we are not amused, to force a split. Most of the time this happens with little conscious thought; but it nonetheless happens as a constant murmur through the interactions of our daily lives. Viewed in this way, the development and maintenance of our social relations are a continually unfolding prosody across all our semiosis, at times rising or lowering in intensity, but nonetheless always there.

The interpersonal function of language is thus ever-present and an integral part of the core of our linguistic system (Halliday, 1978). Tenor, the interpersonal dimension of context, has been one of the key means through which we conceptualize the maintenance of our social relations in SFL. But as we noted in Chapter 1, the centrality of the social in our semiotic life has meant that throughout the history of SFL, tenor has been made to do many at times incommensurate things (Doran et al., 2024). It has been used, for example, to classify different interpersonal contexts (e.g., Halliday, 1978); it has been used to describe the people involved and their social relationships, whether stable or temporary roles (e.g., Gregory, 1967; Halliday & Hasan, 1985; Hasan, 2016); it has been used to understand the general dimensions upon which people can relate, including their statuses and affective involvement (e.g., Eggins & Slade, 1997/2004; Hasan, 2016; Martin, 1992; Poynton, 1990a); and it has been considered in terms of the underlying social values that are imbued in some domain (e.g., Halliday & Matthiessen, 2014). In addition, though typically not in writing, tenor is in fact often used as a conversational shorthand in SFL circles for social relations in general.

This focus and diversity of approaches to tenor emphasize the rich and multifaceted nature of language in relation to society – something we need to grasp in all its complexity if we wish to build a truly *social* semiotic theory (Halliday, 1978; Hodge & Kress, 1988). While this complexity has long been recognized and descriptions formulated, SFL theory itself has not always kept pace. Stemming at least from the early work of Hasan (e.g., 1973) and advanced through its long interaction with social theory (e.g., Bernstein, 1971, 1973, 1975, 1990, 1996/2000), there has been a recognition of the need of an increasingly expansive theory to account for the role of language in society. With the development of dimensions of instantiation (Halliday, 1991a; Matthiessen, 1993), which conceptualizes the relation between the systemic potential of language and the instance of text, and individuation (Martin, 2010), which conceptualizes the relation between the reservoir of meaning in a language community and the repertoire of an individual (cf. Bernstein, 1996/2000), we are now in a stronger position to move towards a richer understanding of the interconnection between language and society. We embarked on this book project because we felt that SFL had not yet reached its potential in this regard.

Accordingly in this book we have taken a step towards mobilizing the full power of SFL theory as a genuinely social theory of language. Rather than trying to account for all of social relations in one place in the model (as in many previous accounts), it has focused on tenor as a *resource* for enacting social relations.[1] The full system of tenor proposed in this book is given in Figure 6.1.

In doing so, it has privileged the need for a model of tenor that can explicitly link with interpersonal resources in language and with genre patterns. The upshot of this is that room has been made for the aspects of language and society that have often been encapsulated within tenor to be conceptualized elsewhere – through other dimensions of the theory. For example, the parameters of status and contact (Poynton, 1990a) can be further developed as principles of co-selection and arrangement within instantiation. Social roles, interpersonal relationships, and community values can be explored as arenas of cooperation and struggle within individuation – where there is considerable potential for SFL to build upon sociological work by Maton (e.g., 2014), Bernstein (e.g., 1996/2000), and Bourdieu (e.g., 1993). In addition the temporary speech roles that occur in dialogue, people's feelings, and the play of voices can be investigated through discourse semantics (e.g., Berry, 1981a; Martin & White, 2005). And the range of verbal action that we

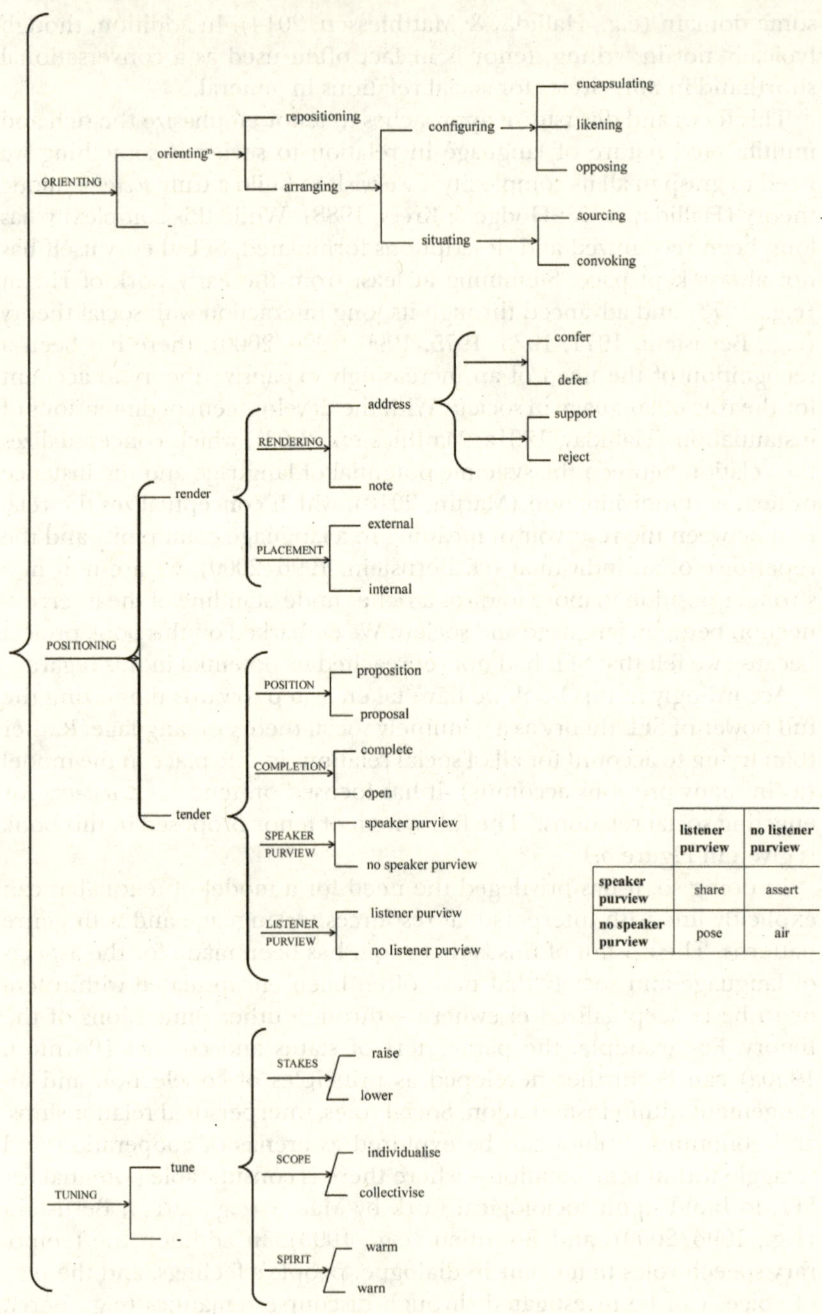

Figure 6.1 Full system of tenor as a resource

participate in all the time (such as instructing, planning, narrating, etc.; Hasan, 1999) can be researched through genre. This is of course an enormous program of work – one that cannot be detailed in a single book. But we have aimed to make explicit what we can do with tenor in the realization hierarchy, and use that, along with field, mode, and rich descriptions of language and other semiotic systems, as the basis for exploring all the rest.

This means that when negotiating social relations, tenor does not walk alone. This is our focus in this closing chapter. Tenor is realized through an enormous array of linguistic, paralinguistic, and multimodal resources; it works closely with resources of field and mode; and it realizes the sets of genres we use to get along with our everyday life. Sections 6.2–6.5 provide an overview of this redistribution of theoretical and descriptive responsibility. First, we look "below" – at how we realize tenor through language and paralanguage such as voice quality and gesture. The goal will be to show just how much interpersonal work is done through linguistic and paralinguistic resources in our talk. Next we look "around" – at how tenor cooperates with field and mode to organize our texts. And then we will look "above" – to see how our model of tenor helps us understand the genres used to organize our social life. To round out the book, we look "across" – to other dimensions of the theory that we are only just beginning to explore – and suggest some avenues for future research. This is our vision of what a truly *social* and *semiotic* theory of language in context needs to encompass.

6.2 Looking Below: Tenor, Language, and Paralanguage

Through this book, we have illustrated a broad range of resources that different choices in tenor can draw upon to realize their meanings. In this section we will bring these together to focus on the amount of interpersonal work that goes on in everyday chat. For this, we will explore a brief excerpt from a conversation between mothers of children with disabilities; they are discussing their experiences and, at times, the guilt that is pervasive in motherhood discourse.[2] We will see that in this face-to-face conversation, the mothers draw on a full multimodal suite of resources to realize their interpersonal meanings – they use language across discourse semantic, lexicogrammatical, and intonational resources. And they use paralanguage – bringing facial expressions, bodily movements and gestures, as well as their voice quality into the picture. The result is a rich and integrated negotiation of their social relations with the others in the conversation, as well as with those being talked about and the play of voices that are presumed in every instance of language.

In Text 6.1, we have divided the text phonologically into tone units, marked by //...//, and feet marked by /.../ (Halliday & Greaves, 2008). We have also specified the tone choice at play, where tone 1 indicates a lowering tone (typical of a statement), 2 indicates a rising tone (typical of a yes-no question), 3 indicates a flat or slightly rising tone (typical of a list), 4 indicates a fall-rise tone (often to indicate uncertainty or qualification), and 5 is a rise-fall tone (often to indicate surprise or commitment); an asterisk * indicates the foot where the main pitch movement occurs (the tonic foot), and bolding indicates the salient syllable in that foot; a caret ^ indicates a silent beat, and the hash # marks an overlap between two speakers.[3]

Renee: //3 I don't / have any other */ **chil**dren right / now
//2 so I */ **should** feel /^ I / guess [LAUGH]
//3 more */ **pres**sure to
*//3 **do** more with / him I
//3 just / ^ / ^ / ^ it's that / whole letting him be a */ **kid** like //

Unknown: #//3 ^ mm */ **mm** //

Renee: #//3 trying to / let – / have a */ **ba**lance we do a
*//3 **lot** of / therapies with / him and
//4 so for */ **me** it's kinda like
//3 I don't know if that's / my little */ **break** he
//3 gets to / go do his / therapies with his */ **the**rapist and then at
*//4 **home**
*//53 **I** help – I / make him / do things on his */ **own** and
//4 help him do stuff like */ **that** but as a
*//4 **gen**eral rule it's
//4 kinda like well / I'm gonna give you a / break when you're at */ **home** 'cause I
*//5 **do** send you to go
*//5 **work**
//5 so */ **much** I / feel like //

Michele: //1 ^ yeah / yeah you have to be a */ **kid** //

Renee: *//3 **yeah** //

Text 6.1 Mum chat

Throughout this text Renee discusses the help she gives her son with his therapies. She does this as part of a larger conversation with three other mothers on the topic of "Mum Guilt with Therapies" (the title of the video). Throughout this excerpt, Renee enacts her meanings along two lines. First, she discusses her feelings about the help she gives her son and the principles that underpin her decisions. This is enacted via a series of propositions about her feelings and by and large represents the meanings she negotiates outwardly with the other mothers, who react supportively. At the same time, Renee construes her relationship with her son in the form of a series of proposals regarding how she organizes and supports her son with his therapies. This line of negotiation, which can in some sense be considered "embedded" within the first line of negotiation, works to nuance in particular the purview that she or her son have over his actions as a child. These two tracks of meaning offer a view of Renee's social world and how she enacts her relationships both in praesentia, with the other mothers, and in absentia, with her son. At the same time, Renee negotiates each of these strands of meaning in relation to the background of social values and expectations that go along with being a mother in general – and being a mother of a child with a disability more specifically. In this section, we will illustrate how she negotiates these meanings by drawing on the tenor resources introduced in this book and how they are realized linguistically and paralinguistically. Our analysis will necessarily be selective rather than exhaustive; but it will provide an indication of just how much semiotic work we do in everyday conversation.

Much of Renee's focus in her reflection on mum guilt is on the feelings she has in relation to her son and to the general expectations on her as a mother. After explaining that she doesn't have any other children, she tenders the idea that, because of this, she should feel more pressure to do more with him.

(6.1)	//3 I don't / have any other */ **chil**dren right / now //2 so I */ **should** feel /^ I / guess [LAUGH]//3 more */ **pres**sure to *//3 **do** more with / him	tender: proposition

The use of *should* makes clear that there is a background expectation on her as a mother – with respect to her feeling she needs to do more with her son. Grammatically speaking this arises due to the fact that *should* realizes modalized obligation (Halliday & Matthiessen, 2014). At the same time, noting that she *should* feel pressure opens up the possibility that she *does not* in fact feel this pressure. Viewed from the perspective of tenor, Renee sets up a tension between different propositions with different purview – she asserts that she *should* feel more pressure to do more with him (an internal view of her statement), but she leaves open (airs) the proposition about whether she in fact does feel this pressure (an external view).

(6.2) //2 so I */ **should** feel /^ I / guess [LAUGH] //3 more */ **pres**sure to *//3 **do** more with / him I

proposition: assert	proposition: air
that I should feel more pressure	that I do feel more pressure

This tension is highlighted by the fact that when she says *I guess,* she lets out a little nervous laugh. This laugh defers the tension, making it clear that her not feeling more pressure may go against the shared expectation on mothers, but that she is Ok with this. Nonetheless, Renee is not strident about her position at this stage. She indicates this by lowering the stakes of what she is saying both linguistically and paralinguistically. Linguistically her *I guess* suggests that what she is saying is tentative and personal. Paralinguistically, the laughter she couples it with is a very brief and very quiet burst, which lowers its force; and it is unvoiced with an open mouth – which Knight (2011) suggests often indicates a negative self-judgment. Taken together, this indicates we might interpret this laughter as invoking nervousness (or, in terms of discourse semantic attitude, negative security). This reading of nervousness is reinforced by her facial expression, where she suddenly raises her eyes and eyebrows, and tightens her lips around her open mouth – what Ngo et al. (2022, p. 122) interpret as indicating negative security.[4] In this one message, then, Renee makes clear through her linguistic and paralinguistic resources that she is pushing against societal expectations about how she should feel in relation to her son, but that this resistance is personal and tentative. This confluence of resources for lowering stakes is visualized in Figure 6.2.

While these initial meanings are tentative, the ones that follow are more strident. Here, Renee more directly rejects the idea that she should feel more pressure to do more with her son, by opposing it to the idea of *letting him be a kid.*

Tenor: STAKES	*I should feel* – ***I guess* [LAUGH]** ↓ **[stakes]** – *more pressure to do more with him I* ***just***↓ **[stakes]**		
Discourse semantics: ENGAGEMENT CONTINUITY	*I guess* heteroglossic entertain *just* Counterexpectancy: diminish		
Voice quality: VOCAL AFFECT	*[LAUGH]* short burst, quiet, unvoiced, open negative security (nervousness)		
Face expression: FACIAL AFFECT	/^	*I*	*/guess//*
	negative security (nervousness)		

Figure 6.2 Lowering stakes through language, voice quality, and facial expression

(6.3) //2 so I */ **should** feel / ^ I / guess [LAUGH] //3 more */ **pressure** to *//3 **do** more with / him I
|| **[opposition]**

//3 just / ^ / ^ / ^ it's that / whole letting him be a */ **kid** like //

Tenor: RENDERING	*I //3 just / ^ / ^ / ^* [reject] *it's that / whole letting him be a */ **kid** like //*			
Discourse semantics: CONTINUITY	*just* counterexpectancy			
Face expression: FACIAL AFFECT	*/just* [reject]	/^ pursing lips → negative affect (antipathy)	/^ shaking head Disagreement	/^ →

Figure 6.3 Rejection through language and facial expression, 1

Tenor: RENDERING	*I should feel* [reject] – *I guess* [LAUGH]– *more pressure to do more with him*		
Face expression: FACIAL AFFECT	 I negative affect (disdain) [reject via facial expression]	***/ should**	feel

Figure 6.4 Rejection through language and facial expression, 2

The opposition between *feeling more pressure to do more with him* and *it's that whole letting him be a kid* is explicitly marked through the continuity item *just.* In the three silent beats that follow (indicated by /^/^/^/), Renee rejects the idea that she should feel more pressure, by drawing on a suite of paralinguistic resources (Figure 6.3) – she purses her lips for two beats, once again indicating a negative attitude of some sort (Ngo et al., 2022), perhaps *negative happiness: antipathy* drawing on Martin and White's terms (2005, p. 49); and she shakes her head as an emblem for "no."

Renee in fact flagged this rejection a little earlier. When she said she *should* feel more pressure, she furrowed her brow on *should,* and partially closed her eyes and pursed her lips, which parallels much of what Ngo et al. (2022) call *disdain,* but what might be more usefully interpreted as invoking a general rejection. These resources for rejection are illustrated in Figure 6.4.

Coupling with this rejection, the opposition also allows Renee to flip the stakes of meanings. Whereas Renee lowered the stakes of her not feeling more pressure by the use of *just* and the linguistic and paralinguistic resources noted above, she significantly raises the stakes of the idea of *letting him be a kid.* She does this first verbally by using explicit graduation (*it's that whole*), and second by using three silent beats. These beats strongly demarcate the two opposed positions (Cléirigh, 1998) and add significant "textual weight" to the information being given and a sense of anticipation for what is to come (Smith, 2008, p. 285). In terms of discourse semantics, this indicates that the *it's that whole letting him be a kid* is being positioned as a likely Hypertheme for what's to come.

(6.4) // so I / should feel/ ^ I / guess [LAUGH]↓ **[stakes]** //3 more / pressure to // do more with / him I

|| **[opposition]**

// just ↓ **[stakes]** / ^ / ^ / ^ ↑ **[stakes]** it's that / whole ↑ **[stakes]** letting him be a / kid like //

The emphasis with which Renee puts forward the idea of *letting him be a kid* allows her to trump her feelings of nervousness at not feeling the pressure that is expected. Her raising of the stakes, combined with the fact that the phrase *letting him be a kid* is an idiom, suggests that it functions as what Stenglin (2004) calls a bonding icon – that is, an iconized instance of ideation, in this case iconizing the activity of letting him be a kid (Carr, 2023, 2025; Stenglin, 2004); this bonding icon holds central place in the network of values that underpin motherhood. Its centrality is seemingly recognized by one of the other mothers, who immediately backchannels,[5] likely indicating support.[6]

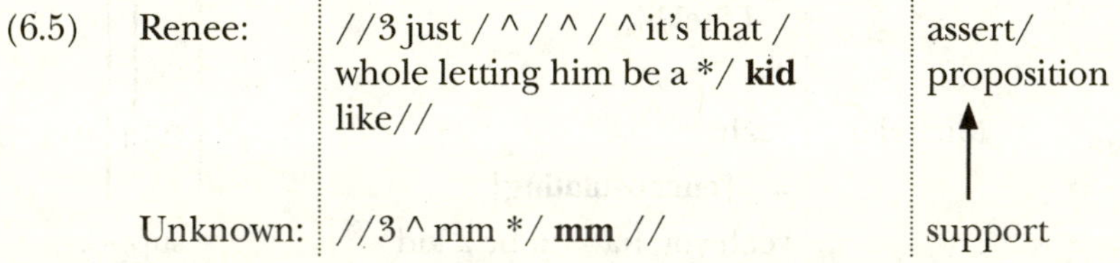

(6.5)	Renee:	//3 just / ^ / ^ / ^ it's that / whole letting him be a */ **kid** like//	assert/ proposition ↑
	Unknown:	//3 ^ mm */ **mm** //	support

The *letting him be a kid* bonding icon sets up the rest of the excerpt, as Renee elaborates on what this means for her. In terms of the system of ORIENTING, it functions to encapsulate a whole series of likened and opposed positions (largely sourced by Renee to herself), before another mother, Michele, supports her stance and once again encapsulates it as *you have to be a kid.*

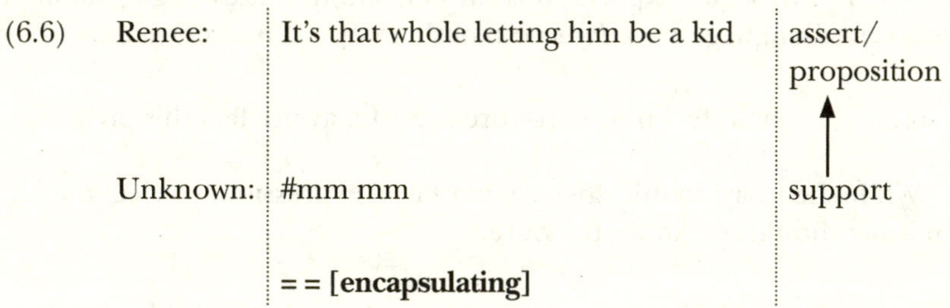

(6.6)	Renee:	It's that whole letting him be a kid	assert/ proposition ↑
	Unknown:	#mm mm	support
		== **[encapsulating]**	

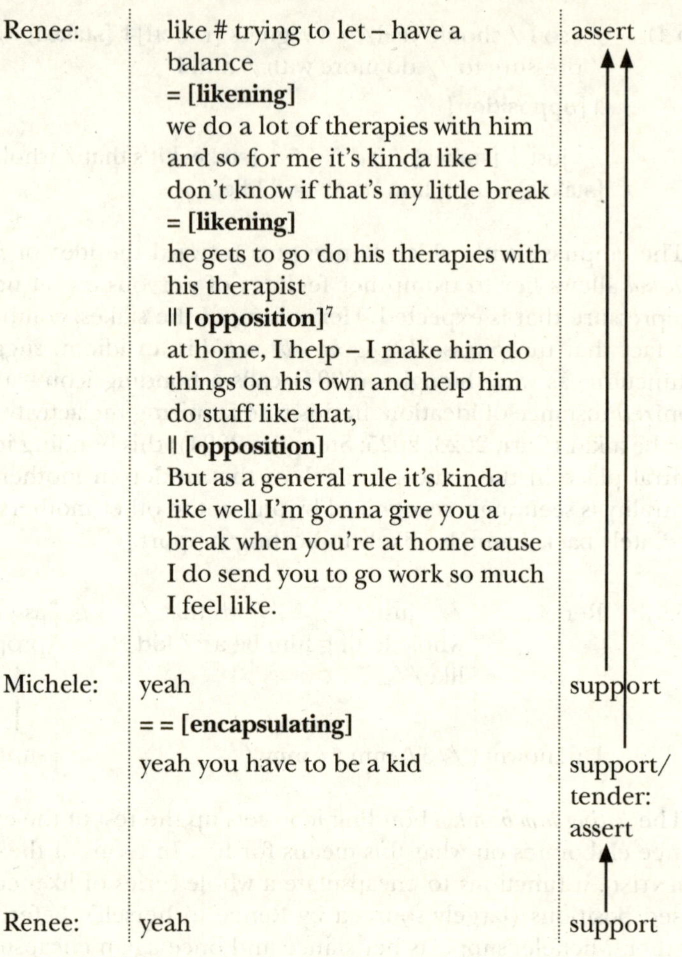

Renee:	like # trying to let – have a balance	assert
	= **[likening]**	
	we do a lot of therapies with him and so for me it's kinda like I don't know if that's my little break	
	= **[likening]**	
	he gets to go do his therapies with his therapist	
	ǁ **[opposition]**[7]	
	at home, I help – I make him do things on his own and help him do stuff like that,	
	ǁ **[opposition]**	
	But as a general rule it's kinda like well I'm gonna give you a break when you're at home cause I do send you to go work so much I feel like.	
Michele:	yeah	support
	= = **[encapsulating]**	
	yeah you have to be a kid	support/ tender: assert
Renee:	yeah	support

Building this up logogenetically, when Renee negotiates her feelings in relation to social expectations on her, she first uses engagement resources of language (*should*) to establish an opposition between:

(6.7)	I should feel more pressure . . .	I may not feel this pressure

While she is saying this, she uses her facial expression to reject the idea that she should feel more pressure.

(6.8)	I should feel more pressure . . . [reject]	I may not feel this pressure

She immediately follows this up with *I guess*, which is a linguistic resource of engagement, coupled with a laughter, voice quality, and a facial expression that both defer and lower the stakes of the tension between these two propositions.

(6.9)	I should feel more pressure . . .	I may not feel this pressure
	[reject]	
	[defer + ↓ stakes]	

She then brings these positions together (and further lowers their stakes) to oppose them to the idea of *the whole letting him be a kid*, through the use of the continuity marker *just*.

(6.10)	I should feel more pressure . . .	I may not feel this pressure	it's that whole letting him be a kid
	[reject]		
	[defer + ↓ stakes]		

While doing this, Renee uses silent beats, a shake of her head, and her facial expression to again reject her initial proposition and raise the stakes of *letting him be a kid* in conjunction with the graduation *the whole*.

(6.11)	I should feel more pressure . . .	I may not feel this pressure	it's that whole letting him be a kid
	[reject]		
	[defer + ↓ stakes]		
	[reject]		[↑ stakes]

Then finally, another mother chimes in to show support for the idea that *letting him be a kid* is important.

(6.12)	I should feel more pressure . . .	I may not feel this pressure	it's that whole letting him be a kid
	[reject]		
	[defer + ↓ stakes]		
	[reject]		[↑ stakes]
			[support] (from other mother)

As this illustrates, in even such a short stretch of language, Renee and the other mother are drawing on a wide range of linguistic and embodied resources to negotiate their feelings with each other and with background social expectations. And they do this in a nuanced yet highly coherent manner with which everyone in the conversation aligns.

As we mentioned above, Renee also works to construe her relationship with her son. Throughout, she makes clear she is the source of much of the care for her son, often using circumstances of accompaniment (e.g., *with him*) and the extended grammar of agency (*letting him be a kid*).

I should feel more pressure *to do more with him*
it's that whole *letting him be a kid*
like trying to *let – have a balance*
we do a lot of therapies with him
he gets to go do his therapies with his therapist
I help – I make him do things on his own
And [I] *help him do stuff like that*
I'm gonna give you a break when you're at home
I do send you to go work

In each of these instances, Renee construes herself or her son's therapist as being involved in what her son does. She does this, though, by nuancing the degree of control she or her son has over these actions – what we can interpret in terms of purview.

She initially construes the work she is expected to do as being something that she does *with him.* This at first glance positions the proposal as being *shared* between her and her son – both have responsibility and purview over doing things.

(6.13)	I should feel – I guess – more pressure *to do more with him*	proposal/share [doing more with him]

This analysis, however, is a simplification. If we unpack the purview of this proposal, we can catch a glimpse of the mire of complexity through which mothers wade when construing their relationship with their children. As noted above, in terms of who does the action (the external purview), the Circumstance of accompaniment *with him* makes clear that it is shared – they *both* do the action together. But in terms of who initiates the action/proposal (the internal purview), the purview is squarely with the mother only, as indicated by the agency *I should do more with him* (as opposed to *we should do more together*) – it is only Renee as the mother who is given responsibility for her son doing his therapies.

As Renee moves through her explanation of how she supports her son, she regularly shifts the purview for his therapy. When she presents the general principle of letting her son be a kid, for example, she shifts the (external) purview onto him alone. Renee *lets* her son be a kid (as above, the internal purview is with her), but it is up to him to determine whether that's what he will do.

(6.14)	it's that whole *letting him be a kid*	proposal/pose [letting him be a kid]

She construes the relationship once more this way (though changes tack before completing her sentence):

(6.15)	trying to *let – have a balance*	proposal/pose [let have a balance]

Before she shifts back to having a shared purview over the action through *with him* once more:

(6.16)	*We do a lot of therapies with him*	proposal/share [doing therapies with him]

In the next stretch, Renee sets up a series of oppositions comparing how she manages his therapies with the therapist versus at home, allowing her to vary the purview in relation to the different positions she is putting forward. First, when her son is at the therapist, she positions it as something he *gets to do* with the therapist. Externally, this is once more a shared action – this time between her son and her therapist. But internally, the *gets to do* suggests it is her son who has purview over whether he wants to do this.[8]

(6.17)	*He gets to do his therapies with his therapist*	proposal/share [external] [doing therapies with his therapist] proposal/pose [internal] [gets to do his therapies]

She then compares this to the situation at home: *at home, I help – I make him do things on his own and help him do stuff like that.* Here, Renee's intonation (tone 5) and facial expression indicate that she is countering the idea that she does nothing with her son (which would significantly clash with the social expectations). So linguistically she sets up the idea that he does do his therapies *on his own* (her son's purview), but shifts between "helping" him do this (in which case there is shared purview) and "making" him do this (in which case the internal purview is entirely on her as the mother).

Finally, she comes to her main point – namely that at home she *gives him a break.* This puts the purview back on her son to make a decision, before construing the trip to the therapist as *sending him to go work,* which puts all of the internal purview back onto her as the mother. At the same time, through the metaphor "work," she rejects this time with the therapist (to which Michele agrees, *yeah, yeah you have to be a kid*).

As we can see, throughout this stretch Renee is not only negotiating how she feels in relation to the other mothers and to the background expectations she has to manage; she is also construing her relationship with her son. As the analysis indicates, this relationship is not a static one that is unchanging; rather it is one that regularly has to be negotiated – in terms of the relative authority and control she must impose as a mother vis-à-vis the autonomy and control that her son needs in his life. At every step of the way, Renee is in a sense positioned between a rock and a hard place; she has to negotiate all aspects of their lives.

In this section, we have provided a snapshot of how different components of tenor come together to organize our social relations and have illustrated some of the range of possible ways this is done. In terms of what SFL calls its *trinocular vision,* we have explored tenor from "below" – from the perspective of the resources drawn on to realize tenor. In the next section, we will look "around" – in terms of how tenor engages with adjacent meanings, focusing in particular on another register variable field. This allows us to see that it is not just our social meanings that are being negotiated at all times, but also the ways we construe phenomena (alongside of course the ways we organize our information).

6.3 Looking Around: Tenor, Field, and Mode

Tenor is not of course the only region of meaning that we draw upon in our lives. It gives value to things and negotiates our social world; but it does this in conjunction with other resources. These include resources for organizing our experiential world (which we describe in SFL in terms of field) and resources for organizing text itself (which we describe in terms of mode). In this section, we consider the interplay of tenor and field as values are invested in events and things.

The text we will consider is a biographical recount (Coffin, 2006; Martin & Rose, 2008) published in a report from a major Australian public inquiry (known as a Royal Commission) into a long-running government scheme known as Robodebt (Commonwealth of Australia, 2023). The Robodebt scheme was a system for assessing possible overpayments of welfare. Its controversial nature arose due to the fact that it used an automated system (the *robo* part of the term Robodebt) involving income averaging, whereby a person's income in a small period of time was taken to be indicative of their income over a longer period of time. The system was nominally established to crack down on welfare fraud and was hailed by the government of the time as likely to save $1.7 billion over five years (Commonwealth of Australia, 2023, p. xxix; Martin & Rose, 2008). As part of this system, if someone was judged to have been overpaid as a result of this calculation, they were issued with a notice that they had to repay this amount (the *debt* component of Robodebt). The scheme resulted in over 800,000 instances of possible debt being identified. Its methodology, however, was deeply flawed, and an enormous proportion of the "debts" identified were incorrect. This was highlighted in November 2020, when the government settled a class action suit, reimbursed $746 million to 381,000 people, and wrote off debts to the tune of $1.75 billion (Commonwealth of Australia, 2023, p. xxix; Martin & Rose, 2008).

The Robodebt scheme was a shameful policy that was driven by political agendas on both sides of Australian politics. It gained traction due to the political benefit that came from demonizing welfare recipients and was exacerbated by a depleted Kafkaesque bureaucracy designed to make it as difficult as possible to gain welfare support. As the Commissioner Janet Holmes (Commonwealth of Australia, 2023) noted:

> Robodebt was a crude and cruel mechanism, neither fair nor legal, and it made many people feel like criminals. In essence, people were traumatised on the off-chance they might owe money. It was a costly failure of public administration, in both human and economic terms. (p. xxix)

Among a wide range of traumatizing effects, Robodebt was implicated in multiple suicides by those who had been sent debt letters. The biographical recount we consider tells the story of one person, Jarrad Madgwick, who died in this way – as told by his mother,

Kathleen Madgwick (Commonwealth of Australia, 2023, pp. 339–340) (As this text deals with suicide, if any reader would prefer to avoid it, you can skip to Section 6.4.). It takes us through the sequence of events leading up to Mr. Madgwick's death, focusing in particular on a series of administrative failures and the impersonal pressures that the Department of Human Services (DHS) and Centrelink (Australia's welfare service centre) placed on Mr. Madgwick – with little consideration for his situation and in spite of his dutiful compliance at every step of the way.

For our purposes, this text illustrates the tightrope that an official report such as this must walk – in terms of being "factual" with respect to presenting the events of the case, while at the same time being very clear in its scathing negative judgment of the system that Mr. Madgwick was caught up in. It does this through an interaction between resources of field and of tenor. In Table 6.1 we have divided the text into the stages and phases characteristic of a biographical recount. Following an Abstract that overviews the case and an Orientation that provides details about Mr. Madgwick's situation when the process began, the Record of Events steps through a set of episodes in the interaction between Mr. Madgwick and the DHS. Following this excerpt, there is another stage, a Re-orientation, that interprets a number of the aspects of this case (though, due to space constraints, we have not included it here).

Each episode in this recount steps through a series of events that Mr. Madgwick was involved in. From the perspective of field (Doran & Martin, 2021), these events are known as *activities.* For example, in the second episode, a series of activities are presented that construct Mr. Madgwick's attempts at applying for a Newstart Allowance (a common type of welfare payment in Australia). In the following, we have presented the series of events in the sequence they occurred, rather than the sequence they are presented in the text (with this sequence indicated by ^); and we have unpacked nominalizations (itemized activities in this text; Hao, 2020; Martin & Rose, 2008) where necessary.

> Mr Madgwick applied for Newstart on 1 May 2019 [Mr. Madgwick's application]
>
> ^
>
> He purportedly missed a telephone call.
>
> ^
>
> Mr Madgwick's initial application . . . was rejected
>
> ^

Table 6.1 A biographical recount of Jarrad Madgwick (Commonwealth of Australia, 2023, pp. 339–340)

Abstract	**Kathleen Madgwick** Kathleen Madgwick told the Commission about the death of her only child, Jarrad Madgwick. He died by suicide on 30 May 2019. He was 22 years of age. He had received notifications under the CUPI phase of the Scheme.
Orientation	From the end of 2017 into 2018, Mr Madgwick held a traineeship in Victoria and was receiving Newstart Allowance. Bullying forced him to leave the traineeship in late 2018. He found work in hospitality, which he had difficulty maintaining, and was living in his car.
Record of Events *episode 1*	In April 2019, he returned to live with Ms Madgwick in Queensland, but she had lost her job, and both were forced to apply for Newstart Allowance. Mr Madgwick was completely without money, with some traffic fines to pay, and his mother was in no position to support him financially.
episode 2	Mr Madgwick's initial application for Newstart on 1 May 2019 was rejected after he was said to have missed a telephone call. He re-applied, explaining that his phone was disconnected. His application was again rejected on 30 May 2019 because he had not provided documents. Telephoning DHS that morning, he was told it was because he had not supplied a BSB number, despite DHS already being in possession of all of his bank details. However, with his mother's help, he was able to have the application reinstated. Immediately after the reinstatement, Mr Madgwick was in a better frame of mind. He understood his claim was being processed and he was hopeful of a priority payment the following week.
episode 3	Ms Madgwick knew her son was struggling, penniless and reliant on her for the most basic things. What she did not know was that on 27 May 2019, DHS had commenced a review in relation to Mr Madgwick for the 2017–2018 financial year and had informed him through his myGov account that there was a discrepancy between his declared earnings and ATO PAYG income amounts, indicating a potential overpayment.
episode 4	On 28 May, as directed, Mr Madgwick entered payslip information for his traineeship income online. For some reason, although he had already responded, he was sent a letter through his myGov account the following day telling him he had to "check and update" the same ATO information. The online system advised Mr Madgwick that "the review would be processed" and that "a provisional debt outcome" had been determined in the amount of $1,795.85 for the period 28 April 2018 to 22 June 2018. Services Australia says that the provisional assessment would have been displayed to Mr Madgwick when he finished entering his income information online, although it cannot say precisely when that was. From what happened later, it seems he either did not see it or did not grasp its contents at that time.

(Continued)

Table 6.1 (*Continued*)

episode 5	Ms Madgwick gave evidence that around 5pm on 30 May 2019, the same day on which they had been in contact with DHS about his Newstart Allowance, Mr Madgwick told her that he would not get paid the allowance, because he owed Centrelink $2,000.
episode 6	He said, "I will never get out of debt." He was distressed and angry, and later that evening left the house. When he was not home by morning, Ms Madgwick went looking for him and found his body in a nearby park.

ATO = Australian Taxation Office, BSB = Bank State Branch, CUPI = Check and Update Past Income, DHS = Department of Human Services, PAYG = Pay As You Go

> He re-applied,
> ^
> explaining that his phone was disconnected.
> ^
> His application was again rejected
> ^
> He telephoned the DHS.
> ^
> He was told it was because he had not supplied a BSB number, despite DHS already being in possession of all of his bank details.
> ^
> With his mother's help, he was able to have the application reinstated.
> ^
> Immediately after the reinstatement, Mr Madgwick was in a better frame of mind. He understood his claim was being processed and he was hopeful of a priority payment the following week.

This second episode encompasses a series of small moments that constitute Jarrad Madgwick's initial engagement with the DHS. In terms of the construction of the text, it focuses explicitly on the steps that Mr. Madgwick took and DHS's responses in terms of the "facts" of the case. But this stretch of course does more than this. Reading it as an outsider, there is a sense of frustration that builds through the first series of events as Mr. Madgwick's multiple applications are rejected, before a sense of relief kicks in when his mother is able to help and have the application reinstated. This valuation is developed through resources of tenor.

The rising frustration is signalled through repeated tenor choices that negatively render the DHS' actions – in bold below. The repetition of Mr. Madgwick's initiatives and subsequent rejections is emphasized throughout, and works to raise the stakes (as underlined).

Mr. Madgwick's initial application for Newstart on 1 May 2019 was rejected after **he was said to** have missed a telephone call.	rejection of DHS's reasoning via *he was said to* [heteroglossic distance]
He re-applied, explaining that his phone was disconnected. His application was again rejected on 30 May 2019 because he had not provided documents.	raising stakes through emphasis on repetition [raising force]
Telephoning DHS that morning, he was told it was because he had not supplied a BSB number, **despite** DHS **already** being in possession of all of his bank details.	rejection of DHS's reasoning via *despite* + *already* [disclaim countering]

Relief arrives when Mr. Madgwick's mother is able to support him. The shift is marked by *however*, underscoring the contrast between Mr. Madgwick's applications being rejected and reinstated. Interpersonally, as is commonplace with such markers, there is a switch from a prosody of rejection to a prosody of support (in bold).

> *However*, with his mother's help, he was **able to** have the application reinstated. Immediately after the reinstatement, Mr Madgwick was in **a better frame of mind**. He understood his claim was being processed and he was **hopeful** of a priority payment the following week.

This is a biographical recount that unfolds as episodes of time and is concerned with judging behaviour (in this case, the DHS' behaviour; Martin & Rose, 2008). The episode just noted (Episode 2) illustrates this text's affinity with story genres. As the above analysis suggests, the text at times puts forward a series of activities coloured by tenor resources that build frustration in similar ways to how longer story genres often involve a series of worsening problems that build tension (Rose, 2020). This tension is then released by presenting activities that parallel the typical solution phases that occur in stories. The fact that this biographical recount focuses on very specific activities in a manageably short period of time affords this more story-like feel. More broadly, it illustrates the tightrope this text must walk between presenting a "factual" account of the events leading up to Mr. Madgwick's death (as befits a formal governmental inquiry) while at the same time illustrating the personal trauma that this program put people under by way of negatively judging the government's policy.

While the second episode ends with a relatively positive solution, the other episodes in the historical recount unfortunately do not. They combine a long series of activities with a prosody of rejection, largely sourced to Mr. Madgwick towards his debt and the DHS – which are positioned as the cause of his death. Each set of activities and the tenor resources that are used with them work to amplify this prosody of rejection and raise its stakes, culminating with Mr. Madgwick's death.

Although this text focuses on one specific instance, this prosody rejecting the program and the DHS occurs across the whole report, as indicated by the subheadings from the chapter in which it is situated (Mr. Madgwick's story occurs within section 2.9 of Chapter 10).

Chapter 10: Effects of Robodebt on Individuals
2.1 Barriers to engagement with Centrelink
2.2 Stigma
2.3 The effects of unfair accusations
2.4 Financial effects
2.5 Withholding payments from recipients
2.6 The use and threat of garnishee notices
2.7 The use of Departure Prohibition Orders
2.8 Distress, trauma, anxiety and mental ill-health
2.9 Deaths resulting from the Scheme
2.10 Loss of faith in the government

Although we cannot explore it in detail here, these subheadings also illustrate the interaction that occurs between tenor and mode – the latter providing resources for composing texture (Doran et al., 2024). In this instance, the prosody rejecting Robodebt is foregrounded in the subheadings functioning as Hyperthemes throughout the text (Martin & Rose, 2007).

As significant work on affiliation in SFL has emphasized in recent years (e.g., Logi & Zappavigna, 2022), interpersonal meaning (in our case tenor) does not occur on its own. We do not just support or reject in general, but support or reject specific things. To develop a full understanding of how texts manage to build their meaning, it is important that we come to grips with the interaction among tenor, field, and mode. Another way that this can be done is by looking from "above" – in terms of how tenor, field, and mode resources realize genres. It is to this we turn in the next section.

6.4 Looking Above: Tenor and Genre

In the previous section, we saw that tenor resources work to build meaning within biographical recounts, and that the prosodies of feeling involved can parallel those found in story genres. This has been a recurring theme throughout the book – namely the role of tenor resources in realizing different genres. Now that we have introduced each component of tenor, we can pull this together as Table 6.2. This table canvasses a range of persuasive genres, informative genres, and story genres that we have noted so far in the book. It reviews their genre staging, the tenor resources that distinguish them, and other relevant resources from field. For the genre analysis, we have drawn on Martin and Rose (2008) and Metropolitan East Disadvantaged Schools Program (1989, 1994, 1996).[9]

As Table 6.2 suggests, some families of genres can be distinguished primarily in terms of how they draw on tenor resources. Persuasive texts, for example, can be distinguished in terms of whether they give a series of likened arguments for multiple opposed sides (discussions) or only one side (expositions and challenges). Within the one-sided persuasive texts, we can distinguish between whether they are rejecting and opposing a position (challenge) or are supporting such a position (expositions), and if supporting, whether this position is a proposition that in some sense describes the world (analytical exposition) or a proposal that calls for action (hortatory exposition) (Martin & Rose, 2008; Metropolitan East Disadvantaged Schools Program, 1989, 1996).

Informative genres, on the other hand, involve less delicate distinctions in tenor. Other than a primary distinction between the enabling genres of procedure and protocol that are organized as proposals and describing genres of explanations and reports that are organized around propositions, the more delicate distinctions are realized through field. Explanations, for example, are distinguished from reports by primarily being realized through a momented activity organized through relations of implication whereby activity occurs as a necessary result of the previous activity; reports, on the other hand, are more typically focused on items. Subtypes of explanations and reports are thus by and large distinguished in terms of the particular configurations that occur among the activities and items that realize them. Similarly, procedures can be

Table 6.2 Some Genres, their Stages, and their Typical Realizations through Resources of Tenor and Field

Genre Family	Genre	Stages	Typical Tenor Resources	Field Resources
Persuasive genres	Discussion	Issue	Tendered position encapsulating	Wide range of field resources Encapsulated position typically foregrounded through mode
		Arguments for	Opposed positions	
		Arguments against		
		Recommendation	One side rendered with support	
	Analytical exposition	Position	Tendered proposition encapsulating	Wide range of field resources Encapsulated proposition typically foregrounded through mode
		Arguments	Likened positions rendering support	
		Reinforcement	Encapsulating previous positions	
	Hortatory exposition	Appeal	Tendered proposal encapsulating	Typically activities in field Encapsulated proposal typically foregrounded through mode
		Arguments	Likened positions rendering support	
		Reinforcement	Encapsulating previous positions	
	Challenge	Position challenged	Tendered position	Wide range of field resources Original and opposed position typically foregrounded through mode
		Rebuttal arguments	Likened positions opposing and rejecting original position	
		Antithesis	Tendering opposed position	
Informative genres	Procedural recount	Aim	Proposals	Producing items
		Equipment		Series of items
		Steps		Momented activities in an expectancy series
	Protocols	Goal		Distinct unmomented activities
		Regulations		

	Explanations	Phenomenon Explanation sequence	Propositions	Activities, with relations between activities determined by subtype of explanation
	Reports	Classification Description		Items and properties, with relations between items dependent on subtype of report
Response genres	Personal response	Orientation Text description Comment	Renders text sourced to author + tenders propositions about author's feelings about text	Variable in field
	Review	Context Text description Judgment	Renders text, typically not sourced to author, + tenders propositions about text	Variable in field
	Interpretation	Text evaluation Text synopsis Reaffirmation of text evaluation	Renders text + orienting resources to build constellation of text's message or theme	Presents two fields – that of the book symbolizing a message or theme
	Critical response	Text evaluation Text deconstruction Challenge to text evaluation	Renders text Tenders positions sourced to text Rejects previous positions + tenders opposed positions	Presents two fields – that of the book symbolizing a message or theme

(Continued)

Table 6.2 (*Continued*)

Genre Family	Genre	Stages	Typical Tenor Resources	Field Resources
Stories	Recount	Orientation Record Re-orientation	Propositions + renderings throughout in reaction, comment, reflection phases	Momented activity in expectancy series, with no or minimal problematic events
	Narrative	Orientation	Propositions	Momented activity in expectancy series
		Complication	Opposed (counter-expectant) propositions + renderings in reaction/comment/reflection phases	Interrupted by new momented expectancy series
		Resolution	Opposed (counter-expectant) proposition + renderings in reaction/comment/reflection phases	Interrupted by new momented expectancy series
	Unresolved stories (anecdotes, exempla, observations)	Orientation	Propositions	Momented activity in expectancy series
		Event	Opposed (counter-expectant) propositions	Interrupted by new momented expectancy series
		Response	Rendering of event (with subtypes of genre coordinating with different renderings)	Variable in field

distinguished from protocols due to the fact that procedures present a momented activity involving expectancy, whereas protocol presents a series of distinct activities that are not typically momented in field (Martin & Rose, 2008).

In contrast to each of these, the family of response genres is more concerned with *rendering* another text, whether in terms of support or rejection (Martin, 1992; Metropolitan East Disadvantaged Schools Program, 1994). How the different response genres are distinguished is based upon how they develop this rendering. Personal responses typically source their renderings to the author and focus on tendering positions about the author's feelings. By contrast, reviews are more impersonal in that they focus less on presenting positions about the author's feelings but rather focus more on rendering the text itself. Interpretations and critical responses differ from these in that they typically set up a more elaborated constellation surrounding the text in terms of its "message" (Hasan's theme; (Hasan, 1989, 2011). In this regard, they typically draw more heavily on a wider range of orienting resources than personal responses or reviews. Interpretations and critical responses can be distinguished in terms of whether in general terms they uncritically support the themes of the text they are considering (interpretations) or whether they reject these themes and present an opposed set of positions (critical responses).

Turning to story genres, the interaction between tenor and field is crucial to making the "point" of a real or imaginative "re/telling." In the case of recounts, which tell the story of a relatively unproblematic event, the relation is straightforward – in terms of field, a recount presents a series of momented activities in an expectancy relation with one another; and in terms of tenor, there are propositions that are interspersed with some rendering. What the rendering is, and from whose perspective it is (i.e., what the sourcing is), will depend on the types of phase chosen. Some may involve reactions as characters respond emotionally to the events of the story, others may involve reflections as a character interprets events, and others may involve comments where the narrator interprets events (Rose, 2020).

Recounts are distinguished from other story genres such as narratives, anecdotes, exempla, and observations, in that these other story genres involve an activity that is special in some way. In terms of field, this means that the expectancy series established in the Orientation is interrupted by an unpredicted activity. In terms of tenor, this interruption establishes a counter-expectant opposition between what would be a "normal" set of events and what actually happened. In broad terms, narratives are distinguished from anecdotes, exempla, and observations by virtue of the fact that they involve some form of Resolution to the Complication. Anecdotes, exempla, and observations, on the other hand, focus instead on rendering the unexpected event (Martin & Rose, 2008, Metropolitan East Disadvantaged Schools Program, 1994). As with recounts, a more nuanced view of these relations would require a focus on the phases that occur within the stages of genres and the choices in tenor and field that realize them.

The genres presented above cover ones that have relatively discrete stages unfolding one after another. In terms of Eggins and Slade's (1997/2004) characterization of spoken language, they are the genres that make up the "chunks" of casual conversation. As we have illustrated throughout this book, conversation also involves longer stretches of chat that cannot be chunked as easily into discrete stages. This book provides tools for characterizing such chat in ways that offer a pathway to a better articulated genre description.

For example, returning to Kristy and her mother's conversation, the key feature of this excerpt is that they put forward opposing proposals. In this way, the text is agnate to a discussion genre where two sides are put forward and contrasted – or, perhaps more specifically, agnate to some sort of hortatory discussion where the sides are proposals for action. However, unlike discussions, Kristy and her mother do not put forward a set of arguments for their case; rather they work to restate and refine their proposals – and in the case of Kristy's mother, interpret why Kristy is pushing for her particular proposal. Similarly, each proposal is not presented once and is then discretely followed by the opposed proposal; it's not a formal debate genre. Rather the proposals are bandied to and fro. Within each proposal, these recurrences are related through likening, while between the proposals, they are related through opposing. The key feature, then, is opposing proposals that are iterated and likened as the excerpt unfolds – before culminating in a position that brings the parties together. From the perspective of genre, we could perhaps call this a *negotiation* genre, with Sides resolved in a Solution (agnate perhaps to successful business meetings and agnate deliberations).

It may be useful at this point to clarify the complementarity of analyses at the levels of tenor and of genre for this mothering text. From the perspective of tenor, there are distinct proposals that are iterated and related by likening. In this sense, the structure is a univariate one, expanded by adding more proposals. In contrast, at the more abstract level of genre, each of these likened proposals in fact realizes a single "Side" of the negotiation. The Sides come and go throughout the conversation across stretches of varying length; and stage boundaries are not clear until the negotiation resolves in a Solution. In this sense, we can

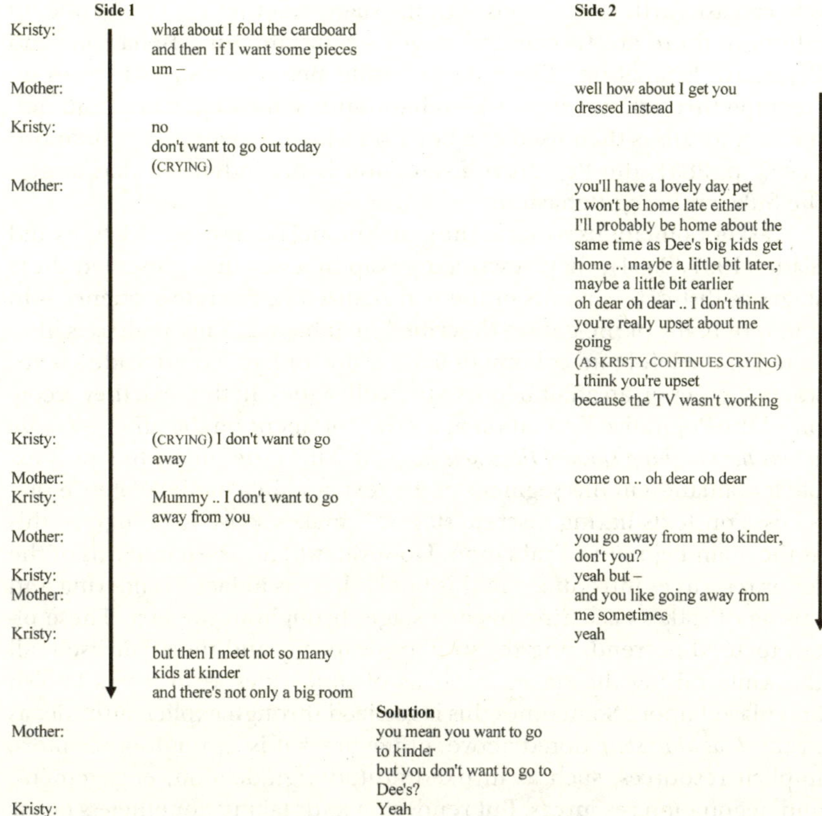

Figure 6.5 Tentative negotiation genre, with prosodic Sides followed by a Solution

consider the genre staging as non-segmental – each Side unfolds in an open-ended way and cuts across units that realize it. This is tentatively illustrated in Figure 6.5, where the Sides are laid out opposite one another (and interrupting segments associated with Ruth are excluded).

Our book also provides tools for exploring the gossip genre described by Eggins and Slade (1997/2004). They consider gossip to be the closest genre to the relatively free-flowing chat segments that made up around half their data (1997/2004, pp. 269–270). To account for gossip, they set up five main typifying stages. Beginning and ending the genre were what they called a "Third person focus" stage, which deals with who was being talked about and the judgments involved; the genre ends with a Wrap-up that offers a final culminative comment on the target's character and behaviour. Throughout, they note that anyone can ask further questions within a stage that they called a Probe. In addition, there are two central stages – Substantiating Behaviour and Pejorative Evaluation. The Substantiating Behaviour stage focuses on stepping through "an event which highlights some departure from normality and this is then used as a hook on which to hang the evaluation" (1997, p. 285); the Pejorative Evaluation is the judgment that targets the Substantiating Behaviour.

The key point for us is that in the genre model being used by Eggins and Slade (1997/2004), they described gossip in a way that presented these stages as distinct segments of the text realized in discrete sequence – in line with many of the genres described in Table 6.2. This analysis is illustrated in the left-hand column of 6 using one of Eggins and Slade's texts, which focuses on an affair between two colleagues. In this text, they recognized the Pejorative Evaluation as a brief comment on the affair – *I mean it was the laughing stock of the whole hospital.* This is definitely the most explicit evaluation in this segment of the text, and in a model of genre that focuses on texts having discrete stages, it makes sense to recognize this as the main Pejorative Evaluation. However, when viewed in terms of the tenor resources introduced in this book, there is in fact a rendering and raising of stakes occurring in each stage throughout the text. These often focused on rendering the woman's capacity and the affair itself, all the while raising the stakes in terms of how widespread it was known and played upon. Sometimes this is realized through explicit attitude, as in the *laughing stock* noted above; other times it is through other more implicit resources, such as invoked attitude, graduation, engagement, and negotiation resources. But rendering and staking nonetheless occur throughout. The rendering and stakes-raising focused on the affair or the people in it are shown in bold in Figure 6.6.

As the bolding reveals, this rendering and raising of stakes occurs in every stage that Eggins and Slade (1997/2004) recognize; it is not confined to a single discrete segment of the text. For this reason, we can perhaps better interpret the Pejorative Evaluation stage as being a prosodically realized stage through the text. This is shown on the right. The perspective on the "point" of the genre accounts for the dispersed rendering and its wide range of discourse semantic realizations; in addition, as for the negotiation between Kristy and her mother reviewed above, it allows for the fact that a text can expand indefinitely – which in fact is what Eggins and Slade's discussion shows (the text in Figure 6.6 is just an excerpt of a larger text). It also allows us to recognize the line *I mean it was the laughing stock of the whole hospital* as part of the Substantiating Behaviour, tendering as it does one of the events that make what happened "gossipable." In this sense, we can recognize that the gossip text can be expanded

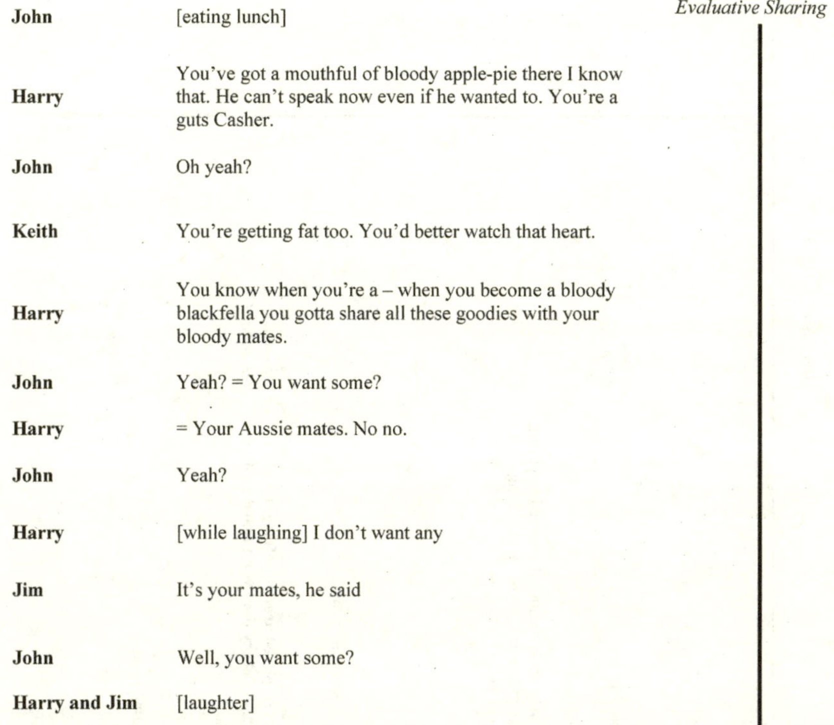

		Evaluative Sharing
John	[eating lunch]	
Harry	You've got a mouthful of bloody apple-pie there I know that. He can't speak now even if he wanted to. You're a guts Casher.	
John	Oh yeah?	
Keith	You're getting fat too. You'd better watch that heart.	
Harry	You know when you're a – when you become a bloody blackfella you gotta share all these goodies with your bloody mates.	
John	Yeah? = You want some?	
Harry	= Your Aussie mates. No no.	
John	Yeah?	
Harry	[while laughing] I don't want any	
Jim	It's your mates, he said	
John	Well, you want some?	
Harry and Jim	[laughter]	

Figure 6.6 Genre analysis of gossip

through two complementary principles. Pejorative Evaluation can be extended prosodically, realized opportunistically throughout the text (and likely show continuous rendering through facial expression and voice quality)[10] – until the conversation shifts to another genre. Alternatively or in addition, the Substantiating Behaviour can extend the text by adding more behaviour to be judged – and this expands serially as more and more events are added as targets for evaluation.

Moving beyond the gossip genre, an orientation to prosodic structure also helps us come to grips with the chat phases of casual conversation. An example of such chat, again from Eggins and Slade (1997/2004, p. 117), is given in Figure 6.7. In this text, a group of mates at work are chatting and teasing each other in ways that signify relatively close solidarity between them – casual racism and all. As Eggins and Slade note, a difficulty for traditional stage-oriented genre analysis is that in this example and the larger conversation it is excerpted from, there

Eggins and Slade Genre Analysis	Speaker	Text	Alternative Analysis	
Third Person Focus	**Jo**	We had… there was an **affair**. **A classic**. **A classic** was here. There was **an affair** going on between the cook	*Third Person focus*	*Pejorative Evaluation* ↓
	Sue	== **Oh yeah**		
	Jo	== and this other girl you know.		
Substantiating behaviour (1)		I mean, she'd come over, **any excuse**, she'd be over.	*Substantiating Behaviour (1)*	
Pejorative Evaluation		I mean it was the **laughing stock** of the **whole** hospital		
Substantiating Behaviour (2)		and we'd **got to the stage** where we'd **really play on it** because if we need **anything** from the other side we'd sort of ring up and say "Oh Anna, if you're not doing anything." And she'd **run**, you know. **Whatever** you == wanted		
Probe	**Sue**	== Did she know that you knew?	*Probe*	
	Donna	**I don't == think so**		
	Jo	== **No, I don't think she was that cluey**		
	Donna	**No I don't think she was aware** of the fact that so **many** people == knew		
	Jo	**Yeah**		
Substantiating Behaviour (3)	**Donna**	She'd come in and… **[laughs]** I reckon she got **so pissed around left right and centre**, just to keep her out of the kitchen. Because **every time you turned around**, and she'd wear, she'd	*Substantiating Behaviour (2)*	
	Sue	**Yeah**		
	Jo	**I know.** Then **all of a sudden** she started wearing makeup.		
Wrap-up		It was **a real classic**.	*Wrap-up*	
	Donna	A girl that never really wore make-up.		

Figure 6.7 Genre analysis of chat

is not a discrete staging that we typically find in other genres. That is, there is not a sequence of distinct "chunks" of the text that follow easily predictable patterns.

Nonetheless, Eggins and Slade do show that chat has at least two clear distinguishing features. It is dialogic (or in this case multilogic), and it heavily foregrounds interpersonal meaning (Eggins & Slade, 1997/2004, p. 20). From the perspective of mode, this means there is necessarily a back and forth between people (i.e., dialogue); and from the perspective of tenor, this means that there is continual rendering. For chat to keep going, there has to be dialogue and there has to be rendering. If at some point in a conversation there is no response from anyone and no evaluation, then the conversation peters out into a potentially embarrassing silence – positioning interlocutors to think of something to talk about or perhaps bring the interaction to a close.

So, despite the fact that chat in general does not display distinct stages, it does have a very clear principle of organization – namely, a prosody of rendering that is engaged with by multiple people throughout. For this reason, we could perhaps recognize the structure as involving a prosody of Evaluative Sharing, as illustrated on the right-hand side of 7 (for further discussion of a prosodic perspective on genre, see Martin [1995, 1996, 2000b] and Cranny-Francis & Martin [1991]).

This prosodic Evaluative Sharing perspective is only minimally descriptive; it is useful for distinguishing chat texts from other previously described genres, such as a narrative that includes an Orientation, Complication, and Resolution.[11] What is clear is that chat genres in fact bring together a wide range of different ways of talking. In Figure 6.7, mates are focused on ribbing one another – teasing, banter, and "taking the piss." In terms of rendering, there is constant rejection coupled with deferral (laughter). Interaction of this kind is unlikely to lead to a lasting schism, though; the barbs are tendered and rendered to bring the mates together. In terms of SPIRIT, despite the negative rendering, they are not warning but warming.

This perhaps gets us to a crucial issue that we can only touch on here. As the description of the text above as *ribbing*, *teasing*, *banter*, and *taking the piss* illustrates, we have a large commonsense vocabulary for different types of chat. Indeed, we all know full well what it is like to be told off or to be praised, to be flirted with or brushed off, to bond or to have someone give us a piece of their mind. We need of course to be wary of commonsense descriptors when developing a technical linguistic description. But the variety and richness of this vocabulary suggest that there are in fact distinct ways of talking that are backgrounded in models of genre that focus on particulate analysis alone. From the perspective of tenor, it is likely that most genres of conversation are organized through nuanced interactions among rendering, spirit, and stakes, among others, and so can be described from a complementary prosodic perspective.

Over thirty years ago, Cate Poynton lamented the backgrounding of interpersonal meaning in broader linguistic theory, which in general favours an ideational perspective (Poynton, 1990b). Although SFL has always acknowledged the interpersonal as a central component of language and the last few decades have massively expanded SFL's descriptive apparatus in this regard, our exploration of the resources of tenor, especially in relation to conversational genres, suggests we have further to go.

6.5 Looking Across: Tenor, Social Relations, and the Social Semiotic

Poynton's frustration with the marginalization of the interpersonal was related to its centrality in understanding the nexus between the individual and the social (women and society in particular). The way we engage with the wider world is heavily dependent on the emotionally charged and values-based ways of thinking that we carry with us at all times and the interactions we have every day. In this book we have aimed to develop a model of tenor as a resource for enacting sociality – in other words, resources for putting forward meanings and reacting to them, resources for connecting meanings into larger complexes of values, and resources for modifying and augmenting the stakes, scope, and spirit of these meanings. As we noted in the first chapter, these resources are not the only perspective on tenor afforded by different aspects of SFL.

One complementary perspective is that described extensively by Poynton herself (Poynton, 1984, 1985/1989, 1990a, 1990b, 1996; Poynton & Lee, 2009) – the relations of social distance (contact) and hierarchy (status) that organize how we see people. As introduced in Section 1.3.2, Poynton outlined these variables as having distinct principles of manifestation. In terms of status (the relation of hierarchy), people of relatively equal status are afforded a reciprocity of choice. That is, they will tend to have the same set of options available to them at any time. Those in unequal positions will tend to have a distinct set of choices available to them, with those in the "higher status" position tending to have more options. Looking a final time at the conversation between Kristy and her mother, we can see this principle at play. Initially, Kristy and her mother take up similar choices in terms of purview, with each tendering a proposal that is left open for the other to agree to. In this sense, they each maintain a posture of relatively equal status (described by Hasan as being typical of middle-class families). This continues through the phase when Kristy is crying about not wanting to go out. But rather than simply telling her she has to go out, Kristy's mother tries to suggest reasons why she might like it. Then, once Kristy gets annoyed at Ruth, the pretence of equal status is removed – with Kristy's mother taking up choices only available to her, telling Kristy off (*don't get cranky*). This simultaneously rejects Kristy's anger at Ruth and gives Kristy no purview over how she can relate to her sister. In this sense, Kristy's mother brings the full range of choices afforded to her as an interlocutor with higher status – choices that at first seem to position her as "equal," before drawing where necessary on choices that make it clear their status is not the same.

Kristy:	what about I fold the cardboard
	and then if I want some pieces um –
Mother:	well how about I get you dressed instead
Kristy:	no
	don't want to go out today [CRYING]
Mother:	you'll have a lovely day pet
	I won't be home late either
	I'll probably be home about the same time as Dee's big kids get home . . . maybe a little bit later, maybe a little bit earlier
	oh dear oh dear . . . I don't think you're really upset about me going
	[AS KRISTY CONTINUES CRYING] I think you're upset
	because the TV wasn't working
	Ruth wants to go on the potty [AS RUTH CALLS]
Kristy:	[CRYING] I don't want to go away
Mother:	come on . . . oh dear oh dear
Kristy:	Mummy . . . I don't want to go away from you
Mother:	you go away from me to kinder, don't you?
Kristy:	yeah but –
Mother:	and you like going away from me sometimes
Kristy:	yeah
	but then I meet not so many kids at kinder
	and there's not only a big room
Mother:	you mean you want to go to kinder
	but you don't want to go to Dee's?
Kristy:	yeah

[TO RUTH] don't!
Mother: oh she's trying to be nice
don't get cranky

Poynton also proposed linguistic manifestations of social distance – namely that people who are closer to each other tend to have a relatively wide range of meanings open to them (what she called proliferation) and at the same time do not need to be as explicit about these meanings as would be the case for those who do not know each other as well (what she called contraction). Alongside the shifts in status, these two principles, contraction and proliferation, are also illustrated in Kristy and her mother's conversation. One way this happens is through the range of different Vocatives deployed (which Poynton highlighted as a crucial resource in this regard) – in this text, the names *Mummy* and *pet* – clear markers of this close relationship. More subtle is the fact that they can each comfortably share their negative feelings and the rejections that go with it. Each rejects the other, and Kristy cries and cries, but this does not result in a "break" between them – because it is safe to proliferate such feelings in a relationship of this kind. Similarly, the men in Figure 6.7 can rib each other as sharply as they do because they are in relatively close contact to one another.

A third complementary perspective on tenor that needs to be brought into the picture involves the social roles and relations that affect the way we talk (Halliday & Matthiessen, 2014) – at a relatively local level (e.g., the way we talk as a mother-child pair) or at a much more global level (e.g., the way we talk in relation to our economic class). In some discussions of tenor in SFL, there is a suggestion that we can simply "wire in" various demographic features and suggest there is a relatively straight realizational path from, say, *mother* and *daughter* to the language being spoken. But what we have tried to show through this book is that being a mother involves a wide range and diverse set of options. In other words, how a mother means is immensely varied and contested and constantly undergoing change. It intersects with the genres, situations, communities, and feelings we have at all times.

Ultimately, then, what we need is a theory of language and semiosis that can manage the complexity of everything we need to say – in Halliday's (1978) terms, a model of the social semiotic that takes seriously both the social and the semiotic. SFL has worked hard over more than six decades to expand its horizons in this regard. This book is another step along this path. We invite you to join us in pushing this engaging enterprise a few steps further.

Glossary

In this glossary, terms that are part of the tenor system in this book have been marked with an asterisk *. Those that are introduced or explained in other publications are given references; where there is no reference, the term can be taken as being explained in Halliday and Matthiessen (2014).

APPRAISAL – an interpersonal discourse semantic system covering resources for expressing and exchanging feelings, stances, evaluations, and so on (see ATTITUDE); points of view, intersubjective positioning, and dis/alignment with other voices (see ENGAGEMENT); and ramping up/toning down or sharpening /softening meanings (see GRADUATION). See Martin and White (2005).

ATTITUDE – interpersonal discourse semantic resources for organizing feelings and opinions, including emotional reactions, judgments of behaviour, and evaluations of things. Part of the more general system of APPRAISAL. See Martin and White (2005).

CONJUNCTION/CONNEXION – a discourse semantic resource for connecting events and longer stretches of discourse across text. Halliday and Hasan (1967) position CONJUNCTION as a system of cohesion within the lexicogrammar; Martin (1992) interprets this as a discourse semantic system (which we follow here); Hao (2020) renames this system CONNEXION so as to distinguish the discourse semantic relation from the word class (conjunctions) that often realize it. In this book we follow Hao's terminology. An important distinction for this book is between external connexion and internal connexion:

- external connexion is oriented towards linking events in terms of how they present experience (or more technically, how they orient to field): for example, *First Jim wrote some entries in the glossary. Next Yaegan wrote the rest and then Michele sorted out the references.*
- internal connexion is concerned with linking text as stretches of discourse: for example, *It was clear which entries were written by who. First, they differed in length. Second, their examples were different.*

contact – a parameter that considers the relative social distance between people, from relatively close and intimate to relatively distant and unfamiliar. Typically considered an interpersonal dimension of tenor (though see Chapter 1), the key work in SFL is by Poynton (1985, 1990) (who calls this parameter *distance*). Building on work by Brown and Ford (1961) on American address systems, among others, Poynton suggests that closer contact tends to involve a greater proliferation of meanings between people (e.g., a wider set of names used and a wider set of feelings being shared). An additional principle for contact suggested by Poynton is that of contraction – the closer people are, the less explicit they need to be in their meanings. Contact is also called social distance (e.g., Hasan, 2020) or solidarity (e.g., Martin & Rose, 2007).

context – a cover term for systems construing field, enacting tenor, and composing mode, and in models such as the one used in this book, which unfold through the staging of a genre (Martin & Rose, 2008).

*convoking – where meanings are oriented towards someone, or where something or someone is being brought into the position. An archetypal example is via Vocatives: *Do you think this example works, Jim?* Within the system of ORIENTING. See Chapter 4.

diatype – the particular set of language choices used due to choices in field, tenor, and mode. The term is taken from Gregory (1967). In this book it is distinguished from register, where register is the cover term for field, tenor, and mode itself. This usage is distinct from Halliday's use of the term register, which is closer to our diatype, with context being the cover term for field, tenor, and mode in Halliday's model.

discourse semantics – a stratum of resources realized through lexicogrammar comprising ideation, connexion, negotiation, appraisal, identification, and periodicity. See Martin (1992) and Martin and Rose (2007).

*encapsulating – where a set of meanings are oriented as being within other meanings, interpersonally speaking. An archetypal example is where an introduction puts forward some general positions that encapsulate more elaborated points given later in a text. Within the system of ORIENTING. See Chapter 4.

ENGAGEMENT – interpersonal discourse semantic resources for organizing the range of voices at play in discourse, such as for organizing points of view, intersubjective positioning, and dis/alignment with other voices. Makes a general distinction between monoglossia, where there is no acknowledgment of other voices, and heteroglossia, where there is an indication that other voices are at play. Part of the more general system of APPRAISAL. See Martin and White (2005) and White (2003).

exchange structure – an interpersonal discourse semantic structure for exchanges in dialogue. There can be action exchanges, where the primary thing being negotiated is a physical action (indicated by the function A1), or knowledge exchanges where the primary thing being negotiated is information (indicated by the function K1). Exchange structure makes a distinction between primary actor or knower, who has responsibility for doing the action or giving the information and who is indicated by 1 (e.g., K1, A1, Dk1, Da1, etc.), and secondary actor or knower, who is the one responsible for prompting or reacting to the action or information and who is indicated by 2 (e.g., K2, A2, K2f, A2f, etc.). Exchange structure also makes a distinction between moves that occur before the primary knowledge or action is given, called *delayed* moves because they delay the primary negotiation and so marked by *D* (Dk1, Da1), and moves that follow the primary knowledge or action that is given, marked by *f* (e.g., K2f, A2f, K1f, A2f). Part of the discourse semantic system of NEGOTIATION at a rank above SPEECH FUNCTION. See Berry (1981a, 1981b) and Martin (1992).

field – contextual resources for construing phenomena as activity, the classification and composition of items, and related properties. See Doran and Martin (2021).

genre – resources for staging social processes realized through choices for field, tenor, and mode. See Martin and Rose (2008).

GRADUATION – resources for turning up or down the force of an evaluation or for sharpening or softening its focus. See Martin and White (2005) and Hood (2010).

grammatical metaphor – a relationship between discourse semantics and lexicogrammar whereby the lexicogrammar symbolizes rather than directly encodes meaning, including the realization of complexes as clauses (e.g., *The attack was followed by a declaration of war*) and figures as groups (e.g., *the attack, a declaration of war*), indirect speech acts (e.g., *Could you pass me some paper, please?*), and subjectively explicit (e.g., *I reckon they'll win*) and objectively explicit (e.g., *<u>It's certain</u> they'll win*) modalities.

ideational – a metafunction concerned with construing experience of the world inside us and around us.

identification – discourse semantic resources for introducing entities and keeping track of them in texts. See Martin (1992). Called REFERENCE by Halliday and Hasan (1976) and considered as one dimension of the lexicogrammatical system of cohesion.

individuation – the scale of belonging conditioning the allocation of semiotic resources across society and the ways they are drawn on to affiliate language users as personae in communities.

instantiation – the cline of abstraction relating meaning potential (*system*) to its actualization in texts (*instance*).

interpersonal – a metafunction concerned with enacting social relations of power and solidarity.

intonation – phonological resources for carrying the tone of an utterance and highlighting news (Halliday, 1970; Halliday & Greaves, 2008).

lexicogrammar – a stratum of resources realizing discourse semantics, organized by rank (e.g., clause, group, word, morpheme) and metafunction (ideational, interpersonal, textual).

*likening – where a set of meanings are oriented as being to some degree similar to each other or on the same side of an opposition. Within the system of ORIENTING. See Chapter 4.

metafunction – different types of meaning (ideational, interpersonal, and textual) constituting systems of choice across ranks and strata.

MODALITY – lexicogrammatical resources for assessing probability, usuality, obligation, inclination, and ability. Makes a generalized distinction between modalization, which is typically oriented to propositions and is concerned with probability (e.g., *Jim's possibly going to get annoyed by all the examples that involve him*) and usuality (*He generally prefers the use of real examples*); and modulation, which is typically oriented to proposals, including obligation (*I probably shouldn't put extended jokes in each of the examples*), ability (*But I can if I want to*), and inclination (*and I am determined to*).

mode – contextual resources for organizing information flow – that is, pulse (waves of prominence), demarcation (boundary marking), and distribution (meaning here or there); see Doran et al. (2024).

MOOD – lexicogrammatical resources for distinguishing moves in interactions (e.g., declarative, exclamative, or interrogative).

NEGOTIATION – discourse semantic resources for organizing exchange structure. See exchange structure, and Martin (1992).

*opposing – where meanings are oriented as being opposed to each other. Within the system of ORIENTING. See Chapter 4.

*ORIENTING – a generalized system for relating positions to each other, via likening, opposing, source, convoking, encapsulating, or repositioning. See Chapter 4.

paralanguage – systems of meaning converging with spoken language, including gesture, facial expression, bodily stance, and movement. See Ngo et al. (2022).

PERIODICITY – a discourse semantic system managing waves of theme and news. See Martin and Rose (2007).

*POSITIONING – a generalized tenor system for tendering positions and rendering them. See Chapters 2 and 3.

*proposal – a position being tendered where there is typically some action involved. See Chapter 2. The term is adapted from Halliday's (e.g., Halliday & Matthiessen, 2014) use of proposal as a cover term for semantic resources used in the exchange of goods and services (e.g., commands and offers) and other analogous meanings across lexicogrammar and semantics.

*proposition – a position being tendered, typically oriented to giving information. See Chapter 2. The term is adapted from Halliday's (e.g., Halliday & Matthiessen, 2014) use of proposition, often as a cover term for semantic resources used in the exchange of information (e.g., statements and questions) and other analogous meanings across lexicogrammar and semantics.

*PURVIEW – a system focused on resources for indicating who is interpersonally tied to the meanings being tendered. The system indicates that there can be speaker purview or no speaker purview, listener purview or no listener purview, as well as internal purview and external purview. Within the broader system of POSITIONING. See Chapter 3. Related to what conversation analysis discusses in terms of epistemic authority (e.g., Heritage & Raymond, 2005) and deontic authority (Stevanovic & Peräkylä 2012).

register – cover term for field, tenor, and mode resources. Distinguished in this book from diatype, which are the language features that occur due to choices in field, tenor, and mode (see diatype). This usage is distinct from Halliday's use of the term register, which is closer to our diatype, with the cover term for field, tenor, and mode in Halliday's model being context.

*rendering – resources for reacting to or indicating our feelings, opinions, or evaluations about other meanings. A primary choice within the system of POSITIONING. See Chapter 2.

*repositioning – where one position is presented as another. For example, a proposition can be repositioned as a proposal, as in *Tell me what entries I missed* (as opposed to the non-repositioned *What entries did I miss?*). See Chapter 3.

*scoping – where the ambit of a meaning is either broadened or narrowed. A position can be individualized, and so narrowing its scope, or collectivized, and so broadening its scope, along a cline of more or less individualizing or collectivizing. Within the system of TUNING. See Chapter 5.

*sourcing – where meanings are oriented as being from the perspective of someone or something (i.e., as being "theirs" in some sense). An archetypal example is through projection or an Emoter: *Jim thinks I should stop doing this; I hope Michele likes it.* Within the system of ORIENTING. See Chapter 4.

*SPEECH FUNCTION – an interpersonal discourse semantic system for different types of moves in discourse, such as command, question, statement, and offer.

*spiriting – where a meaning is adjusted to be read more or less favourably (e.g., adjusting the "vibe" of the meaning or the "tone" of how it was said). A position can be said in a warming spirit, and so making the meanings more favourable, or in a warning spirit, and so less favourable, along a cline of warmer or less warm spirit. Within the system of TUNING. See Chapter 5.

*staking – where a meaning is calibrated in terms of interpersonal risk (e.g., how significant is the meaning? How tenuous is its standing?). Stakes can be higher or lower along a cline of interpersonal risk. Within the system of TUNING. See Chapter 5.

status – a parameter that considers the relative social hierarchy between people, from relatively equal to relatively unequal. Typically considered an interpersonal dimension of tenor (though see Chapter 1). Key work in SFL is by Poynton (1985, 1990). Building on work by Brown and Gilman (1960) on pronominal use across language, Poynton suggests that more equal status tends to involve more reciprocal selection of meanings and more unequal status tends to involve less reciprocal selection of meanings.

stratification – levels of abstraction, that is, phonology, lexicogrammar, discourse semantics, and register (and genre in the model of context assumed here).

TAGGING – resources for establishing expectations about the kind of response expected from addressees (e.g., *Stop it, will you/won't you/can you/can't you?*).

*tendering – resources for putting forward meanings. A primary choice within the system of POSITIONING. See Chapters 2 and 3

*tenor – a resource for enacting social relations, including positioning (render and tender), tuning (stakes, scope, and spirit), and orienting (repositioning and arranging).

textual – a metafunction concerned with managing information flow.

TONE – intonation resource adjusting the key of an utterance. Primary distinctions in tone in English are: falling (tone 1), rising (tone 2), level (tone 3), falling rising (tone 4), rising falling (tone 5), and two compound tones: falling-level (13) and rising falling–level (53). See Halliday (1970) and Halliday and Greaves (2008).

*TUNING – a system for adjusting meanings interpersonally, covering resources for modifying the stakes, scope, and spirit of meanings. See Chapter 5.

Vocatives – names used to elicit a response from a particular addressee.

Notes

1 Negotiating Social Relations: A Systemic Functional Perspective

1 As this terminological distinction has often led to confusion, it would perhaps be useful to use Gregory's (1967) suggestion of "diatype" for the skewing of probabilities in the systems of language by choices in field, tenor, and mode (i.e., Halliday's "register"), and leave *register* as the cover term for field, tenor, and mode. It is of course worth emphasizing that there is a substantive difference in the model of social context presumed here and that of Halliday's in that this model divides context into register (field, tenor, and mode) and genre as distinct strata, whereas Halliday's only has field, tenor, and mode.

2 This is not to say that social constructs such as femininity or being a woman are not enacted by language and semiosis – they of course are. Cloran (1989) illustrates this quite strikingly in terms of the semiotic enactment of gender as part of Hasan's semantic variation project. But being a woman does not entail a strict set of realizations in the interpersonal metafunction of language that if used indicate femininity, while if others are used indicate masculinity or other gender identities (the most obvious reflex of grammatical gender, *he/she* in English, is only a tiny part of what gender identity entails, and is one that is heavily contested). Rather, femininity must be considered a vast and constantly evolving social arena of collaboration and contestation that requires we draw on the full force of our social semiotic theory to understand it – not just one component such as tenor.

3 In fact Chilton (1978; see also Martin, 1992), when presenting networks for tenor (what he calls "role relationships") that are remarkably similar in certain components to Hasan's (2020) tenor network four decades later, notes explicitly that "the categories . . . will not necessarily be those of the sociologist" (p.).

4 Both the contact and affect dimensions (cf. Eggins & Slade's [1997] contact and affective involvement) are anticipated in Pearce (1972), who writes that alongside formality, tenor "deals with such questions as the permanence or otherwise of the relationship and the degree of emotional charge in it" (p. 186).

5 Poynton's notation for clined systems has been adjusted here, following Martin et al. (2013).

6 One additional system, INTERDEPENDENCY (comprising resources for reconstruing and interrelating phenomena), will not be reviewed here.

7 For a comparable approach to modelling mode as a resource for organizing information, see Doran et al. (2024), who suggest DISTRIBUTION, PULSING, and DEMARCATION as key systems.

8 We have anonymized all identifying information such as names and places in this video transcript.

9 With thanks to Brad Smith for the phonological analysis of this text and of many of the examples throughout this book.

10 Available from the authors on request.

2 Negotiating Tenor: Rendering Meaning in Dialogue and Monologue

1 We have made some very slight adaptations to this text for ease of reading, including filling in some small stretches where the original transcription was not clear, and removing some of the annotations in Hasan's original text. However, these do not affect the analyses presented in this book.

2 Berry (1981a, pp. 139–145; 2017) makes a distinction between proposition completion moves that put forward a proposition (often through declaratives or answers to questions) and what she calls proposition base moves (typically realized by either polar or *wh-* interrogatives) that establish the "base" from which the response can complete the proposition. Using Berry's examples:

Son:	Which English cathedral has the tallest spire?	proposition base
Father:	Salisbury.	proposition completion
Son:	Oh.	proposition support
Son:	Is John coming?	proposition base
Father:	Yes.	proposition completion
Son:	Oh.	proposition support

Berry's model groups together polar interrogatives and *wh-* interrogatives as realizing the same discourse element. But when looked at from the perspective of rendering, the two types of interrogatives tend to do distinct things, with polar interrogatives being more similar to declaratives in this regard. Like declaratives, propositions tabled by polar interrogatives can be either supported or rejected (i.e., they can be rendered), whereas the propositions put forward by *wh-* interrogatives cannot – *wh-* interrogatives can only be rendered as linguistic acts (as we will discuss in Chapter 3). Accordingly, we distinguish between open propositions that cannot have their propositional content rendered, which are often realized grammatically through *wh-* interrogatives (i.e., they can only be a proposition base in Berry's terms), and closed propositions, often realized by polar interrogatives and declaratives, where their propositional content can be rendered. This allows an easier understanding of the interaction between evaluation and dialogue structure, extending beyond a focus on dialogue structure alone. Nonetheless, as we hope is clear throughout this chapter, Berry's model has been fundamental to the development of both our model of tenor (much of it via Zhang's [2020a, 2020b, 2020c] work in this regard) and the interpersonal discourse semantics presented in Martin (1992). Indeed, Berry's ideational tier anticipates a number of features of our model by four decades.

3 The meaning of such backchannelling is heavily dependent on their phonological realization in terms of both tone and phonemic choice (Gardner, 2001). For example, in this instance, the backchannel is said on tone 3 (Halliday & Greaves, 2008), a relatively flat tone, which indicates a less certain response. If it were said on tone 1 (a falling tone), it could potentially be read as support, agreeing with the other speaker (though it could still be read as neutral; Gardner, 2001, pp. 99ff.). Comparable variation occurs for paralanguage, such as nodding, where the choice of rendering type depends on the timing and form of the nod (Muntigl et al., 2012). Indeed most distinctions introduced in this chapter are heavily sensitive to phonological (and paralinguistic) patterns; however, for reasons of space, we will only explore the most crucial tone choices where relevant. See our final chapter for an analysis that includes phonological patterns.

4 Kristy renders both lines of *You know if you eat too much I say you're a little pig* and *I say you're a little piggy-wig* together, drawing on what we will refer to in Chapter 4 as likening. We have shown this by having the arrow connect to a brace in Example (2.8). This relates to Eggins' (1990, p. 271) observation of "cumulative" relations between moves, where some moves relate to more than one prior move.

5 An alternative interpretation is that Kristy is doing what Kartika-Ningsih (2019) calls a vocalizing move. This interprets Kristy's repetition of what her mother says as simply practicing the word, rather than supporting what her mother has said. Under this interpretation, Kristy's *silly donkey* would be tendering a meaning to be either supported as correct or rejected as incorrect by her mother. In order to distinguish these two interpretations, we would need information about the intonation, which Hasan's published data does not include.

6 More specifically, Martin (1992, p. 72) allows for this to be analyzed as a challenge conflated with a justification. But this does not solve the problem of the boundary between exchanges.

7 Whether this in fact involves tendering depends on whether the *come on* here involves some sort of proposal (that, e.g., Kristy's mother actually wants Kristy to come to her) or whether this is just an idiomatic rejection with no sense of a proposal. Without intonation or video to see the paralanguage, we cannot tell, so we have taken the *come on* here in literal terms as a command realized through an imperative, and thus both a rendering of Kristy's proposal and a tendering of a new one.

8 Speaking strictly, a denial such as this tenders two opposed positions and rejects one of them. We will discuss resources for opposing positions in Chapter 4.

9 Zhang (2020c), working on Khorchin Mongolian, suggests a similar parallel viewed from the perspective of discourse semantics, interpreting the equivalent of *No* in terms of heteroglossic denial.

10 There is a question here as to whether *no I won't* additionally tenders a negative proposition, as we argued for the full clauses in Examples (2.20)–(2.22) and (2.24). Our interpretation is that replaying the Subject and Finite without the Residue, as is done in *no I won't*, means the turn is not putting forward any new proposition, and so is best read as simply rendering – reacting to what was said previously. A new proposition is tendered only when there is some adjustment of the Mood (Subject and Finite) – what Halliday calls a shift in the modal responsibility (Halliday & Matthiessen, 2014) – or the specification of Residue (Martin, 1992, pp. 461ff.). This is because any further rendering involving the same strategy will simply replay the Mood of the initial position: *you will be home late as well / no I won't / yes you will / no I won't*, and so on. Having said that, some instances with this configuration would tender a new proposition, such as either if the primary tone was placed on the Subject and Finite to suggest some sort of contrast: *you will be home late as well / no **I** won't*; or if the Mood Adjunct and Mood are given on different tone groups: *//no//^ I won't//*. Ultimately, evidence as to whether there is a new proposition being tendered will depend on how it is negotiated in the following discourse.

11 We can see this by the fact that when rejecting this statement using polarity such as *No, it doesn't*, this could be read as rejecting either that *The UNSW Diversity Toolkit claims* or that *the word settlement ignores the reality of*...
12 This example also illustrates the role of engagement in realizing internal rendering. Here the *Of course* is not rendering an opinion on whether they support or reject Indigenous lands being stolen, but rather is supporting this as a linguistic act – that is, supporting it as true. We can contrast this with an external support – *Fortunately, Indigenous lands were stolen* – which is definitely not what is being said. Heteroglossia when used for rendering is often used for internal rendering in this sense, functioning as it does to manage the play of voices.
13 We could also analyse *maybe a little bit later, maybe a little bit earlier* as two further positions about the time, *noting* the possibility of both *a little bit later* and *a little bit earlier.*
14 An exemplum is one type of story genre that revolves around a moral judgment in relation to a set of events, and has a typical structure of Orient ation^Incident^Interpretation (Martin & Rose, 2008, p. 62).
15 Here we are taking the most explicit rendering, where Kollontai's hyperbolic metaphor of purses being stuffed with gold and credit notes most directly realizes positive attitude (judgment of capacity). In this sense, it realizes support within tenor. But by virtue of her political positioning, Kollontai by no means considers this wealth a good thing. This means that for those who know her political stance, this stretch can be read as being infused with sarcasm. But being written, not spoken, no formal features appear to be indicating this – one must know her authorial position. For this reason, for those whose reading involves sarcasm, a second-level analysis can be suggested, that Kollontai is rejecting her explicit positive support (what we can interpret in terms of Szenes' [2021] notion of *recoupling*), but doing so as a deferral (as through laughter) – her explicit support wrinkles against established bonds that only those who closely affiliate with her political positioning share. It is not until the final paragraph of this excerpt that Kollontai confers a rejection by calling the bourgeoisie *humbugs* and *hypocrites.*
16 Here Kollontai is using scare quotes to, in terms of engagement, distance herself from this term, which from the perspective of tenor indicates that she rejects the term.

3 Positioning Others: Tendering in Text

1 Here we need to stress that we are describing the resources for English, and so are not dealing with assessment and stance systems that occur across languages (e.g., for Korean, see Kim et al., 2023).

2 This parallels the distinction made by Berry (1981a) between her proposition base (e.g., *Why is it?*), which provides "a basis for the completed proposition by predicting the form of the completed proposition" (p. 140), and her proposition completion (e.g., *It changes direction*), which completes what is established in the proposition base. As noted in Chapter 2, Berry extends this distinction to include polar interrogatives, which we do not.

3 Here, the best interpretation for how this fits is that she is using *cream* to mean the colour – that flour is a cream colour.

4 This iterative repositioning can be compared to iterative reconstruals of meaning in field that occur in highly technical discourse, such as in medicine (Chen, 2024; Doran & Martin, 2021; Martin & Unsworth, 2024). It reminds us of just how interpersonally oriented classroom discourse is, in terms of constant evaluation, commanding, and dialogue.

5 Viewed in terms of the relationship between different strata of language (following Martin [1992, p. 40], drawing on Levinson, 1983, p. 290), the sequence of responses shift from lower to higher strata and rank: the *yeah* responds to the grammatical interrogative (*can you give*), while the *sure* responds to the speech function of a command (*give us an example*), and the *since I've been working* . . . responds to the knowledge exchange (K2) that the interviewer initiates.

6 Note that while repositioning and interpersonal grammatical metaphor are related, there is not a one-to-one relation. Repositioning is a relation within tenor, realized through discourse semantics, while grammatical metaphor is a relation between (discourse) semantics and lexicogrammar. For example, linguistic services are not typically grammatical metaphors. They grammatically involve a command in the semantics, and so are congruent; the command just happens to be to use language. But the exchange they set up in discourse semantics involves a tension between action (proposal) and knowledge (proposition). The relation is at a higher stratum than grammatical metaphor deals with. This relation is comparable to the ideational distinction Hao (2020) makes between activity entities in discourse semantics and ideational grammatical metaphors. Activity entities, such as *phagocytosis,* typically realize activities reconstrued as items in field (Doran & Martin, 2021) and cannot be unpacked – in other words, we cannot say, "The phagocyte phagocytoses the lysosome." Comparable ideational grammatical metaphors, such as *invasion,* are figures within discourse semantics, which means they can be unpacked – that is, we can say, "Germany invades France."

7 For Halliday and Matthiessen (2014), modulated clauses "are statements of obligation and inclination made by the speaker in respect of others. . . . Such statements of obligation function **as propositions**, since to the person addressed they convey information rather than goods-&-services. . . .

Modal clauses are thus in principle ambiguous as between proposition and proposal" (p. 178; boldface in original). Under the current model, we would clarify this by saying they realize proposals that have been repositioned as propositions.

8 This is generalized across Zhang's (2021) discussion of speaker and listener positioning in terms of who "knows" the information being discussed, and for proposals, Zhang's (2024) responsibility-based model of moves in action exchanges. This model of purview relates in particular to what Zhang (2020c) calls the "spatial" dimension of conversation. Here, the spatial dimension refers to the expansion or contraction of the dialogic space (in relation to ENGAGEMENT in appraisal; Martin & White, 2005; White, 2003), in terms of allowance for other voices. Zhang's temporal dimension, concerned with whether the expansion or contraction of the dialogic space is looking prospectively to what will be said next (typically the next move by another speaker), or retrospectively to what has been said previously, impinges on our tender versus render distinction. Rendering typically works in dialogue retrospectively (though as we have seen in relation to engagement, this is not always the case), while variation in purview discussed here typically occurs prospectively (though once again, with room for variation in relation to engagement, as we will discuss in Section 3.6). Zhang's work provides a crucial link between the dialogic exchange of conversation and the dialogism that occurs in the play of voices (i.e., between NEGOTIATION and APPRAISAL) that this chapter and Chapter 2 seek to model, as well as an SFL interpretation of what in conversation analysis is often described in terms of epitemic and deontic authority (Heritage & Raymond 2005; Stevanovic & Peräkylä 2012). Indeed Zhang's work also suggests that options in purview might best be considered as a cline of more or less speaker and listener purview, rather than a binary choice, though we do not have scope to explore this here.

9 Instances of projection involving first person – *I think, I believe,* and so on – that involve what Halliday and Matthiessen (2014, p. 689) call explicit subjective modality present a special case that brings in a number of other factors arising from the possibility of interpersonal metaphor, variations in tense (present *I think* vs. present-in-present *I am thinking*), and, from the perspective of tenor, the interaction among purview, rendering, and stakes (Chapter 5). Accordingly, we will set these aside here.

10 With apologies for re-using these terms in different ways in this book.

4 Building Values: Establishing Meanings to Share

1 This is in contrast to *epistemological* constellations that organize technical, procedural, empirical, and "content"-based meanings, and so on (Maton,

2014). See Maton and Doran (2021) for an exploration of epistemological constellations, and Doran and Martin (2021) for an SFL-based perspective in terms of field.

2 At the time of writing, this article was available from https://web.archive.org/web/20161017160823/http://www.essentialkids.com.au/development-advice/advice/top-5-reasons-for-mummy-guilt-and-how-to-combat-them-20140327-35kg6#ixzz4dMLCuMdu.

3 The distinction between the emphasis on the individual in Kristy and her mother's conversation and the emphasis on the collective in this discussion can be described through a system called TUNING, introduced in Chapter 5.

4 Here we need to emphasize the distinction between the resources we have introduced here (sourcing and convoking), which mark where a position comes from and who it is directed at, from more general parameters of status and contact (Martin, 1992; Poynton, 1990a) that are often used to characterize reader-writer relations. All texts, whether or not they draw on sourcing and convoking, enact status and contact relations; but this is accomplished by drawing on a raft of different linguistic resources well beyond convocation.

5 In terms of LCT's constellations, the use of *disclaim: denial* relies on there being a set of presumed positions within the constellation underpinning the text that are acknowledged only to be rejected (Doran, 2020a). By contrast, the use of internal connexion to oppose two stated positions allows for each position and their place in the constellation to be built from scratch, rather than be presumed.

6 Here we are using the Australian English dialect, where *but* regularly occurs at the end of a clause as part of the New.

7 The nature of implicit connexion is that it does not fully commit the meanings it puts forward. Thus this could alternatively be read as an implicit internal additive connexion of addition (Martin, 1992, p. 221), through something like *in addition* or *furthermore*. Either way, this would realize likening in terms of the model being developed here.

8 Here we have left out the rejection + opposition between lines i and ii, as it surrounds the possibility of having Allenby there, rather than whether they need Allenby. Eggins (1990, p. 2:133) accounts for this by establishing distinct countering relations between lines i and ii and lines i and iii.

9 This is likened to the *still but*, and so is opposed to *I like David a lot*.

10 This turn shifts gears somewhat, especially with the 10-second pause. But it is on broadly the same topic of David or his sister. In this case, if needed, we can broadly abduce a likening relation that could be glossed as "[On a similar topic] you met his sister, . . ." although due to the pause and the shift, we have not analysed it as likening here.

11 This could in fact be read as either likening or opposing, depending on the intonation. It would be likening if it were being used to support the argument that Jill is brighter than David, in which case *precocious* would be

being used contrastively with *academically bright*; it would be opposing if it were being used to in fact rescind the previous comment that Jill is brighter than David. As Eggins and Slade call this an "elaborating" move (1997, p. 171), it suggests likening, and so we have analysed it thus here.

12 This is a general strategy in improvisational comedy, where performers should go with and extend what other performers suggest, so as to build scenarios and dialogue in the performance, rather than rejecting them and shutting down possibilities.

13 With thanks to Lorenzo Logi for suggesting this relation.

14 There are in fact two things the student does to flag the coming points. First, they put forward specific positions that encapsulate the points that will be made: *we should have advertisements in newspapers and magazines* and *some people argue ads should not be put in newspapers and magazines.* Second, they flag that there are going to be further points given to justify this by using the semiotic entity *reasons* (*Here are some reasons why* . . . and *for these various reasons*). We consider the first of these strategies that specify the positions being put forward to be encapsulating within tenor. By contrast, we consider the use of "reasons" to flag that some justifications will come as part of mode – what we might call *distributing*, as it flags that meaning is being distributed to different parts of the text. This distinction allows us to see different types of higher level periodicity in terms of what resources they draw on in tenor and/or mode. It is because of this that we do not include the opening sentence of the text – *There are many reasons for both sides of the question, "Should we have printed advertisements?"* – as encapsulating the following positions. Rather than synthesizing distinct points, it draws on the semiotic entities *reasons* and *both sides of the question* to distribute meaning.

5 Tuning: Adjusting the Meanings We Share

1 For an overview of the economic and political logics of digital platforms, see Gillespie (2018).

2 This corpus was collected using the Twitter API between April 23, 2017,and March 13, 2019. The total unfiltered corpus was 5,920 tweets. This was cleaned to remove repeated tweets, as well as tweets that appeared to have been posted by bots, resulting in a corpus of 3,055 tweets (107,586 words).

3 It also arguably indicates collectivization in terms of scope, in terms of an emblem for "We can do it!": https://en.wikipedia.org/wiki/We_Can_Do_It!

6 Resources for Negotiating Social Relations

1 More specifically, it has viewed tenor from the perspective of the realization hierarchy – where tenor is one component of the stratum of register (following Martin's conceptualization of strata; Martin & Rose,

2008) – tenor as a set of resources for enacting social relations. We can take a complementary view of tenor from the perspective of instantiation, where it encapsulates a set of underlying principles for organizing and arranging choices in terms of status and contact, or from the perspective of individuation, where it captures domains of sociality such as our specific social roles and relationships and the values that underpin these, as arenas of variation, contestation, and collaboration. Doran et al. (2024) attempt to open space for a multiperspectival view in this regard.

2 At the time of writing, the video can be found here: https://www.youtube.com/watch?app=desktop&v=dDRWgLDodmo – the time we are focusing on is from 0:00 to 0:49. We recommend watching this video as you read to get a feel for the meanings at play that can only be approximated in a written transcript. With thanks to the ExceptionalFamily YouTube account for permission to use this video.

3 With thanks to Brad Smith for the phonological analysis and helpful comments, which we have slightly simplified here for presentation purposes.

4 More specifically, Ngo et al. (2022) suggest this is an indication of fear. But given the relatively brief nature of this facial expression and its not particularly expansive movements, the more general analysis of negative security coupled with lowering force suggests nervousness may be the better interpretation.

5 It seems that backchannelling is a common marker of a recurrent bond or bonding icon being mentioned in a text, as others recognize as well as note and rally around key meanings to show solidarity. If this observation is in fact widely generalizable, it offers a means of "seeing" these values as they develop in spoken discourse – values that are notoriously implicit (Doran, 2020b; Maton, 2014).

6 We say *likely* support here, because the camera does not include the other mother in the frame, and so we cannot be sure – it alternatively could simply be a noting. To be confident of this, we would need to see the paralanguage, such as the nodding or facial expression.

7 The opposition is indicated here by both the shift in place – from being with his therapist to being at home – and via the tone 4 that is on *home,* which constitutes the whole tone group.

8 The "gets to do" perhaps also suggests that the son likes doing his therapies – that he both has purview and supports the action. There is also a feeling here that, because up until now the mother has had purview over whether her son does the therapies or not, it is in fact the mother who "releases" the purview onto her son, giving her responsibility once more.

9 A range of Disadvantaged Schools Program (DSP) materials are available at https://educationalsemiotics.wordpress.com.

10 Martin (2000b) makes a related point about the prosodic potential of what he calls "appraisal telos."

11 As far as narratives are concerned, it is instructive to compare Labov and Waletzky (1967), who recognize a distinct Evaluation stage located between Complication and Resolution, with Labov (1972) who comments, "But it would be a mistake to limit the evaluation to d-e [to a particular stage of the text; YJD/JRM/MZ], since evaluative devices are distributed throughout the narrative. We must therefore modify the scheme of Labov and Waletzky (1967) by indicating E [Evaluation] as the focus of waves of evaluation that penetrate the narrative" (p. 369). This description suggests waves of evaluation emanating from the Evaluation to colour the Complication and Resolution – a prosody in SFL terms.

References

Abetz, J., & Moore, J. (2018). "Welcome to the mommy wars, ladies": Making sense of the ideology of combative mothering in mommy blogs. *Communication, Culture and Critique, 11*(2), 265–81. http://dx.doi.org/10.1093/ccc/tcy008

Adami, E. (2014). Retwitting, reposting, repinning; reshaping identities online: Towards a social semiotic multimodal analysis of digital remediation. *LEA-Lingue e Letterature d'Oriente e d'Occidente, 3*, 223–43.

Ariztimuño, L.I., Drefyus, S., & Moore, A.R. (2022). Emotion in speech: A systemic functional semiotic approach to the vocalisation of affect. *Language, Context and Text, 4*(2), 335–74. https://doi.org/10.1075/langct.21012.ari?locatt=mode:legacy

Bartlett, T. (2021). Interpersonal grammar in Scottish Gaelic. In J.R. Martin, B. Quiroz, & G. Figueredo (Eds.), *Interpersonal grammar: Systemic functional linguistic theory and description* (pp. 257–84). Cambridge University Press. http://dx.doi.org/10.1017/9781108663120

Bateman, J.A. (2007). Towards a grande paradigmatique of film: Christian Metz reloaded. *Semiotica, 167*, 13–64. https://doi.org/10.1515/SEM.2007.070

Beddington, E. 2024. Birth changes women's bodies for ever – and we need to get real about it. *The Guardian.* https://www.theguardian.com/commentisfree/article/2024/aug/18/birth-changes-womens-bodies-for-ever-and-we-need-to-get-real-about-it

Bernstein, B.B. (1971). *Class, codes and control: Volume 1. Theoretical studies towards a sociology of language.* Routledge & Kegan Paul.

Bernstein, B.B. (1973). *Class, codes and control: Volume 2. Theoretical studies towards a sociology of language.* Routledge & Kegan Paul.

Bernstein, B.B. (1975). *Class, codes and control: Volume 3. Theoretical studies towards a sociology of language.* Routledge & Kegan Paul.

Bernstein, B.B. (1990). *Class, codes and control: Volume 4. Theoretical studies towards a sociology of language.* Routledge & Kegan Paul.

Bernstein, B.B. (2000). *Pedagogy, symbolic control, and identity: Theory, research, critique* (2nd rev. ed.). Rowman & Littlefield. (Original work published in 1996)

Berry, M. (1981a). Systemic linguistics and discourse analysis: A multi-layered approach to exchange structure. *Studies in Discourse Analysis, 1,* 20–145.

Berry, M. (1981b). Towards layers of exchange structure for directive exchanges. *Network, 2,* 23–32.

Berry, M. (2017). Challenging and supporting moves in discourse. In S. Neumann, J. Wegener, P. Fest, P. Niemietz, & N. Hützen (Eds.), *Challenging boundaries in linguistics: Systemic functional perspectives* (pp. 255–80). Peter Lang.

Bourdieu, P. (1993). *The field of cultural production.* Columbia University Press.

Bouvier, G. (2015). What is a discourse approach to Twitter, Facebook, YouTube and other social media: Connecting with other academic fields? *Journal of Multicultural Discourses, 10*(2), 149–62. https://doi.org/10.1080/17447143.2015.1042381

Brown, R., & Ford, M. (1961). Address in American English. *Journal of Abnormal and Social Psychology, 62,* 375–85. https://doi.org/http://doi.org/10.1037/h0042862

Brown, R., & Gilman, A. (1960). The pronouns of power and solidarity. In T.T. Sebeok (Ed.), *Style in language* (pp. 253–76). MIT Press.

Carlyle, T. (1841). *The works of Thomas Carlyle in thirty volumes: Volume 4. On heroes, hero-worship, and the heroic in history.* Chapman and Hall.

Carr, G. (2023). *With respect to consent: The language of sex education* [Unpublished PhD thesis]. Department of Linguistics, The University of Sydney. http://www.isfla.org/Systemics/Print/Theses/Carr-2023-phd.pdf

Carr, G. (2025). *The language of sex education: With respect to consent.* Bloomsbury.

Chen, L. (2024). *Knowledge-building in tertiary medical science* [Unpublished PhD thesis]. Department of Linguistics, The University of Sydney. https://hdl.handle.net/2123/32685

Chilton, P.A. (1978). On the theory of register. *Nottingham Linguistic Circular, 7*(2), 113–30.

Christie, F. (2002). *Classroom discourse analysis.* Continuum.

Cléirigh, C. (1998). *A selectionist model of the genesis of phonic texture: Systemic phonology & universal Darwinism* [Unpublished PhD thesis]. Department of Linguistics, The University of Sydney. http://www.isfla.org/Systemics/Print/Theses/CleirighThesis/Preliminaries.pdf

Cloran, C. (1989). Learning through language: The social construction of gender. In R. Hasan & J.R. Martin (Eds.), *Language development: Learning language, learning culture* (pp. 111–51). Ablex.

Coffin, C. (2006). *Historical discourse: The language of time, cause and evaluation.* Continuum.

Commonwealth of Australia. (2023). *Royal Commission in the Robodebt scheme: Full Report*. Commonwealth of Australia. https://robodebt.royalcommission.gov.au/system/files/2023-09/rrc-accessible-full-report.PDF

Cranny-Francis, A., & Martin, J.R. (1991). Contratextuality: The poetics of subversion. In F. Christie (Ed.), *Literacy in social processes: Papers from the inaugural Australian Systemic Linguistics Conference held at Deakin University, January 1990* (pp. 286–344). Centre for Studies in Language in Education, Northern Territory University.

Darlington, R., & Hospodaryk, J. (1993). *Understanding Australian history*. Heinemann.

Donegan, M. (2022). Roe v Wade has been overturned. Here's what this will mean. *The Guardian*. https://www.theguardian.com/commentisfree/2022/jun/24/overturning-roe-story-is-women-unfreedom

Doran, Y.J. (2018). *The discourse of physics: Building knowledge through language, mathematics and image*. Routledge.

Doran, Y.J. (2020a). Cultivating values: Knower-building in the humanities. *Estudios de Lingüística Aplicada, 37*(70), 169–98. http://doi.org/10.22201/enallt.01852647p.2019.70.965

Doran, Y.J. (2020b). Seeing values: Axiology and affording attitude in Australia's 'invasion'. In J.R. Martin, K.A. Maton, & Y.J. Doran (Eds.), *Accessing academic discourse: Systemic functional linguistics and legitimation code theory* (pp. 151–76). Routledge.

Doran, Y.J. (2024). Interpreting history: Valuing events in a postcolonial world. In J. Hao & J.R. Martin (Eds.), *The discourse of history: A systemic functional perspective* (pp. 73–94). Cambridge University Press.

Doran, Y.J., & Martin, J. (2021). Field relations: Understanding scientific explanations. In K. Maton, J.R. Martin, & Y.J. Doran (Eds.), *Teaching science: Knowledge, language, pedagogy* (pp. 105–33). Routledge.

Doran, Y.J., Martin, J.R., & Herrington, M. (2024). Rethinking context: Realisation, instantiation and individuation in SFL. *Journal of World Languages, 10*(1). http://dx.doi.org/10.1515/jwl-2023-0051

Dreyfus, S.J. (2012). Life's a bonding experience: A framework for the communication of a non-verbal intellectually disabled teenager. *Journal of Interactional Research in Communication Disorders, 4*(2), 249–71. http://doi.org/10.1558/jircd.v4i2.249

Eggins, S. (1990). *Keeping the conversation going: A systemic-functional analysis of conversational structure in casual sustained talk* [Unpublished PhD thesis]. Department of Linguistics, The University of Sydney. https://ses.library.usyd.edu.au/bitstream/handle/2123/1003/KEEPING%20THE%20CONVERSATION%20GOING%20VOL%201.pdf?sequence=4&isAllowed=y

Eggins, S., & Slade, D. (2004). *Analysing casual conversation*. Equinox. (Original work published in 1997)

Feez, S., Iedema, R., & White, P.R.R. (2010). *Media literacy*. Adult Migrant Education Service. https://hdl.handle.net/1959.11/5571

Firth, J.R. (1964). *The tongues of men, and speech*. Oxford University Press.

Gardner, R. (2001). *When listeners talk: Response tokens and listener stance*. John Benjamins.

Gee, J.P. (2005). Semiotic social spaces and affinity spaces: From the Age of Mythology to today's schools. In D. Barton & K. Tusting (Eds.), *Beyond communities of practice: Language power and social context* (pp. 214–32). Cambridge University Press.

Gillespie, T. (2018). *Custodians of the internet: Platforms, content moderation, and the hidden decisions that shape social media*. Yale University Press.

Gregory, M. (1967). Aspects of varieties differentiation. *Journal of Linguistics, 3*(2), 177–89. http://doi.org/10.1017/S0022226700016601

Halliday, M.A.K. (1970). *A course in spoken English: Intonation*. Oxford University Press.

Halliday, M.A.K. (1973). *Explorations in the functions of language*. Edward Arnold.

Halliday, M.A.K. (1978). *Language as social semiotic: The social interpretation of language and meaning*. Edward Arnold.

Halliday, M.A.K. (1985). *An introduction to functional grammar*. Edward Arnold.

Halliday, M.A.K. (1991a). The notion of "context" in language education. In T. Le & M. McClausland (Eds.), *Language education: Interaction and Development. Proceedings of the International Conference held in Vietnam April 1991* (pp. 1–24). University of Tasmania.

Halliday, M.A.K. (1991b). Towards probabilistic interpretations. In E. Ventola (Ed.), *Recent systemic and other functional views on language* (Trends in Linguistics: Studies and Monographs, pp. 39–61). de Gruyter.

Halliday, M.A.K. (2006). *Computational and quantitative studies*. Bloomsbury.

Halliday, M.A.K., & Greaves, W.S. (2008). *Intonation in the grammar of English*. Equinox.

Halliday, M.A.K., & Hasan, R. (1976). *Cohesion in English*. Longman.

Halliday, M.A.K., & Hasan, R. (1985). *Language, context, and text: Aspects of language in a social-semiotic perspective*. Deakin University Press.

Halliday, M.A.K., & Martin, J.R. (1993). *Writing science: Literacy and discursive power*. Falmer.

Halliday, M.A.K., & Matthiessen, C.M.I.M. (1999). *Construing experience through meaning: A language-based approach to cognition*. Cassell.

Halliday, M.A.K., & Matthiessen, C.M.I.M. (2014). *Halliday's introduction to functional grammar*. Routledge.

Hao, J. (2020). *Analysing scientific discourse from a systemic functional linguistic perspective: A framework for exploring knowledge building in biology*. Routledge. http://dx.doi.org/10.4324/9781351241052

Hao, J., & Martin, J.R. (2024). *The discourse of history: A systemic functional linguistic perspective.* Cambridge University Press. https://doi.org/10.1017/9781009024884

Hasan, R. (1973). Code, register and social dialect. In B. Bernstein (Ed.), *Class, code and control: Applied studies towards a sociology of language* (Vol. 2, pp. 253–92). Routledge & Kegan Paul.

Hasan, R. (1983). *A semantic network for the analysis of messages in everyday talk between mothers and their children* [Mimeo]. Macquarie University.

Hasan, R. (1989). Semantic variation and sociolinguistics. *Australian Journal of Linguistics, 9*(2), 221–75. http://doi.org/10.1080/07268608908599422

Hasan, R. (1999). Speaking with reference to context. In M. Ghadessy (Ed.), *Text and context in unctional linguistics* (pp. 219–328). Benjamins.

Hasan, R. (2009). Sample mother-child dialogues. In J.J. Webster (Ed.), *Semantic variation: Meaning in society and in sociolinguistics* [CD-ROM]. Equinox.

Hasan, R. (2011). *Verbal art: A social semiotic perspective.* Equinox.

Hasan, R. (2014). Towards a paradigmatic description of context: Systems, metafunctions, and semantics. *Functional Linguistics, 1*(1), 9. http://doi.org/10.1186/s40554-014-0009-y

Hasan, R. (2016). *The collected works of Ruqaiya Hasan: Volume 4. Context in the system and process of language* (J. Webster, Ed.). Equinox.

Hasan, R. (2020). Tenor: Rethinking interactant relations. *Language, Context and Text, 2*(2), 213–333. http://dx.doi.org/10.1075/langct.00029.has

Hasan, R., Williams, G., Cloran, C., & Lukin, A. (2005). Semantic networks: The description of linguistic meaning in SFL. In R. Hasan, C.M.I.M. Matthiessen, & J. Webster (Eds.), *Continuing discourse on language: A functional perspective* (Vol. 2, pp. 697–738). Equinox.

Heritage, J., & Raymond, G. (2005). The terms of agreement: Indexing epistemic authority and subordination in talk-in-interaction. *Social Psychology Quarterly, 68*(1), 15–38. http://doi.org/10.1177/019027250506800103

Hodge, R., & Kress, G. (1988). *Social semiotics.* Polity.

Hood, S. (2010). *Appraising research: Evaluation in academic writing.* Palgrave Macmillan.

Hood, S. (2022). Graduation in research writing: Managing the dial demands of objectivity and critique. In D. Caldwell, J.S. Knox, & J.R. Martin (Eds.), *Appliable linguistics and social semiotics: Developing theory from practice* (pp. 23–40). Bloomsbury.

Hood, S., & Forey, G. (2008). The interpersonal dynamics of call-centre interactions: Co-constructing the rise and fall of emotion. *Discourse & Communication, 2*(4), 389–409. http://dx.doi.org/10.1177/1750481308095937

Humphrey, S., & Vale, E. (2020). *Investigating model texts for learning.* Primary English Teachers Association of Australia.

Iedema, R., Feez, S., & White, P.R.R. (1994). *Media literacy (Write it Right Literacy in Industry Research Project – Stage 2)*. Metropolitan East Disadvantaged Schools Program. (Republished as Feez, S., Iedema, R. & White, P.R.R. [2008]. *Media literacy.* New South Wales Adult Migrant Education Service.)

Jackson, G. (2021). Axiological constellations in literary response writing: Critical SFL praxis in an ELA classroom. *Language and Education, 35*(5), 446–62. http://doi.org/10.1080/09500782.2020.1856132

Jovanovic, D., & Van Leeuwen, T. (2018). Multimodal dialogue on social media. *Social Semiotics, 28*(5), 683–99. http://doi.org/10.1080/10350330.2018.1504732

Kartika-Ningsih, H. (2019). Implementing the Reading to Learn bilingual program in Indonesia. In K. Rajandran & S.A. Manan (Eds.), *Discourse of Southeast Asia: A social semiotics perspective* (pp. 145–63). Springer.

Kim, M., Martin, J.R., Shin, G.-H., & Choi, G.H. (2023). *Korean grammar: A systemic functional approach.* Cambridge University Press. http://dx.doi.org/10.1017/9781009019941

Knight, N.K. (2008). "Still cool . . . and American too!": An SFL analysis of deferred bonds in internet messaging humour. In N. Nørgaard (Ed.), *Systemic functional linguistics in use* (Odense Working Papers in Language and Communication, Vol. 29, pp. 481–502). University Press of Southern Denmark. https://doi.org/10.35360/NJES.78

Knight, N.K. (2010a). *Laughing our bonds off: Conversational humour in relation to affiliation* [Unpublished PhD dissertation]. University of Sydney. https://ses.library.usyd.edu.au/handle/2123/6656#

Knight, N.K. (2010b). Wrinkling complexity: Concepts of identity and affiliation in humour. In M. Bednarek & J.R. Martin (Eds.), *New discourse on language: Functional perspectives on multimodality, identity, and affiliation* (pp. 35–58). Bloomsbury.

Knight, N.K. (2011). The interpersonal semiotics of having a laugh. In S. Dreyfus, S. Hood, & M. Stenglin (Eds.), *Semiotic margins: Meaning in multimodalities* (pp. 7–30). Continuum.

Knight, N.K. (2013). Evaluating experience in funny ways: How friends bond through conversational humour. *Text & Talk, 33*(4–5), 553–74. http://dx.doi.org/10.1515/text-2013-0025

Kollontai, A. (1997). Working woman and mother. In A. Holt (Ed.), *Alexandra Kollontai: Selected writings* (pp. 127–39). Norton. (Original work published in 1916)

Kress, G., & Van Leeuwen, T. (2021). *Reading images: The grammar of visual design.* Routledge.

Labov, W. (1972). The transformation experience in narrative syntax. In *Language in the inner city: Studies in the black English vernacular* (pp. 354–96). University of Pennsylvania Press.

Labov, W., & Waletzky, J. (1967). Narrative analysis. In J. Helm (Ed.), *Essays on the verbal and visual arts* (pp. 12–44). University of Washington Press.

Lemke, J.L. (1995). *Textual politics: Discourse and social dynamics.* Taylor & Francis.

Leppänen, S., Peuronen, S., & Westinen, E. (2018). Superdiversity perspective and the sociolinguistics of social media. In A. Creese & A. Blackledge (Eds.), *The Routledge handbook of language and superdiversity* (pp. 30–42). Routledge.

Levinson, S.C. (1983). *Pragmatics.* Cambridge University Press.

Logi, L. (2021). *Impersonation, expectation and humorous affiliation: How intermodal impersonation and linguistic expectation are employed by stand-up comedians to create humour* [Unpublished PhD thesis]. The University of New South Wales.

Logi, L., & Zappavigna, M. (2021). Impersonated personae – Paralanguage, dialogism and affiliation in stand-up comedy. *Humor, 34*(3), 339–73. https://doi.org/10.1515/humor-2020-0023

Logi, L., & Zappavigna, M. (2022). Analysing ambient affiliation. In D. Caldwell, J. Knox, & J.R. Martin (Eds.), *Appliable linguistics and social semiotics: Developing theory from practice* (pp. 325–40). Bloomsbury.

Mackenzie, J., & Zhao, S. (2021). Motherhood online: Issues and opportunities for discourse analysis. *Discourse, Context & Media, 40,* 100472. https://doi.org/10.1016/j.dcm.2021.100472

Martin, J.R. (1984). Language, register and genre. In F. Christie (Ed.), *Children writing: A reader* (ECT Language Studies, pp. 21–30). Deakin University Press.

Martin, J.R. (1992). *English text: System and structure.* Benjamins.

Martin, J.R. (1995). Text and clause: Fractal resonance. *Text, 15*(1), 5–42. https://doi.org/10.1515/text.1.1995.15.1.5

Martin, J.R. (1996). Types of structure: Deconstructing notions of constituency in clause and text. In E.H. Hovy & D.R. Scott (Eds.), *Computational and conversational discourse: Burning issues – An interdisciplinary account* (pp. 39–66). Springer. https://doi.org/10.1007/978-3-662-03293-0

Martin, J.R. (1999). Modelling context: A crooked path of progress in contextual linguistics (Sydney SFL). In M. Ghadessy (Ed.), *Text and context in functional linguistics* (CILT Series IV, pp. 25–61). Benjamins.

Martin, J.R. (2000a). Beyond exchange: Appraisal systems in English. In S. Hunston & G. Thompson (Eds.), *Evaluation in text: Authorial stance and the construction of discourse* (pp. 142–75). Oxford University Press.

Martin, J.R. (2000b). Factoring out exchange: Types of structure. In M. Coulthard, J. Cotterill & F. Rock (Eds.), *Working with dialogue* (pp. 19–40). Niemeyer.

Martin, J.R. (2007a). Construing knowledge: A functional linguistic perspective. In F. Christie & J.R. Martin (Eds.), *Language, knowledge & pedagogy: Functional linguistic and sociological perspectives* (pp. 34–64). Continuum.

Martin, J.R. (2007b). Genre and field: Social processes and knowledge structures in systemic functional semiotics. In L. Barbara & T. Berber Sardinha (Eds.), *Proceedings of the 33rd International Systemic Functional Congress* (pp. 1–35). PUCSP. http://www.pucsp.br/isfc

Martin, J.R. (2008a). Innocence: Realisation, instantiation and individuation in a Botswanan town. In N.K. Knight & A. Mahboob (Eds.), *Questioning linguistics* (pp. 32–76). Cambridge Scholars Publishing.

Martin, J.R. (2008b). Tenderness: Realisation and instantiation in a Botswanan town. *Odense Working Papers in Language and Communication, 29*, 30–58.

Martin, J.R. (2010). Semantic variation: Modelling system, text and affiliation in social semiosis. In M. Bednarek & R.J. Martin (Eds.), *New discourse on language: Functional perspectives on multimodality, identity, and affiliation* (pp. 1–34). Continuum.

Martin, J.R. (2011). Multimodal semiotics: Theoretical challenges. In S. Hood & S. Dreyfus (Eds.), *Semiotic margins: Meaning in multimodalities* (pp. 243–68). Continuum.

Martin, J.R. (2012, November). Heart from darkness: Apocalypse Ron. *Revista Canaria de Estudios Ingleses, 65*(Special issue on The Evaluative Uses of Language: The Appraisal Framework), 67–99.

Martin, J.R. (2014). Evolving systemic functional linguistics: Beyond the clause. *Functional Linguistics, 1*(3), 1–24. https://doi.org/10.1186/2196-419X-1-3

Martin, J.R. (2017). Revisiting field: Specialized knowledge in secondary school science and humanities discourse. *Onomázein, 1*(Special Issue on Systemic Functional Linguistics and Legitimation Code Theory on Education and Knowledge), 111–48. http://dx.doi.org/10.7764/onomazein.ne2.05

Martin, J.R. (2020). The effability of semantic relations: Describing attitude. *Journal of Foreign Languages, 43*(6), 2–20.

Martin, J.R. (2021a). Pedagogic discourse: Marshalling register variation. *Revista Signos, 54*(107; Special Issue in Honour of Giovanni Parodi), 771–98. https://doi.org/10.4067/S0718-09342021000300771

Martin, J.R. (2021b). *Secular communion: The carrot and the stick* (paper presented at the Australian Systemic Functional Linguistics Association Conference, Brisbane, The University of Queensland, 29 September–1 October).

Martin, J.R. (2024). Coordinating meaning: Scaffolding teaching/learning in pedagogic discourse. In J. Hao & J.R. Martin (Eds.), *The discourse of history: A systemic functional perspective* (pp.). Cambridge University Press. https://doi.org/10.1017/9781009024884

Martin, J.R., & Cruz, P. (2021). Interpersonal grammar in Tagalog: Assessment systems. In J.R. Martin, B. Quiroz, & G. Figueredo (Eds.), *Interpersonal grammar: Systemic functional theory and description* (pp. 130–59). Cambridge University Press. https://doi.org/10.1017/9781108663120

Martin, J.R., Maton, K., & Matruglio, E. (2010). Historical cosmologies: Epistemology and axiology in Australian secondary school history discourse. *Revista Signos: Estudios de lengua y literature, 43*(73), 433–63. http://dx.doi.org/10.4067/S0718-09342010000500003

Martin, J.R., & Matruglio, E.S. (2020). Revisiting mode: Context in/dependency in Ancient History classroom discourse. In J.R Martin, K. Maton, & Y. Doran (Eds.), *Accessing academic discourse: Systemic functional linguistics and legitimation code theory* (pp. 89–113). Routledge. (Original work published in 2013)

Martin, J.R., & Rose, D. (2007). *Working with discourse: Meaning beyond the clause* (2nd rev. ed.). Bloomsbury. (Original work published in 2003)

Martin, J.R., & Rose, D. (2008). *Genre relations: Mapping culture.* Equinox.

Martin, J.R., & Unsworth, L. (2024). *Reading images for knowledge building: Analyzing infographics in school science.* Routledge.

Martin, J.R., Wang, P., & Zhu, Y. (2013). *Systemic functional grammar: A next step into the theory–axial relations* (W. Pin & Z. Youngsheng, Trans. and extensions). Beijing Higher Education Press.

Martin, J.R., & White, P.R.R. (2005). *The language of evaluation: Appraisal in English.* Palgrave.

Martin, J.R., Zappavigna, M., & Dwyer, P. (2010). Negotiating evaluation: Story structure and appraisal in Youth Justice Conferencing. In A. Mahboob & N.K. Knight (Eds.), *Appliable linguistics* (pp. 44–75). Continuum.

Maton, K., & Doran, Y.J. (2021). Constellating science: How relations among ideas help build knowledge. In K. Maton, J.R. Martin, & Y.J. Doran (Eds.), *Teaching science: Knowledge, language, pedagogy* (pp. 49–75). Routledge.

Maton, K.A. (2014). *Knowledge and knowers: Towards a realist sociology of education.* Routledge.

Matthiessen, C.M.I.M. (1993). Register in the round: Diversity in a unified theory of register analysis. In M. Ghadessy (Ed.), *Register analysis: Theory and practice* (pp. 221–92) Pinter.

Matthiessen, C.M.I.M. (1995). *Lexicogrammatical cartography: English systems.* International Language Sciences.

Metropolitan East Disadvantaged Schools Program. (1989). *The discussion genre.* Metropolitan East Disadvantaged Schools Program.

Metropolitan East Disadvantaged Schools Program. (1994). *Exploring literacy in School English.* Metropolitan East Disadvantaged Schools Program.

Metropolitan East Disadvantaged Schools Program. (1996). *Exploring literacy in school history: Write it right: Resources for learning.* Metropolitan East Disadvantaged Schools Program.

Muntigl, P. (2004). *Narrative counselling: Social and linguistic processes of change.* John Benjamins.

Muntigl, P. (2009). Knowledge moves in conversational exchanges: Revisiting the concept of primary vs. secondary knowers. *Functions of Language, 16*(2), 225–63. http://doi.org/10.1075/fol.16.2.03mun

Muntigl, P., Knight, N., & Watkins, A. (2012). Working to keep aligned in psychotherapy: Using nods as a dialogic resource to display affiliation. *Language and Dialogue, 2*(1), 9–27. http://doi.org/10.1075/ld.2.1.01mun

Ngo, T., Hood, S., Martin, J.R., Painter, C., Smith, B., & Zappavigna, M. (2022). *Modelling paralanguage using systemic functional semiotics: Theory and application.* Bloomsbury. http://dx.doi.org/10.5040/9781350074934

NSW Public School Cookery Teachers' Association. (1970). *The commonsense cookery book: Metric edition.* Angus & Robertson.

O'Donnell, M. (1990). A dynamic model of exchange. *Word, 41*(3), 293–327. http://doi.org/10.1080/00437956.1990.11435825

Painter, C., Martin, J.R., & Unsworth, L. (2013). *Reading visual narratives: Image analysis of children's picture books.* Equinox.

Pearce, J. (1972). Diversity in writing. In J. Pearce & G. Thornton (Eds.), *Exploring language* (Schools Council Program in Linguistics and English Teaching, pp. 177–87). Edward Arnold.

Poynton, C. (1984). Names as vocatives: Forms and functions. *Nottingham Linguistic Circular, 13*, 1–34.

Poynton, C. (1989). *Language and gender: Making the difference.* Oxford University Press. (Original work published in 1985)

Poynton, C. (1990a). *Address and the semiotics of social relations: A systemic-functional account of address forms and practices in Australian English.* University of Sydney.

Poynton, C. (1990b). The privileging of representational and the marginalising of the interpersonal: A metaphor (and more) for contemporary gender roles. In T. Threadgold & A. Cranny-Francis (Eds.), *Feminine/masculine and representation* (pp. 231–55). Routledge.

Poynton, C. (1996). Amplification as a grammatical prosody: Attitudinal modification in the nominal group. In M. Berry, C. Butler, & R.P. Fawcett (Eds.), *Meaning and form: Systemic functional interpretations* (Meaning and Choice in Language: Studies for Michael Halliday, pp. 211–27). Ablex.

Poynton, C., & Lee, A. (2009). Debating appraisal: On networks and names. In H. Chen & K. Cruickshank (Eds.), *Making a difference: Challenges for applied linguistics* (pp. 21–36). Cambridge Scholars Publishing.

Queensland Studies Authority. (2011). *The world's best animal is . . . NAPLAN – literacy: Sample texts for teaching persuasive writing.* Queensland Studies Authority.

Randwick City Council. (n.d.). *Why is it called Wedding Cake Island?* Informational Plaque, Coogee, NSW, Australia.

Ravelli, L. (2000). Beyond shopping: Constructing the Sydney Olympics in three-dimensional text. *Text, 20*(4), 489–515. http://dx.doi.org/10.1515/text.1.2000.20.4.489

Rose, D. (2018). Pedagogic register analysis: Mapping choices in teaching and learning. *Functional Linguistics, 5*(1), 3. http://doi.org/10.1186/s40554-018-0053-0

Rose, D. (2020). The baboon and the bee: Exploring register patterns across languages. In J.R. Martin, Y.J. Doran, & G. Figueredo (Eds.), *Systemic functional language description: Making meaning matter* (pp. 273–306). Routledge.

Schegloff, E.A. (2007). A tutorial on membership categorization. *Journal of Pragmatics, 39*(3), 462–82. http://doi.org/10.1016/j.pragma.2006.07.007

Smith, B.A. (2008). *Intonational systems and register: A multidimensional exploration* [Unpublished PhD thesis]. Department of Linguistics, Macquarie University. http://www.isfla.org/Systemics/Print/Theses/SmithBradPhD.pdf

Stenglin, M. (2004). *Packaging curiosities: Towards a grammar of three-dimensional space* [Unpublished PhD thesis]. The University of Sydney. https://ses.library.usyd.edu.au/handle/2123/635#

Stenglin, M. (2022). Binding and bonding: A retrospective and propsetive gaze. In D. Caldwell, J. Knox, & J.R. Martin (Eds.), *Appliable linguistics and social semiotics: Developing theory from practice* (pp. 309–24). Bloomsbury.

<BBOK>Stevanovic, M. & Peräkylä, A. (2012). Deontic authority in interaction: The right to announce, propose, and decide. *Research in Language and Social Interaction, 45*(3), 297–321.

Swales, J. (1986). Citation analysis and discourse analysis. *Applied Linguistics, 7*(1), 39–56. http://doi.org/10.1093/applin/7.1.39

Szenes, E. (2021). The linguistic construction of business decisions: A systemic functional linguistic perspective. *Language, Context and Text, 3*(2), 335–66. http://dx.doi.org/10.1075/langct.20008.sze

Tann, K. (2010a). Imagining communities: A multifunctional approach to identity management in texts. In *New discourse on language: Functional perspectives on multimodality, identity, and affiliation* (pp. 163–94). Continuum.

Tann, K. (2010b). *Semogenesis of a nation: An iconography of Japanese identity* [Unpublished PhD thesis]. Department of Linguistics, The University of Sydney. http://hdl.handle.net/2123/7611

Tann, K. (2013). The language of identity discourse: Introducing a systemic functional framework for iconography. *Linguistics & the Human Sciences, 8*(3). http://dx.doi.org/10.1558/lhs.v8i3.361

Tilakaratna, N.L. (2016). *Reviving the nation: The discursive construction of national identity in Sri Lankan English language textbooks* [Unpublished PhD thesis]. Department of Linguistics, The University of Sydney. http://hdl.handle.net/2123/15750

Trew, T. (1979). Theory and ideology at work. In R. Fowler, B. Hodge, B. Kress, & T. Trew (Eds.), *Language and control* (pp. 94–116). Routledge and Kegan Paul.

Van Leeuwen, T. (1999). *Speech, music, sound.* Palgrave.

Varis, P., & Blommaert, J. (2015). Conviviality and collectives on social media: Virality, memes, and new social structures. *Multilingual Margins: A Journal of Multilingualism from the Periphery, 2*(1). http://dx.doi.org/10.14426/mm.v2i1.50

Ventola, E. (1987). *The structure of social interaction: A systemic approach to the semiotics of service encounters.* Frances Pinter.

Wang, P. (2021). Interpersonal grammar in Mandarin. In J.R. Martin, B. Quiroz, & G. Figueredo (Eds.), *Interpersonal grammar: Systemic functional linguistic theory and description* (pp. 96–129). Cambridge University Press. http://dx.doi.org/10.1017/9781108663120

Warren, N. (2003). *Excel HSC physics.* Pascal.

White, P.R.R. (1998). *Telling Media Tales: The News Story as Rhetoric.* PhD Dissertation, The University of Sydney.

White, P.R.R. (2003). Beyond modality and hedging: A dialogic view of the language of intersubjective stance. *Text & Talk, 23*(2), 259–84.

White, P.R.R. (2020). Attitudinal alignment in journalistic commentary and social-media argumentation: The construction of values-based group identities in the online comments of newspaper readers. In M. Zappavigna & S. Dreyfus (Eds.), *Discourses of hope and reconciliation: On J.R. Martin's contribution to systemic functional linguistics* (pp. 21–38). Bloomsbury.

White, P.R.R. (2022). The appraisal framework and analyses of journalistic discourse: Objectivity, subjectivity and attitudinal positioning. In D. Caldwell, J.S. Knox & J.R. Martin (Eds.), *Appliable linguistics and social semiotics: Developing theory from practice* (pp. 295–308). Bloomsbury.

Wignell, P., Martin, J.R., & Eggins, S. (1989). The discourse of geography: Ordering and explaining the experiential world. *Linguistics and Education, 1*(4), 359–91. http://doi.org/10.1016/S0898-5898(89)80007-5

Williams, R. (1958). *Culture and society: 1780–1950.* Vintage.

Zappavigna, M. (2014a). Ambient affiliation in microblogging: Bonding around the quotidian. *Media International Australia, 151*(1), 97–103. http://doi.org/10.1177/1329878X1415100113

Zappavigna, M. (2014b). Enacting identity in microblogging. *Discourse and Communication, 8*(2), 209–28. http://doi.org/10.1177/1750481313510816

Zappavigna, M. (2015). Searchable talk: The linguistic functions of hashtags. *Social Semiotics, 25*(3), 274–91. http://doi.org/10.1080/10350330.2014.996948

Zappavigna, M. (2016). Social media photography: Construing subjectivity in Instagram images. *Visual Communication, 15*(3), 271–92. http://doi.org/10.1177/1470357216643220

Zappavigna, M. (2018). *Searchable talk: Hashtags and social media metadiscourse.* Bloomsbury.

Zappavigna, M., & Logi, L. (2024). *Emoji and social media paralanguage.* Cambridge University Press.

Zappavigna, M., & Martin, J.R. (2018a). #Communing affiliation: Social tagging as a resource for aligning around values in social media. *Discourse, Context & Media, 22*(Special Issue on the Discourse of Social Tagging), 1–64. http://dx.doi.org/10.1016/j.dcm.2017.08.001

Zappavigna, M., & Martin, J.R. (2018b). *Discourse and diversionary justice: An analysis of ceremonial redress in Youth Justice Conferencing.* Palgrave.

Zappavigna, M., & Zhao, S. (2017). Selfies in 'mommyblogging': An emerging visual genre. *Discourse, Context & Media, 20,* 239–247. http://dx.doi.org/10.1016/j.dcm.2017.05.005

Zhang, D. (2020a). Dialogic positioning in Khorchin Mongolian: The temporal and spatial dimensions of propositional engagement in conversations. *Lingua, 244,* 1–16. http://doi.org/10.1016/j.lingua.2020.102920

Zhang, D. (2020b). *Negotiating interpersonal meaning in Khorchin Mongolian: discourse and grammar* [Unpublished PhD thesis]. The University of Sydney. https://hdl.handle.net/2123/22835

Zhang, D. (2020c). Towards a discourse semantic characterisation of the modal particles in Khorchin Mongolian: A case study of an interaction. *Journal of Pragmatics, 158,* 13–32. http://doi.org/10.1016/j.pragma.2019.12.013

Zhang, D. (2021). Dynamism in knowledge exchanges: Developing move systems based on Khorchin Mongolian interactions. *Discourse Studies, 23*(3), 386–413. http://doi.org/10.1177/1461445620982113

Zhang, D. 2024. Towards a responsibility-based model of the move system in discourse semantics: reasoning from above. *Lingua. 309,* 103796. https://doi.org/10.1016/j.lingua.2024.103796

Zhao, S., Djonov, E., & van Leeuwen, T. (2014). Semiotic technology and practice: A multimodal social semiotic approach to PowerPoint. Text & Talk, *34,* 349–75. http://dx.doi.org/10.1515/text-2014-0005

Zhao, S., & Flewitt, R. (2020). Young Chinese immigrant children's language and literacy practices on social media: A translanguaging perspective. *Language and Education, 34*(3), 267–85. http://doi.org/10.1080/09500782.2019.1656738

Zwicky, A.M. (1974). *Hey, whatsyourname. Papers from the Regional Meeting of the Chicago Linguistic Society, 10,* 787–801.

Index

activity, 13, 16–18, 201, 204–5, 217, 226; see also field
aggregation, 13, 15–16; see also mass
appraisal, 7–8, 12, 28, 31, 176–7, 215–216, 227, 231, 239, 241; attitude, 22–3, 32, 34–5, 43, 51–3, 56–7, 59–60, 104, 114, 161, 166, 186–7, 208, 215, 225, 235; engagement, 22–3, 29, 33, 49, 51, 55–7, 59, 62, 90, 92, 101, 105, 122, 128, 161, 190–1, 198, 200, 208, 215–216, 225, 227, 245; graduation, 25, 152, 159, 161, 166, 170–1, 177, 188, 191, 208, 215, 217, 237; see also discourse semantics
association, 16, 20, 67, 160; contraction, 12, 15, 162, 213, 216, 227
attitude, 22–3, 32, 34–5, 43, 51–3, 56–7, 59–60, 104, 114, 161, 166, 186–7, 208, 215, 225, 235; see also appraisal

classification, 9, 11, 13, 18, 203, 217; see also field
composition, 18, 217; see also field
connexion, 7–8, 101, 105, 120, 126–8, 130, 132, 137, 215–216; see also discourse semantics
contact, 9, 12, 14, 15, 181, 212–213, 216, 222, 230
contraction, 12, 15, 162, 213, 216, 227; see also association
convoking, 106, 115–119, 121, 144, 164–5, 216, 218; see also orienting

discourse semantics, 5, 25, 35, 43, 64, 81, 181, 188, 220, 223–4, 226, 245; appraisal, 7–8, 12, 28, 31, 176–7, 215–216, 227, 231, 239, 241; connexion, 7–8, 101, 105, 120, 126–8, 130, 132, 137, 215–216; ideational meaning, 6, 13, 68, 101, 104; identification, 7–8, 216–217; negotiation, 7–8, 28–9, 31, 33, 36, 49, 54, 61–3, 89, 92, 100, 114, 123, 151–4, 160, 183, 185, 206–8, 216–218, 227; periodicity, 7, 45, 138, 216, 218, 229

encapsulating, 25, 106, 138–40, 145–8, 190, 202, 216, 218, 229; see also orienting
engagement, 22–3, 29, 33, 49, 51, 55–7, 59, 62, 90, 92, 101, 105, 122, 128, 161, 190–1, 198, 200, 208, 215–216, 225, 227, 245; see also appraisal

field, -1, 4–9, 11–13, 16–17, 19–20, 27, 102, 105, 136, 156, 183, 194–6, 201–6, 215–217, 219, 221, 226, 235; activity, 13, 16–18, 201, 204–5, 217, 226; classification, 9, 11, 13, 18, 203, 217; composition, 18, 217; item, 18, 52, 187; momented activity, 17, 201, 204–5; property, 16, 19; technicality, 13, 15–16; unmomented activity, 17; see also register

graduation, 25, 152, 159, 161, 166, 170–1, 177, 188, 191, 208, 215, 217, 237; see also appraisal

iconization, 13, 15–16, 59, 103–4, 160; see also mass
ideational meaning, 6–8, 13, 15–16, 19, 33, 35–6, 68, 101, 103–4, 136–7, 140, 189, 216–218, 223, 226; see also discourse semantics
identification, 7–8, 216–217; see also discourse semantics
information unit, 224, 230; see also information (textual meaning)
interpersonal meaning, 6–7, 10, 13, 15–16, 19–20, 22, 31–3, 36, 51–5, 59, 62, 76, 78–9, 81, 84, 88, 94–6, 98, 103–4, 116, 126, 138, 151–2, 154, 159, 162, 167–8, 171–3, 176, 178, 180–1, 183, 200, 210, 215–221, 223, 226–7, 237, 245
intonation, 28, 82, 194, 218, 220, 224
item, 18, 52, 187; see also field

lexicogrammar, 5, 33, 64, 81, 215–220, 226
likening, 25, 106, 113, 120, 126, 132–40, 144, 146–9, 176–7, 190, 206, 218, 223, 229; see also orienting

mass, 19, 51, 91–2, 175; aggregation, 13, 15–16; iconization, 13, 15–16, 59, 103–4, 160; technicality, 13, 15–16
modality, 51–3, 60, 62, 91, 152–3, 171–2, 218, 227
mode, 4–9, 11–13, 16, 20, 27, 136, 183, 194–5, 200–1, 210, 216–219, 221–2, 229, 241; see also register
momented activity, 17, 201, 204–5; see also field
mood, 6, 34–5, 60, 62, 94–5, 118, 172, 175, 218, 224

negotiation, 7–8, 28–9, 31, 33, 36, 49, 54, 61–3, 89, 92, 100, 114, 123, 151–4, 160, 183, 185, 206–8, 216–218, 227; see also discourse semantics

opposing, 25, 34, 55, 106, 113, 118, 120–8, 130, 133–8, 140, 144, 149, 163, 186, 201–2, 206, 218, 224, 229; see also orienting
orienting, 27, 79, 101–2, 143, 151, 189, 203, 220; convoking, 106, 115–119, 121, 144, 164–5, 216, 218; encapsulating, 25, 106, 138–40, 145–8, 190, 202, 216, 218, 229; likening, 25, 106, 113, 120, 126, 132–40, 144, 146–9, 176–7, 190, 206, 218, 223, 229; opposing, 25, 34, 55, 106, 113, 118, 120–8, 130, 133–8, 140, 144, 149, 163, 186, 201–2, 206, 218, 224, 229; sourcing, 25, 52, 56, 92, 106, 108–119, 121, 123, 144, 158, 164, 205, 219

periodicity, 7, 45, 138, 216, 218, 229; see also discourse semantics
phonology, -10, 5, 27, 32–3, 39, 62, 220
polarity, 34–6, 60, 81, 173, 176, 225
positioning, 27, 151, 173, 176, 215–216, 245; purview, 22–3, 51, 81, 84, 86–96, 112, 152–3, 185–6, 192–4, 212, 219, 227, 230; rendering, 20–1, 23, 29, 31, 33–6, 39–47, 49, 51, 53–62, 64, 70, 73, 80, 90, 96, 110, 119, 125–6, 130, 136–8, 140, 143–4, 164–7, 175, 202, 205–6, 208–210, 218–219, 222–5, 227; tendering, 20–1, 23, 31, 34–6, 40–3, 49, 51, 54–5, 59–67, 69, 71, 73–4, 77, 79, 81, 87, 89–91, 93,

95–6, 126, 143–5, 165, 172, 202, 205, 208, 212, 218, 220, 224
property, 16, 19; see also field
proposition, 34–5, 44, 49, 51–3, 62–4, 67–74, 76–81, 84, 86–7, 89–96, 109, 118, 135, 146, 166, 170–1, 173, 185–6, 189, 191, 201–2, 204, 219, 222–4, 226–7; see also information (speech function)
purview, 22–3, 51, 81, 84, 86–96, 112, 152–3, 185–6, 192–4, 212, 219, 227, 230; see also positioning

question, 21–2, 31–3, 35, 44–6, 54–6, 60, 64, 68–71, 77–9, 84, 86–8, 95–6, 100–3, 121, 126, 138, 152, 166–7, 172, 178, 184, 208, 218–219, 222, 224, 226, 229; see also information (speech function)

register, 15, 28, 220, 237, 239, 243; field, -1, 4–9, 11–13, 16–17, 19–20, 27, 102, 105, 136, 156, 183, 194–6, 201–6, 215–217, 219, 221, 226, 235; mode, 4–9, 11–13, 16, 20, 27, 136, 183, 194–5, 200–1, 210, 216–219, 221–2, 229, 241
rendering, 20–1, 23, 29, 31, 33–6, 39–47, 49, 51, 53–62, 64, 70, 73, 80, 90, 96, 110, 119, 125–6, 130, 136–8, 140, 143–4, 164–7, 175, 202, 205–6, 208–210, 218–219, 222–5, 227; see also positioning

scoping, 159–64, 167, 219; see also tuning
sourcing, 25, 52, 56, 92, 106, 108–119, 121, 123, 144, 158, 164, 205, 219; see also orienting
spiriting, 159, 161, 173–4, 176, 219; see also tuning
staking, 159, 161, 165–6, 168, 208, 220; see also tuning

statement, 21, 34–5, 45–6, 64, 68–9, 80–1, 90, 92, 121, 154, 184, 186, 219, 225–6; see also information (speech function)
status, 9–12, 15, 76, 79, 92–3, 116, 153–4, 160, 181, 212–213, 220, 230

technicality, 13, 15–16; see also field, mass
tendering, 20–1, 23, 31, 34–6, 40–3, 49, 51, 54–5, 59–67, 69, 71, 73–4, 77, 79, 81, 87, 89–91, 93, 95–6, 126, 143–5, 165, 172, 202, 205, 208, 212, 218, 220, 224; see also positioning
tenor, see status; contact; association; positioning; orienting; tuning
textual meaning, 6–7, 9, 13, 15, 19, 188, 218, 220, 239
theme, 6, 15, 168, 201, 205, 218
tonality, 15; see also information (textual meaning)
tone, 12, 22, 62, 82, 87–8, 90, 151, 173–4, 184, 194, 218–220, 223–4, 230; see also information (textual meaning)
tonicity, 15; see also information (textual meaning)
tuning, 25, 27, 130, 151–3, 156–8, 169, 171, 175, 177–9; scoping, 159–64, 167, 219; spiriting, 159, 161, 173–4, 176, 219; staking, 159, 161, 165–6, 168, 208, 220

unmomented activity, 17; see also field

vocatives, 116, 120, 153–4, 160–1, 173, 213, 216, 220